*Transformations of the State*

Series Editors: **Achim Hurrelmann**, Carleton University, Canada; **Stephan Leibfried**, University of Bremen, Germany; **Kerstin Martens**, University of Bremen, Germany; **Peter Mayer**, University of Bremen, Germany.

*Titles include*:

Achim Hurrelmann, Stephan Leibfried, Kerstin Martens and Peter Mayer (*editors*)
TRANSFORMING THE GOLDEN-AGE NATION STATE

Steffen Mau, Heike Brabandt, Lena Laube and Christof Roos
LIBERAL STATES AND THE FREEDOM OF MOVEMENT
Selective Borders, Unequal Mobility

Lutz Leisering (*editor*)
THE NEW REGULATORY STATE
Regulating Pensions in Germany and the UK



Andreas Kruck
PRIVATE RATINGS, PUBLIC REGULATIONS
Credit Rating Agencies and Global Financial Governance

Michael Dobbins
HIGHER EDUCATION POLICIES IN CENTRAL AND EASTERN EUROPE
Convergence Towards a Common Model?

Moritz Weiss
TRANSACTIONS COSTS AND SECURITY INSTITUTIONS
Unravelling the ESDP

Heinz Rothgang, Mirella Cacace, Simone Grimmeisen, Uwe Helmert, Claus Wendt
THE STATE AND HEALTHCARE
Comparing OECD Countries

Anna Holzscheiter
CHILDREN'S RIGHTS IN INTERNATIONAL POLITICS
The Transformative Power of Transnational Discourse

Kerstin Martens, Alexander-Kenneth Nagel, Michael Windzio and Ansgar Weymann (*editors*)
TRANSFORMATION OF EDUCATION POLICY

Steffen Schneider, Achim Hurrelmann, Zuzana Krell-Laluhová, Frank Nullmeier and Achim Wiesner
DEMOCRACY'S DEEP ROOTS
Why the Nation State Remains Legitimate

Anja P. Jakobi
INTERNATIONAL ORGANIZATIONS AND LIFELONG LEARNING
From Global Agendas to Policy Diffusion

Michael J. Warning
TRANSNATIONAL PUBLIC GOVERNANCE
Networks, Law and Legitimacy

Thomas Rixen
THE POLITICAL ECONOMY OF INTERNATIONAL TAX GOVERNANCE

Hartmut Wessler (*editor*)
PUBLIC DELIBERATION AND PUBLIC CULTURE
The Writings of Bernhard Peters, 1993–2005

Hartmut Wessler, Bernhard Peters, Michael Brűggemann,
Katharina Kleinen-von Kőnigslőw, Stefanie Sifft
TRANSNATIONALIZATION OF PUBLIC SPHERES

Jochen Zimmerman, Jörg R. Werner, Philipp B. Volmer
GLOBAL GOVERNANCE IN ACCOUNTING
Public Power and Private Commitment

Jochen Zimmermann and Jörg R. Werner
REGULATING CAPITALISM?
The Evolution of Transnational Accounting Governance

Peter Starke
RADICAL WELFARE STATE RETRENCHMENT
A Comparative Analysis

Jens Steffek, Claudia Kissling, Patrizia Nanz (*editors*)
CIVIL SOCIETY PARTICIPATION IN EUROPEAN AND GLOBAL GOVERNANCE
A Cure for the Democratic Deficit?

Klaus Dingwerth
THE NEW TRANSNATIONALISM
Transnational Governance and Democratic Legitimacy

Kerstin Martens, Alessandra Rusconi and Kathrin Leuze (*editors*)
NEW ARENAS OF EDUCATION GOVERNANCE
The Impact of International Organizations and Markets on Educational Policy Making

Achim Hurrelmann, Steffen Schneider and Jens Steffek (*editors*)
LEGITIMACY IN AN AGE OF GLOBAL POLITICS

Joan DeBardeleben and Achim Hurrelmann (*editors*)
DEMOCRATIC DILEMMAS OF MULTILEVEL GOVERNANCE
Legitimacy, Representation and Accountability in the European Union

Peter Starke, Alexandra Kaasch, Franca Van Hooren (*editors*)
THE WELFARE STATE AS CRISIS MANAGER
Explaining the Diversity of Policy Responses to Economic Crisis

---

**Transformations of the State**
**Series Standing Order ISBN 978–1–4039–8544–6 (hardback)**
**978–1–4039–8545–3 (paperback)**
(*outside North America only*)

You can receive future titles in this series as they are published by placing a standing order. Please contact your bookseller or, in case of difficulty, write to us at the address below with your name and address, the title of the series and the ISBNs quoted above.

Customer Services Department, Macmillan Distribution Ltd, Houndmills, Basingstoke, Hampshire RG21 6XS, England

---

# Regulating Capitalism?

## The Evolution of Transnational Accounting Governance

Jochen Zimmermann
*Chair of Accounting, University of Bremen, Germany*

and

Jörg R. Werner
*Professor of Accounting, Frankfurt School of Finance and Management, Germany*

palgrave
macmillan

First published 2013 by
PALGRAVE MACMILLAN

Palgrave Macmillan in the UK is an imprint of Macmillan Publishers Limited, registered in England, company number 785998, of Houndmills, Basingstoke, Hampshire RG21 6XS.

Palgrave Macmillan in the US is a division of St Martin's Press LLC, 175 Fifth Avenue, New York, NY 10010.

Palgrave Macmillan is the global academic imprint of the above companies and has companies and representatives throughout the world.

Palgrave® and Macmillan® are registered trademarks in the United States, the United Kingdom, Europe and other countries.

ISBN 978–0–230–27984–1

This book is printed on paper suitable for recycling and made from fully managed and sustained forest sources. Logging, pulping and manufacturing processes are expected to conform to the environmental regulations of the country of origin.

A catalogue record for this book is available from the British Library.

A catalog record for this book is available from the Library of Congress.

# Contents

## Part V Conclusion

# Figures and Tables

## Figures



## Tables

# Acknowledgements

The regulation of the capitalist world is becoming increasingly complex and difficult. This volume is the second book in which we try to understand the embeddedness of the state in the world of accounting and how the role of the state changes in this policy field (Zimmerman et al. 2008). We were privileged to have done this under the auspices of the Collaborative Research Centre 'Transformations of the State' at the University of Bremen. We would like to thank our colleagues, and in particular the Centre's speaker Professor Stephan Leibfried, for the congenial research atmosphere, and the Deutsche Forschungsgemeinschaft for its financial support.

We would like to thank in particular a number of people who helped us during the preparation of this book. We discussed our early ideas with Dr Stephan Abée, Dr Ulf Luthardt and Dr Stefan Veith. We were assisted in the preparation of the text by Dr Jan-Hendrik Hammermeister, Dr Tim-Frederik Oehr and Dr Johannes Schymczyk. Their enthusiasm and diligence provided a constant motivation for us to press ahead. We owe them our gratitude not only for their work but also for the *esprit de corps* that they brought to the accounting department at the time of writing this book and beyond.

*Jochen Zimmermann*
*Jörg R. Werner*
Bremen and Frankfurt

# Abbreviations

| | |
|---|---|
| AAA | American Accounting Association |
| AARC (CDN) | Accounting and Auditing Research Committee |
| ACCA (UK) | Association of Chartered Certified Accountants |
| AcSB (CDN) | Accounting Standards Board |
| AcSC (CDN) | Accounting Standards Committee |
| AcSOC (CDN) | Accounting Standards Oversight Council |
| AG (DE) | Stock Corporation (*Aktiengesellschaft*) |
| AICPA | American Institute of Certified Public Accountants |
| AIM (UK) | Alternative Investment Market |
| AISG | Accountants International Study Group |
| AktG (DE) | Stock Corporation Act (*Aktiengesetz*) BGBl. I 1965, p. 1089 |
| AMF (FR) | Financial Markets Authority (*Autorité des Marchés Financiers*) |
| ANC (FR) | National Standards Authority (*Autorité des Normes Comptables*) |
| AnSVG (DE) | Investor Protection Improvement Act (*Anlegerschutzverbesserungsgesetz*) BGBl. I 2004, p. 2630 |
| APB (US) | Accounting Principles Board |
| ARAB | Accounting Research Advisory Board |
| ARC | Accounting Research Committee |
| ASBJ | Accounting Standards Board of Japan |
| ASB (UK) | Accounting Standards Board |
| ASC (UK) | Accounting Standards Committee |
| ASCG | Accounting Standards Committee of Germany (*Deutsches Rechnungslegungs Standards Committee*) |
| BAC | Business Accounting Council of Japan |
| BADC (JPN) | Business Accounting Deliberation Council |
| BilMoG (DE) | Accounting Law Modernisation Act (*Bilanzrechtsmodernisierungsgesetz*) BGBl. I 2009, p. 1102 |
| BiRiLiG (DE) | Accounting Directives Act (*Bilanzrichtliniengesetz*) BGBl. I 1985, p. 2355 |
| CAC-40 (FR) | leading index of the Paris Stock Exchange |
| CAP (US) | Committee on Accounting Procedure |
| CASE (UK) | Committee on Accounting for Smaller Entities |
| CCAB (UK) | Consultative Committee of Accountancy Bodies |
| CICA | Canadian Institute of Chartered Accountants |
| CIPFA (UK) | Chartered Institute of Public Finance and Accountancy |

| | |
|---|---|
| CNC (FR) | National Accounting Council (*Conseil National de la Comptabilité*) |
| CNCC (FR) | National Institute of Statutory Auditors (*Compagnie Nationale des Commissaires aux Comptes*) |
| COB (FR) | Securities and Exchange Commission (*Commission des Opérations de Bourse*) |
| COFRI (JPN) | Corporation Finance Research Institute |
| CPA (JPN) | Certified Public Accountants |
| CRC (FR) | Accounting Regulation Committee (*Comité de la Réglementation Comptable*) |
| CU (FR) | Emergency Committee (*Comité d'urgence*) |
| DACA | Dominion Association of Canadian Accountants |
| DAI | *Deutsches Aktieninstitut* |
| DRS | German Financial Reporting Standards (*Deutsche Rechnungslegungs Standards*) |
| DTI (UK) | Department of Trade and Industry |
| EC | European Commission |
| ED | Exposure Draft |
| EEA | European Economic Area |
| EEC | European Economic Community |
| EFRAG | European Financial Reporting Advisory Group |
| EIC | Emerging Issues Committee |
| EITF | Emerging Issues Task Force |
| EU | European Union |
| FAF (US) | Financial Accounting Foundation |
| FASAC | Financial Accounting Standards Advisory Council |
| FASB (US) | Financial Accounting Standards Board |
| FASF (JPN) | Financial Accounting Standards Foundation |
| FDI | Foreign Direct Investment |
| FraCourt | French Court |
| FraGov | French Government |
| FRC (UK) | Financial Reporting Council |
| FSAJ | Financial Services Agency of Japan |
| FTSE 100 (UK) | leading index of the London Stock Exchange |
| G4 | Group of Four National Standard Setting Bodies |
| GAAP | Generally Accepted Accounting Principles |
| GASAC | Governmental Accounting Standards Advisory Council |
| GASB | German Accounting Standards Board (*Deutscher Standardisierungsrat*) |
| GDP | Gross Domestic Product |
| GerCourt | German Court |
| GerGov | German Government |
| HDAX (DE) | index of 110 companies with the highest market capitalisation in Germany |

| | |
|---|---|
| HGB (DE) | Commercial Code (*Handelsgesetzbuch*) RGBl. 1897, p. 219 most recent: BGBl. I 2011 pp. 288, 307 |
| IAASB | International Auditing and Assurance Standards Board |
| IAS | International Accounting Standards |
| IASB | International Accounting Standards Board |
| IASC | International Accounting Standards Committee |
| IASCF | International Accounting Standards Committee Foundation |
| ICAEW | Institute of Chartered Accountants of England and Wales |
| ICBAS (JPN) | Investing Committee on Business Accounting Systems |
| IDW (DE) | Institute of Auditors (*Institut der Wirtschaftsprüfer*) |
| IFAC | International Federation of Accountants |
| IFRIC | International Financial Reporting Interpretations Committee |
| IFRS | International Financial Reporting Standards |
| IMF | International Monetary Fund |
| IOSCO | International Organisation of Securities Commissions |
| IPO | Initial Public Offering |
| ISA | International Standards on Auditing |
| JapGov | Japanese Government |
| JFSA | Japanese Financial Services Agency |
| JICPA | Japanese Institute of Chartered Public Accountants |
| KapAEG (DE) | Capital Raising Facilitation Act (*Kapitalaufnahmeerleichterungsgesetz*) BGBl. I 1998, p. 707 |
| KonTraG (DE) | Corporate Sector Supervision and Transparency Act (*Gesetz zur Kontrolle und Transparenz im Unternehmensbereich*) BGBl. I 1998, p. 786 |
| LSE | London Stock Exchange |
| M&A | Mergers and Acquisitions |
| MJDS | Multi Jurisdictional Disclosure System |
| MNE | Multinational Entity |
| MOF | Ministry of Finance |
| MOJ | Ministry of Justice |
| NAFTA | North American Free Trade Agreement |
| NASDAQ (US) | National Association of Securities Dealers Automated |
| Nikkei 225 (JPN) | index of the Tokyo Stock Exchange |
| NYSE | New York Stock Exchange |
| OEC (FR) | Institute of Public Accountants (*Ordre des Experts Comptables*) |
| OECD | Organisation for Economic Cooperation and Development |
| OEEC | Organisation for European Economic Cooperation |

| | |
|---|---|
| OTC | Over the Counter |
| PCG (FR) | National Accounting Code (*Plan Comptable Général*) |
| RIC (DE) | Accounting Interpretations Committee (*Rechnungslegungs Interpretations Committee*) |
| SA (US) | Securities Act |
| SAC | Standard Advisory Council |
| SEA (US) | Securities Exchange Act |
| SEC (JPN) | Securities and Exchange Commission |
| SEC (US) | Securities and Exchange Commission |
| SEL (JPN) | Securities and Exchange Law |
| SIC | Standing Interpretation Committee |
| SME | Small and Medium Sized Entities |
| SOA (US) | Sarbanes-Oxley Act (Pub.L. 107-204, 116 Stat. 745) |
| S&P 100 (US) | leading index of the New York Stock Exchange |
| SWP | Strategy Working Party |
| TNC | Transnational Corporation |
| TransPuG (DE) | Transparency and Disclosure Act (*Transparenz- und Publizitätsgesetz*) BGBl. I 2002, p. 2681 |
| TSE | Tokyo Stock Exchange |
| TSE 60 (CDN) | leading index of the Toronto Stock Exchange |
| TUG (DE) | Transparency Directive Implementation Act (*Transparenzrichtlinien-Umsetzungsgesetz*) |
| UEC | Union Européen des Experts Comptables, Economiques et Financiers |
| UITF (UK) | Urgent Issues Task Force |
| UK | United Kingdom |
| UKGov | UK Government |
| UN | United Nations |
| UNCTAD | United Nations Conference on Trade and Development |
| UNESCO | United Nations Educational, Scientific and Cultural Organisation |
| USA | United States of America |
| USGov | US Government |
| WpHG (DE) | Securities Trading Act (*Wertpapierhandelsgesetz*) BGBl. I 1998, p. 2708 |
| WPK (DE) | Chamber of Public Accountants (*Wirtschaftsprüferkammer*) |
| WPO (DE) | Public Accountant Act (*Wirtschaftsprüferordnung*) |

# Part I

# Introduction

Many people believe that financial reporting is a merely technical matter, something discussed among professional circles but of only minor importance for the state, for society or for the economy as a whole. However, a closer look reveals how important financial reporting and its regulation are for the functioning of businesses and markets. Financial accounting makes an important contribution to general welfare, and consequently nation states have often intervened in accounting regulation. Traditionally, regulation has varied from country to country. Continental European countries have tended to rely more strongly on extensive legal and hierarchical regulation than have Anglo-Saxon ones, which have generally demonstrated more collaborative governance modes: i.e., types of regulation in which private actors – most prominently private standard-setters and other professional organisations – have been embedded within regulatory frameworks. Nevertheless, the different solutions have shared one common feature: they have all been rooted in the nation states in which they operated. However, in an increasingly globalised world, these national solutions have become more and more inefficient and ineffective.

As a consequence, a new constellation of accounting regulation has emerged since the 1990s. The most distinctive feature of this new constellation is the presence of a transnational standard-setter that produces financial reporting rules with global outreach: the International Accounting Standards Board (IASB). Many countries require these rules to be applied when supplying information about the financial position of economic entities or, more technically speaking, for consolidated financial reports.[1] This development marks a vast formal convergence of regulation, both in terms of applicable accounting rules and in accounting governance. However, traditional national accounting rules persist in some, mostly continental, European countries, where they remain applicable when preparing financial statements of private (i.e., unlisted) firms and unconsolidated accounts. This hybridisation has hardly been addressed in the literature, leaving two important questions unanswered. First, what are the underlying causes of the observed changes? And second, are these observable changes indicative of an overall transformation of the state? Chapter 1 aims at laying down some theoretical foundations that will help us to answer both questions in the course of this book. This explanatory framework is based on evolutionary economics. It argues that the recent changes to accounting systems can be explained as reactions of economic agents to exogenous 'shocks' such as globalisation. This has led to changes in national accounting systems. Bounded rationality suggests that these changes should in general lead to a convergence of accounting systems worldwide, due to mimicking, normative pressure or coercion. In the process of change, existing national institutions matter as they have a bearing on the decisions that are made. Thus, different paths and paces of change are likely to emerge. Empirical evidence taken from studies of six countries helps to validate the outlined case.

Chapter 1, which is setting the scene, is organised as follows: first we summarise the evidence relating to changes in accounting regulation (Section 1.1); then in sections 1.2 and 1.3 we develop a general framework that helps explain why some elements of accounting regulation are becoming more similar while others continue to vary from country to country. We argue that evolutionary economics, in particular, combined with neo-institutional thinking provides a comprehensive framework to explain the observed changes.

# 1
# Explaining the Evolution of a New Accounting Framework

## 1.1 Accounting between global convergence and national preference

In recent years a new architecture of accounting regulation has evolved. Most notably, an international private (i.e., transnational) standard-setter has emerged that develops financial reporting standards with global reach – the International Financial Reporting Standards (IFRS). The standard-setter's efforts have been backed by many national governments, which have prescribed the adoption of the transnationally set standards for at least subgroups of firms, particularly those listed on public markets. The reporting demands are supposedly better met by globally uniform, high-quality standards developed by an international professional body. The rapid adoption of international standards has led to an increasing formal convergence of accounting standards across the world and has come about in a rather sudden and abrupt manner, as the notion of the 'global IFRS revolution' suggests (Benzacar 2008; Chua and Taylor 2008).

Even for listed firms, some doubts remain about whether formal convergence of the rules actually goes hand in hand with an actual convergence of accounting practices at company level (Ball 2006). This is even more the case as the revolutionary character of the regulatory changes has very often left reporting firms without any implementation guidance (Schipper 2005). As yet, enforcement mechanisms are also not consistent globally (Ball 2006; Zimmermann et al. 2008a) and the convergence process has largely been confined to the consolidated accounts of listed companies. In most countries, private unlisted companies still have to report following national accounting rules, which has resulted in inconsistencies in the national accounting systems (Werner and Zimmermann 2008). Even more strikingly, unconsolidated 'parent-only' accounts sometimes still have to be prepared in addition to consolidated IFRS accounts (Goncharov et al. 2009). This hybridisation implies that a single organisation has to prepare two different sets of accounts – consolidated group accounts and unconsolidated parent-only accounts – following two different sets of rules: IFRS are used for one, national rules for the other. The reason for this surprisingly robust hybrid solution is that the two accounts are said to serve different purposes: consolidated accounts inform outsiders about the financial position of the economic entity in which they are invested. Where nation states require additional (unconsolidated) accounts according to national rules, they have tied legal consequences to them: most notably, determination of dividend and tax payments.

Over all, unconsolidated accounts are embedded more strongly in the national socio-economic systems and thus are more resistant to harmonisation. The same is true of the reporting practices of small and medium-sized firms which have not outgrown the boundaries of national regulation. Thus, the state of play is that we have increasing transnationalisation on the one hand, but some strongly persistent national differences on the other. These findings will be shown at the country level in Chapter 4, where we analyse regulatory changes in six major Organisation for Economic Cooperation and Development (OECD) countries (Canada, Germany, France, Japan, the UK and the US). We provide evidence that there were, traditionally, substantial differences in accounting regulation across countries, that there has been significant convergence, but that some elements of accounting regulation still vary from one nation state to another. Evidence for these three findings is summarised in the following:

- *Traditional differences in regulation*. Our six countries traditionally relied on different governance models. France, Germany and Japan belong to a group of countries with a long-standing tradition of state-dominated accounting regulation. In the 1970s these countries had accounting rules with strong legal backing, as they were mainly set by parliaments in the form of laws. The incorporation of private actors in standard-setting was of minor relevance. Professional bodies regulated their members' behaviour but held no further powers over accounting regulation. These countries also featured a strong interrelation between financial reporting and tax accounting, and their use of accounting was predominantly payout-oriented (Werner and Zimmermann 2009). In contrast, Canada, the UK and the US represent countries where accounting regulation originated in the private sector and remained dominated by professional self-regulation. Legal backing was traditionally more limited in these countries, as rules were privately set. The legal system in these countries gives little payout relevance to financial reports, as tax and dividends were calculated by other means (Goncharov et al. 2009).
- *Convergence*. Over the last decades, the number of modes of governance has increasingly diminished. Accounting systems strongly reliant on the state have incorporated private actors to enhance market efficiency, while liberal accounting systems have strengthened the legal backing for

accounting rules to provide them with greater legitimacy (Luthardt and Zimmermann 2009). These developments seem to have been largely influenced by harmonised requirements for accounting regulations through globalised financial markets (see Chapter 5). International competition for funds meant that the provision of information for capital markets became an increasingly important accounting function, and today it is featured in the accounting systems of all the six countries in this study. The harmonisation of regulatory needs also initiated the search for a global set of comparable accounting standards. The ongoing internationalisation of accounting standards had a major impact on most accounting systems, as international rules were adopted or mimicked in national ones. A strong tendency for accounting systems to converge can thus be seen in each country.

- *Persistence*. The analysis of the national case studies also reveals differences in the pace of change. With regard to the predominant uses of accounting, convergence is only visible with consolidated accounts. Single accounts in France, Germany and Japan remain largely unaffected by the harmonisation process. Their function as a way of determining corporate payouts remains unaltered, as do the accounting regulations for single accounts. Rapid change took place only in some areas, while others saw only incremental reform. Information-oriented accounting is provided for the economic entity in consolidated accounts, and single accounts, which are relevant for determining corporate payouts, still diverge between countries with different regulatory traditions. For these countries (France, Germany and Japan) a stable level of legal backing points to ongoing differences in the relationship between accounting and tax and company law.

Different paths and differences in the pace of change have not yet been addressed and explained in the literature. Comparative accounting research, the strand of literature to which we contribute, has largely focused on static comparisons: i.e., on comparing accounting systems (and their embeddedness) across countries at a given point in time (Werner and Zimmermann 2009). Differences in legal and financial systems but also in culture are identified as driving differences in accounting systems and their respective modes of governance (Werner 2008). However, there are several research gaps in this strand of literature. First, the role of the state seems to have been largely neglected in previous analyses. Second, static comparisons do not account for changes over time. The main explanation for change in static explanations would be that the variables causing differences in accounting systems – for example, legal and financial systems – change over time. Even though there is some evidence that those legal and financial systems do gradually reconfigure, the consequences for financial reporting have not been explicitly addressed in comparative accounting research. This may be due to the fact that these reconfigurations are incremental rather than revolutionary. Moreover, third, comparative accounting research has not addressed the question of why these incremental changes take place. To the degree that the institutional structures evolve, they seem to be endogenous to more fundamental drivers (or triggers) of change, which have not been identified in previous research. The latter could be related to a fundamental change in the individual national statehood that, fourth, has not been addressed in comparative accounting research.

## 1.2 Explaining the change of accounting systems: A framework for analysis

In the following, we attempt to explain the observed different paths and paces of change in accounting regulation, which can be understood as a process of self-transformation triggered by the decisions of individual or collective actors. The process takes place in two phases:

- Agents react to exogenous 'shocks' such as globalisation, which require decisions to change national accounting systems currently in place. These alterations should generally lead to worldwide convergence of accounting regulation, due to mimicking, normative pressure or coercion.
- In the process of change, existing national institutions matter as they constrain the agents' scope in altering system elements. As a consequence, the exogenous 'shocks' can result in different paths and differences in the pace of change.

The explanatory approach thus calls for an investigation into the role of two distinct types of explanatory variables. First, we consider the influence of variables triggering agents' decisions in regard to general system change (triggering events or exogenous shocks). Here we examine, in particular, the role of globalisation, emerging professional networks and corporate crises. Unconstrained by institutional arrangements, these factors should lead to coercive, normative and mimetic isomorphism of accounting regulation. However, the existing institutional frameworks within countries do limit the agents' decisions and create path dependencies. Thus, we have to take into account a second group of variables that characterise the institutional framework giving rise to path dependencies. Here we analyse the role of national socio-economic systems, in particular the legal and financial system and the type of welfare state in place.

Our framework refers to evolutionary economics, which seems a promising starting point. Evolutionary economics is an approach that helps to explain processes of change by looking at the individual behaviour of agents assumed to act under bounded rationality. The application of evolutionary theory to economic phenomena has produced a lot of research findings in recent years. Meanwhile, it can be regarded as an established school of thought in analysing economic problems (Witt 2008). It is one of the few research paradigms that are not static in nature and thus can be particularly useful when analysing phenomena of economic change or other dynamic processes. While it is often thought that evolutionary theory is, more or less, an adaptation of the Darwinian theory of natural selection, this is not necessarily true for evolutionary economics. The main reason for this is that natural selection does not necessarily extend to 'selection' processes in social systems, because human beings are capable of thoughts and feelings and of social interaction. As Witt (2002) argues, evolutionary economics instead understands evolution as a self-transformation process of a particular system. Even though there does not seem to be a generally agreed definition of evolutionary economics, it is usually built on the following three premises:

- Evolution of economic systems can be understood as a process of self-transformation triggered from within by the learning and innovations of economic agents, who are characterised by bounded rationality.
- Preferences, technologies and institutions are not treated as exogenous but become explicit objects of analysis.
- Evolutionary processes are not erratic but follow regular patterns, on which explanatory hypotheses can be based.

In the following, we briefly outline how the three premises are applied to explain the emergence of a new constellation of accounting regulation. System change is triggered from within by learning and by innovating economic agents who are characterised by bounded rationality. Our explanatory model assumes that regulatory and other economic actors induce change when triggering events occur. Owing to the fact that individual and collective actors are embedded in the systems which are subject to change, system transformation is always self-transformation (Witt 2008). We thus follow an actor-centred view when explaining processes of change, referring to DiMaggio and Powell (1983), who describe the behaviour of economic agents as showing three different ways of institutional learning, which they label as mimetic, normative and coercive (Csigó 2006). In what follows, we outline how these types of institutional learning by economic agents may affect accounting regulation:

- *Coercive isomorphism.* This type of isomorphism stems mainly from pressure by other organisations and by cultural expectations. We argue that coercive isomorphism in accounting regulation stems mainly from reporting demands on globalised capital markets. As projects continue to grow in size, firms need to compete for funds internationally. Self-financing from retained earnings or tapping into national markets is no longer sufficient. Competing for international funds makes it necessary to respond to the demand of financial investors for comparable high-quality information. Financial reports that are hard to understand deter investors, or they require a risk premium. High-risk premiums either devalue the firm or squeeze it out of the capital markets as competing projects from other firms gain preference. Globalised financial markets introduce pressure for financial accounts to look alike, leading to coercive isomorphism. Chapter 5 of this book takes a closer look at the role of coercive isomorphism.

- *Mimetic isomorphism*. In general, mimetic isomorphism refers to the reactions of organisations facing environmental uncertainty or doubts about organisational technologies. They tend to model themselves on other organisations that are considered successful at that time. We argue that, in particular, cases of fraud, accounting scandals and business crises lead to a mimicking reaction by accounting regulators (Chua and Taylor 2008). The reason is that such events raise public doubt about the suitability of national regulation. Regulators react to public concerns by creating new regulation. New regulation, then, is likely to be a transplant of regulation found in other countries that at that time do not suffer from scandals or fraud. There are primarily two paths by which crises can lead to mimetic isomorphism. First, a revision of its own system starts in one country because accounting scandals have occurred there. It may then subsequently adopt reforms modelled on regulation in other countries. Second, the appearance of accounting scandals in another country may alert the home regulator. In both cases uncertainty about the stability of particular elements or about the stability of the system as a whole is the driving force behind the search for different solutions. From a legitimacy perspective, the regulator is threatened by a loss of confidence in his ability 'to maintain or establish effective normative structures in the extent required' (Habermas 1973) after such cases attract public interest. By announcing and implementing reforms, the regulator focuses the public's attention on administrative issues, preventing the institution itself from scrutiny (Sikka and Willmott 1995). Uncertain about which alterations are feasible, the regulator starts to look for sets of apparently better working systems in other jurisdictions, hoping to find adequate reforms for their own arrangements. This leads to the adoption of regulations from other systems. Chapter 6 takes a closer look at the role of mimetic isomorphism.
- *Normative isomorphism*. Finally, normative pressures can be a driver for isomorphic change of organisations. Such pressures are supposed to originate mainly from professions and networks that influence the agents' behaviour. Thus, the background and training of agents belonging to a particular profession may contribute to the emergence of normative isomorphism. The internationalisation of service markets gives rise to

economies of scale for accounting firms: their services can be offered outside their domestic markets if the services meet the customers' expectations. Accounting firms therefore have an interest in making their offerings more homogeneous and also in homogenising the expectations and interests of their clients. This is first done by building networks, in which ideas are exchanged, but becomes even more powerful when these networks can shape the demands of customers: e.g., by interfering with regulation. Chapter 7 takes a closer look at the role of normative isomorphism.

Changes induced by mimetic, normative and coercive learning of agents are in line with the assumption of bounded rationality as the change of structures does not necessarily lead to (global) efficiency. The triggering events for change simply lead to the perception that the regulatory solutions in place are outdated and no longer appropriate to cope with new challenges. Economic agents will thus respond to the triggering events by altering accounting practices and regulation – but without knowing what the best solution (the global optimum) would look like. Bounded rationality thus means that the systems are changed by different patterns of institutional learning.

## 1.3 Institutions as explicit objects of analysis

A country's institutions shape the behaviour of economic agents. Within each country, several 'layers' of institutions exist. North (1990) defines institutions as 'the rules of the game in a society or, more formally, the humanly devised constraints that shape human interactions'. In this respect, the institutions forming the socio-economic system are the most fundamental and relatively stable 'rules of the game' to which we restrict our analysis. Institutions develop to solve predominant coordination problems within economic systems. From an institutional perspective, accounting itself can be regarded as a complementary institution which co-evolves with the more general or underlying institutional structure.

We examine particularly the roles of legal and financial systems in the country in question, but also the type of welfare state, which we regard as a missing link in comparative accounting research (Oehr and Zimmermann 2012). Regulatory and economic actors have to account for the 'top' institutional structures in place as they will directly influence their decision-making: they affect contracting and other agency costs and also shape the demands of voters in relation to the political system and the decisions of regulatory actors. In the following, we outline how institutional structures may impact the paths and paces of accounting change.

- *Impact of legal systems on changes in accounting regulation*. Following on from findings in the law and finance literature (see, e.g., La Porta et al.

1997), it was argued that legal systems and, connectedly, the degree of investor protection explain to a large extent – albeit not exclusively – differences in accounting regulation between countries (Bushman et al. 2004). Legal systems can differ in the way in which equity investors are protected, but also in the way and in the extent to which the accounting system is used to protect stakeholders. On the one hand, the legal system may grant participation and monitoring rights (Siems 2005a). In this case the rules are interventionist and form standardised contracts between management and owners. The focus of the governance will be on long-term orientation. Accounting will have to be aligned by the state to the standardised contracts. On the other hand, the legal system may emphasise self-protection by information. In this case arrangements will be more open and flexible.

- *Impact of financial systems on changes in accounting regulation.* Financial systems refer to financing preferences and institutions in developed capitalist economies. Hackethal et al. (2006) define financial systems as 'comprising both supply and demand, which is determined by the use that nonfinancial or real sector units make of financial services offered by the financial sector'. Typical features of financial systems are thus country-specific financing preferences, the size and depth of capital markets, the proportions of public and private firms and the existence of an active market for corporate control. In outsider economies equity capital is more important than debt capital (Wüstemann 2003), and debt raised on markets is more important than credit raised through banks. Outsider systems show a dispersed ownership/holdership in contrast to the family-dominated and bank-financed entities in insider economies. As a result, the information asymmetries of shareholders in outsider economies are higher. Shares in insider economies are mostly held by well-informed block-holders such as families, other companies or the state. The analogue is true for debt, with a particular role being played by the main financing bank. Hence, nation states as well as the involved private actors have different interests concerning financial reporting. In outsider systems the demand for investor protection is higher, and consequently the basic objective of accounting is to provide useful information for making financial decisions; the basic objective of accounting in insider economies is the protection of creditors.
- *Impact of the type of welfare state on changes in accounting regulation.* Several studies found evidence that culture has an impact on the shape of accounting systems and practices. However, there are serious concerns about using culture as a moderating variable (Baskerville 2003). We thus propose to take a more societal view by looking at the type of welfare state. This is pretty much in line with Bhimani (1999), who argues that relatively permanent societal features influencing a country's institutions and business exist, but that analyses of their mediating influences should

rather focus on the 'effects of societal features such as the educational system, the forms of social stratification, the vocational training programs in place, and the division of labour'. We posit that differences in the type of welfare state explain differences of accounting systems and thus may also affect the ways in which they are altered. Societal motives and value judgements play a substantial role in determining accounting systems. We differentiate between two types of welfare state: residual and institutional. Societal attitudes expressed in both welfare-state models are likely to reflect a country's prevalent aims and goals of accounting. They, in turn, determine how the societally important sets of company accounts are regulated: residual welfare states emphasise the allocative function and leave regulation to private bodies, and institutional welfare states emphasise the distributive nature of accounting and allocate regulation to the state. Convergence occurs only in the area that is irrelevant for the regulatory impetus of the welfare state – i.e., group accounts – as they do not serve a legally binding function.

## 1.4 Summary

This chapter outlines the framework used throughout this book to analyse and explain the recent changes in financial accounting regulation. Our starting point was the idea that there is strong evidence for international harmonisation and new modes of governance. In the new constellation of accounting regulation, private and international actors play a more vital role, indicating a move towards a more transnational type of regulation. Based on a framework informed by evolutionary economics, we showed that the emergence of the new constellation of accounting regulation can be regarded as an outcome of self-transformation triggered by exogenous shocks (globalisation, crises and ideologies, leading to coercive, mimetic and normative isomorphism, respectively). The analysis, however, also reveals that there are persisting differences in accounting regulation and that these differences can be explained by path dependencies triggered by the relative stability of legal and financial systems and of the welfare states (still) in place. While this chapter (and, more generally, this book), on the surface, deals with accounting issues, it can also make a case exemplary for a more fundamental change in the state, for three reasons in particular. First, the drivers of change (globalisation, crises, networking) are general ones that also extend to other policy fields. Their influence is thus likely to extend to further policy fields. Our general prediction would therefore be that the drivers of change generally lead to diminishing regulatory differences between nation states. Second, we have shown that moderating factors – such as legal, financial and welfare systems – still differ at the national level and that the shape of these systems affects (and hinders quick) harmonisation of accounting regimes. Again, this finding seems generalisable. But, more importantly, we find that the identified systems at the national levels are also subject to change. In our view, this directly refers to (and is evidence for) a change of statehood. Third, our evidence suggests that the process of change can be regarded as a process of self-transformation, as changes have been triggered by economic agents. The consequences of the changes, however, have not fully been anticipated; thus, the outcomes of the process do not necessarily reflect what was on the political agenda. This can be seen especially as national regulatory actors at times still try to intervene in accounting regulation, although these efforts are increasingly meaningless. This probably requires a reconfiguration of statehood at a higher, international, level, reinforcing the change of statehood.

However, the new constellation has not yet proved to be stable, and its weaknesses have not fully been addressed. There is probably a lack of legitimisation of the transnational standard-setters that have entered the stage (Luthardt and Zimmermann 2009). Also, the quality of the rules set by these institutions is at stake, particularly in the wake of the recent financial crisis. Very often they do not seem to complement the enduring parts of national regulation. Hence, it remains unclear whether this points to problems of adaptation or to more fundamental construction problems in the new constellation – a question requiring further research. Changes thus might, at least to some extent, be only transitory. Further change is therefore on the cards, and the outcomes in terms of welfare and legitimisation are still unclear.

# Part II

# Accounting between Global Convergence and National Preference

Accounting provides problem solutions not only for economic transactions but also for societal problems such as achieving allocative efficiency and distributional justice. While the logic of economic transactions is more or less uniform and gravitates towards convergence, national preferences for particular solutions may erect barriers to harmonisation. This part of the book provides empirical evidence for convergence, analyses the elements for societal interventions and gives a country-by-country account of harmonisation efforts and successes.

Chapter 2 tells the global success story of accounting harmonisation with the spreading of IFRS. It outlines the economic arguments for convergence at the company level and provides current data on IFRS adoption. It also introduces the ideological foundations on which accounting convergence rests: professional self-regulation and information accounting. Both elements are often merely seen as the modernisation of accounting and a separation of economic activity from the state, but they are also representative for a trend towards neo-liberalism and financialisation in market activities.

The emphasis on self-regulation and information accounting in the wake of neo-liberalism and financialisation can easily cause us to lose sight of other functions that accounting fulfils and that cannot easily be delegated to experts and markets. Chapter 3 therefore sets out the broad range of functions and instruments in accounting. This range is available and potentially important not only to economic actors but also to the state. The state can make use of accounting in number of ways: in company law, to mitigate conflicts between owners, creditors and managers; in securities law, to ensure fair trade on equity and bond markets; and in tax law, to achieve an equitable burden to finance state activities. Chapter 3 demonstrates the linkages between instruments such as company and group accounts, valuation rules based on prudence or full information and the societal functions of conflict resolution, capital market efficiency and tax collection. Conflicting goals will make it likely that a number of reporting instruments will ensue, each regulated in different intensity by the state or professionals respectively.

Chapter 4 sketches the developments of accounting regulation in some detail in six country cases: Canada, France, Germany, Japan, the UK and the US. The countries represent different traditions how they organise their legal, financial and economic systems. The country systems vary in terms of the intensity of state intervention and supra-national integration. The accounting regulation of each of the six countries can be characterised in relation to four features: the predominant use of accounting, its legal backing, the extent of professional self-regulation and the degree of internationalisation. The analysis takes up the instruments and functions from the previous chapters and asks, for instance, whether resolving conflict or informing markets was and is the primary use of accounting. It looks at the intensity of state intervention when considering the legal backing. The capacity for expert-led accounting rules as well as the readiness for convergence is addressed by the latter two aspects.

Part II reveals that accounting converges for capital markets. Information accounting and professional self-regulation are the commonly accepted regulatory type. However, accounting functions and instruments are not harmonised across the board, nor do they converge. States such as France, Germany and Japan which have used accounting for state intervention still rely strongly on nationally regulated accounts. We are witnessing a hybridisation of accounting: globally converged for capital markets but following national preferences in all other areas. Explanations for both developments will be provided in Part III and Part IV respectively.

# 2
# Information Accounting: The Global IFRS Revolution

## 2.1 Introduction: Rationales for a common set of accounting standards

Over the past few years the desire to create a global set of accounting rules has led to an ever increasing use of the IFRS released by the IASB. Today, IFRS are internationally the dominant set of accounting standards. The IASB has come to predominate over other international bodies concerned with international accounting issues, such as the OECD Working Group on Accounting Standards, the UN Intergovernmental Working Group of Experts on International Standards of Accounting and Reporting and the European Union's Accounting Advisory Forum. This development had already been foreseen as long ago as 1976, by Sir Henry Benson, the founding chairman of the IASB's predecessor, the International Accounting Standards Committee (IASC), who predicted that the organisation's standards would become dominant by about the turn of the millennium (Benson 1976). At the time this seemed like wild speculation, or at least hyperbole, but it has become a reality – and within the predicted time span – at least for listed companies.

The rise of IFRS is often analysed with the terminology of convergence. In social and political science, the term 'convergence' defines the tendency of societies or policies to resemble one another ever more closely. The concept is thus related to the development of similarities in structure, process and performance (Kerr 1983; Drezner 2001): for example, convergence towards a common set of legal rules (Coffee 2000a). 'Convergence' can also be used to describe the result of a process that has led to an alignment of national policies over the course of time. In general, convergence occurs by the transfer or the diffusion of policies, programmes and ideas. Transfer connotates the transmission from one system to another (Dolowitz and Marsh 1996), while 'diffusion' describes the interconnected adoption within a larger group (Elkins and Simmons 2005). Hence 'diffusion' refers more to a spatio-temporal proliferation of certain policies than 'transfer', which instead deals with bilateral adoption. While the 'transfer' or 'diffusion' models differ in their account of how convergence occurs, both terms and definitions specify that adoption is voluntary.

Convergence is, first and foremost, triggered by the increasing international interconnections of nation states and societies, visible in economic and political interdependences of markets and nation states, respectively (Holzinger et al. 2007).[1] In such an interconnected world there are advantages to convergence, which mainly stem from welfare gains through standardisation. In this context 'standardisation' describes the process of creating and establishing subject-specific rules for specifications, methods, definitions, procedures or practices (Bowker and Star 2000). If there are different standards at the local level, every nation state gains its own advantages from the local standardisation, but the sum of the gains at the national level is lower than the total possible gains from one single standard. The adoption and diffusion of a single set of standards – be it those of an individual country or those of an international standard-setter – yields joint advantages and larger economies of scale. This gives rise to welfare gains as standardisation overcomes spatial or temporal distances and thus creates comparability, coordination and cooperation beyond national borders (Brunsson and Jacobsson 2000). For accounting standards, the main argument for standardisation is that mutually agreed-upon standards help to reduce transaction costs. Not only do preparers of financial accounts benefit but so do those who use them, such as investors or financial analysts, or auditors and regulating authorities. Generally, it is assumed that over all the costs of information processing will diminish when a shared body of accounting standards is adopted (Barth et al. 2008).

The literature lists multiple benefits for a common set of accounting standards. The first set of arguments revolves around the functioning of capital markets and the ensuing higher liquidity and lower cost of capital. Commonly used accounting standards reduce the burden of cross-listings on international capital markets as companies are not obliged to prepare different sets of financial accounts (Covrig et al. 2007). Furthermore, listing costs can also be lower than on the domestic market if the transaction costs for listings on foreign markets are lower (Stapleton and Subrahmanyam 1977; Daske et al. 2008). Apart from that, cross-listing induces informational advantages such as analyst coverage, media presence or visibility through public scrutiny (Benos and Weisbach 2004). Next to these examples of cost-saving potential, a single set of accounts will further the integration of capital markets. Integration results in lower cost of capital for companies as these costs tend to be higher in segmented than in integrated markets (Errunza and Losq 1985; Alexander et al. 1987). In addition, it would be easier for companies to raise external capital on larger capital markets with probably higher liquidity, which in turn may lower the cost of equity capital as these are usually higher in relatively small and sparsely traded markets. Conversely, the liquidity and efficiency of domestic capital markets could similarly improve if the adopted accounting standards raise the transparency and quality levels of financial reporting. This increase attracts investment inflows and helps expand the investor base, which improves risk-sharing and reduces the cost of capital (Merton 1987).

The second set of arguments revolves around the preparers and deals with a more individualised, non-market-based use of accounts in an international context. It runs as follows. A common set of standards will make it easier for companies with subsidiaries in foreign countries to prepare consolidated accounts. If the same accounting rules apply to all kinds of financial accounts, companies will not have to deal with different national accounting standards. This, in turn, reduces time-consuming as well as costly reconciliation processes for consolidated accounts and slashes accounting expenditures. Common standards allow built-up core capabilities in accounting within companies to be easily transferred and utilised across the globe (Choi and Meek 2008). The same will also apply to auditing companies. Further, a familiar set of accounting standards makes international business relationships with suppliers or customers less difficult. Strategic decision-making by companies in the area of cross-border mergers and acquisitions (M&A) will improve as intra- and inter-sectoral comparability and transparency advances (Wagenhofer 2008). In addition, a decrease in information costs helps promote synergetic cooperation between companies. All these benefits can be expected to be even greater, the more internationally active a company is.

The third set of arguments emphasises how common accounting standards will help facilitation of business activities. Common accounting standards help investors and financial analysts to understand accounts better as corrections in order to make financial reports more internationally comparable are no longer necessary (Ball 2006). Users of financial statements are not constrained by their limited knowledge of different accounting standards. The acquired accounting skills about the common set of standards allow cross-country financial data to be processed. Consequently, the costs of investors and financial analysts using financial information decrease as the time required to understand and convert financial statements declines. Global accounting standards enable investors to filter out more favourable investment opportunities, which allow them to diversify their portfolio investments and thereby reduce risks (Nicolaisen 2005; Ball 2006). Furthermore, the facilitation of cross-border acquisition or divestitures could even increase the takeover premiums which remunerate existing investors (Bradley et al. 1988). All in all, a consistent overall presentation of companies' financial results sustains investor confidence, which could, conversely, be negatively affected if the disclosed financial information varies according to which set of accounting standards are applied (Box 2.1).

**Box 2.1 Company cases of distortive effects**

An example of the distortive effects of applying different national accounting standards to international operating companies is presented by Nobes and Parker (2006). In 1995 the equity of Glaxo Wellcome PLC (UK) reported under UK Generally Accepted Accounting Principles (GAAP) was £91 million, but adjusted to US GAAP the equity rocketed to £8,168 million, which equals a rise of 8,876 per cent.

A much more anecdotal example, which caused a stir in the beginning of the 1990s, was the case of Daimler Benz AG (Germany). In 1993 Daimler Benz AG applied for a listing on the New York Stock Exchange (NYSE) (Radebaugh et al. 1995). To meet the listing requirements, it had to reconcile their German GAAP accounting data to US GAAP, which led to significant differences between the net income and equity reported. Net income reported under German GAAP was DM602 million, and the equity amounted to a total of DM17,584 million. After several necessary adjustments the net income according to US GAAP was minus DM1,839 million (405 per cent lower) and the equity DM26,281 million (49 per cent higher). Investors were irritated by these accounting figures and were beset by doubts about which set of standards gave the true data (Flower 2004).

A more contemporary example of the distortive effects of substantive accounting differences, this time give from US GAAP to IFRS, concerns the consolidated account of Deutsche Bank AG (Germany) from 2007. For instance, Deutsche Bank AG disclosed, previous to the IFRS reconciliation, total assets of €992 billion. Reconciled to IFRS, the total assets increased by approximately 46 per cent to €1,449 billion. As with other similar cases, the effect stems from reclassification and revaluation requirements under IFRS.

These examples show that differences in accounting can severely damage the credibility of the practice in general. Therefore, on the whole, comparability and transparency are the main focus of a common set of accounting standards to optimise global capital allocation (van Zandt 2005; Chua and Taylor 2008).

## 2.2 The genesis of the IASB and IFRS

### 2.2.1 Early macro-level endeavours at standardisation

Early attempts to unify accounting standards were made several decades ago. Already in the late 1940s and early 1950s internationally comparable financial accounts appeared on the agenda (Botzem and Quack 2005b). The discussions were initiated by the announcement of the European Recovery Program (the Marshall Plan) by the US government in 1947 and the formation of the Organisation for European Economic Cooperation (OEEC) in 1948. Both initiatives aimed at a closer transatlantic cooperation, which made a minimum comparability of statistical data about economic development and public expenditures vital especially for the distribution of US financial aid in the course of the Marshall Plan. In this context, the international comparability discussion gained momentum and became part of the agenda of other intergovernmental organisations. In 1953 the OEEC and the United Nations (UN) separately issued standardised systems of national income accounts. The two were finally consolidated in 1956 (Samuels and Piper 1985).

The Marshall Plan also gave a further impulse for international harmonisation to financial accounts at the firm level. The rebuilding of Europe's industries after the Second World War also involved an exchange of ideas between European and US experts, involving politicians, managers and professional experts, such as the accounting profession (Djelic 2001). To that effect, the community concerned with accounting and with the discussion about its global standardisation broadened. Such debates took place primarily at international accounting conferences and were therefore restricted to a small group of academics. The dissemination of US accounting ideas and techniques largely revolved around management accounting issues such as budgeting and costing methods. Nevertheless, the exchange between those experts created an awareness of issues related to financial reporting.

Shortly afterwards, the United Nations Educational, Scientific and Cultural Organisation (UNESCO) proposed the establishment of an International Institute of Accountancy under its patronage (Samuels and Piper 1985). However, this proposal never came to fruition, mainly because of resistance and scepticism on the part of the European accounting professions, who had no confidence in the idea of global cooperation in accounting. However, some professional European accounting associations decided to find their own way of achieving greater comparability of corporate financial statements. So in 1951 the Union Européenne des Experts Comptables, Economiques et Financiers (UEC) was founded, which hosted 27 accounting professions from 19 countries until the late 1970s (Samuels and Piper 1985; Camfferman and Zeff 2007). The original ten accounting bodies were from Austria, Belgium, France, Germany, Italy, Luxembourg, the Netherlands, Portugal, Spain and Switzerland. Twelve years later, in 1963, the accountancy bodies of Denmark, Ireland, Norway, Sweden and the UK joined the UEC. But the UEC's ability to achieve greater comparability of financial accounts remained quite modest.

Some years later, the European Economic Community (EEC) started a programme to harmonise its member states' financial accounting. Although the initiative was largely propelled by public actors, the EEC was supported by the Groupe d'Etudes, which was formed by the EEC in 1966 as advisory group for special issues (Botzem and Quack 2005b). The Groupe d'Etudes provided accounting experts with a supranational forum for cross-border discussion and cooperation. However, this group was restricted to members from the European Economic Community.[2] In the same year, the Accountants International Study Group (AISG) was set up to further international cooperation between accountants in Canada, the UK and the US (Camfferman and Zeff 2007). It was dissolved 11 years later, in 1977, after publishing several comparative studies and comprehensive brochures dealing with accounting issues in the three member countries. The AISG was the initiative of Sir Henry Benson, who was the president of the Institute of Chartered Accountants of England and Wales (ICAEW) and a forward-looking thinker on professional matters. Initially, the AISG consisted of representatives from the Canadian Institute of Chartered Accountants (CICA), the American Institute of Certified Public Accountants (AICPA) and professional accounting associations from the UK. The representatives were principally well-known practitioners from international accounting firms, who represented their accounting body. However, there was no real international collaboration between accountants until 1973, the year in which the IASC was founded, the organisation that eventually developed into today's IASB. Almost simultaneously, an interest in international accounting harmonisation started to grow among academics: the first publications in academic journals started to appear in the mid-1960s, and by now such publications have become more mainstream (Baker and Barbu 2007).

### 2.2.2 The rise of the IASB: The organisational view on accounting

The IASC, the precursor of today's standard-setter, did not emerge spontaneously in 1973. The idea of setting up an international committee for accounting standards originated with Sir Henry Benson (Flower 2004), who proposed and discussed the expansion of the AIGS's activities at a private meeting at the Tenth International Congress of Accountants in Sydney in 1972 (Mennicken and Heßling 2007). The members agreed that the key future task of the AIGS should be the formulation of accounting standards that would gain global acceptance (Véron 2007). Additional members from countries other than Canada, the UK and the US needed to be involved, and the organisational structure had to be strengthened (Camfferman and Zeff 2007). In a second meeting, in December 1972, the same participants considered the idea of not using the shell of the AISG but of creating a new organisation – the IASC – to exist in parallel to the AISG. In March 1973 representatives of accounting bodies from Australia, Germany, Japan, Mexico and the Netherlands were invited to an informal meeting in London, where these ideas were discussed. Following this meeting, the participants met again on 29 June 1973 to finalise and sign an agreement to establish the IASC. Sir Henry Benson was elected chairman of the newly created IASC, which soon eclipsed the AISG's activities.

An implicit motive behind the establishment of the IASC was a desire to counterbalance the harmonisation endeavours of the European Economic Community (EEC). Harmonisation efforts were stepped up with the accession of the UK to the EEC in 1973 (Hopwood 1994). The UK's membership was a game-changer, as the early blueprints of the newly developed European accounting directives were influenced by the Continental European paradigm of accounting, and the UK would have suffered from substantial changes in the accounting landscape. A probably more important reason to establish the IASC, however, was the growing demand for improved and aligned financial accounts for multinational entities (MNE), an aim already outlined in the IASC's first constitution (Haller et al. 2000). From the outset, the IASC pursued the goals of formulating and publishing, in the public interest, accounting standards for financial accounts and of promoting their global acceptance. The Committee extended its view from a narrow American–European focus, in particular to help the newly independent countries of the Commonwealth in developing reliable accounting practices.

The IASC drew its membership from the International Federation of Accountants (IFAC), and from 1983 all members of the IFAC were automatically members of the IASC (Flower 1997). At its peak the IASC therefore included 138 member organisations, from 112 countries. However, within the IASC power was not exercised by all its members but by different organisational units. The board, various steering committees and the Standing Interpretation Committee (SIC, created in 1997) were of particular importance. Within the IASC, the board, as the central decision-making body, had the most extensive responsibilities: it drove the standard-setting process and was, moreover, responsible for defining policy guidelines and working programmes. The board consisted to a large extent of appointed representatives from national professional accounting bodies: altogether three representatives from 16 countries in each case (Wagenhofer 2009). Additionally, some members from non-accountancy organisations – for example, the International Organisation of Securities Commissions (IOSCO) – were on the board, but the majority of members came from the accounting profession. The overall membership count eventually rose to more than 70 members. The technical standard-setting process was largely left to the committees (Haller et al. 2000).

While the technical challenge of transforming the objectives into standards involved only a small group of individuals, all members played quite a significant role: the IASC was heavily dependent on its members' lobbying power to put standards into practice. After all, the IASC was a privately organised meta-organisation which had no powers to put its standards into effect (Flower 2004). The IASC was also powerless to enforce compliance with its standards at the company level, unless the national body responsible for standard-setting in the respective countries had endorsed the standards (Whittington 2005).

To overcome this problem of a lack of authority, the IASC took several actions to improve its image and to expand participation in its standard-setting processes in the late 1980s and 1990s. The aim was to transform the IASC from an organisation controlled by the accounting profession into an independent institution that could be regarded as a legitimate standard-setter. The most fundamental change took place in 2001, when the IASC was completely restructured, since structural and procedural weaknesses had increasingly been seen as militating against the objective of issuing accounting standards with global acceptance (Street 2006). The key initiators of the restructuring were a group of four national standard-setting bodies (G4) which included the standard-setting bodies of Australia, Canada, the UK and the US (Street and Shaughnessy 1998). They pressurised the IASC into making major structural changes by clearly articulating that, if the IASC did not restructure in a satisfactory way, they would set themselves up in opposition by transforming the G4 into an international standard-setting body.

The G4 identified several deficiencies in the IASC's structure (Street 2006). First, the Board was criticised for inefficient decision-making. The total number of those attending board meetings regularly exceeded 70, which was considered too many for efficient decision-making. Second, there were concerns about whether all board members had the appropriate experience and professionalism to work as standard-setters. Third, the standard-setting process was criticised as too time-consuming, partly as it required the votes of 75 per cent of the board to approve the standards. As a consequence, standards suffered from compromises as many different viewpoints had to be incorporated for their approval. A fourth criticism was of the fact that the established framework for standard-setting, which should have been binding or should at least have informed the standard-setting, had often taken a back seat when creating or deciding on standards. The delegates instead followed national interests or their own special ones (Gallhofer and Haslam 2007). Fifth, and finally, the (by and large) marginal inclusion and representation of national standard-setters in the IASC was criticised. In response to these criticisms, in 1997 the IASC set up the Strategy Working Party (SWP) (Martinez-Diaz 2005), which was charged with the task of evaluating the IASC's existing structure and establishing a new organisational structure.

In the debate that followed, the future board structure was of central concern. Two approaches were discussed by the interested parties (Ruder et al. 2005). The first approach conformed to an expert or independence model. The standard-setter's legitimacy would be derived from its independence from special interests and from governmental influence, and its use of standards set by competent individuals serving in the public interest. The second approach conformed to a structure of approval, consensus and geographic representation to overcome the legitimacy problem. While the European Commission (EC) as one of the interest groups preferred the latter option, the independence model was favoured by the G4 and the US, in particular the Securities and Exchange Commission (SEC). In 2001, after several changes to the original proposed structure, the IASC finally agreed on a solution that combined elements from both approaches. But although the new structure constituted a compromise, the infrastructure showed in some important respects parallels to the organisational structure of the US standard-setter, the Financial Accounting Standards Board (Whittington 2005).

The decision in favour of an expert model revealed that the IASC saw the acceptance of their standards on global capital markets as a paramount objective with the US capital markets as an important target (Walton 2004). With the same intention, the strategic target of the constitution was reformulated. The constitution put greater emphasis on the objective of enforceable, high-quality international accounting standards for global capital markets, and the IASB strives for convergence between national accounting standards and its own ones (Flower 2004).[3] The IASB is the main operative body responsible for setting standards independently, but in accordance with the objectives stipulated in the constitution. Moreover, standard-setting is bound to a due process of exposure and consultation (Ruder et al. 2005). In line with the expert approach of standard-setting, the members are chosen for their technical knowledge, and 12 of the 14 members are full-time representatives. To guarantee the independence of the board members, membership requires resignation from other work and a commitment not subsequently to rejoin the previous employer. Moreover, the quorum of the board was reduced from a qualified majority to a simple majority, in order to avoid blocks from minorities.

The IASB is under the supervision of a board of 19 trustees, who are representatives of various interest groups (Whittington 2005). The principal task of the trustees is to make sure that the appointed board represents a broad geographical distribution as well as a balanced mix of former auditors, preparers and users of financial statements. From a legitimacy point of view, an important new feature of the revised organisational structure is the liaison group of national standard-setters. This liaison group has a privileged status in the due process and regularly meets the board members to discuss current and future projects (Street 2006). The group consists of members from the G4 and is complemented by the national standard-setters from France, Germany and Japan, owing to the economic importance of those countries and their commitment to international accounting convergence.

Since this structural reform in 2001, only minor changes to the IASB's organisational structure have been made (Wagenhofer 2009). For instance, in 2005 the liaison structure was modified. The constitution now states that the IASB is allowed to establish partnerships with national standard-setters and institutions concerned with standard-setting, giving the IASB greater flexibility to conduct partnerships with a broader range of parties (IASCF 2005). The disbanding in 2001 of the IASB's former competitor, the G4 working group, shows that the restructuring process had strengthened the IASB's role as an independent international standard-setter.

### 2.2.3 The rise of IFRS: The conceptual view of accounting

In the history of IFRS two approaches towards standard-setting can be distinguished, which roughly coincide with the responsibility of IASC and IASB, respectively, in setting accounting standards: the first approach can be labelled as being descriptive in nature, the second as normative (Beresford 1992).

*Descriptive approach towards standard-setting*

The descriptive phase began with the genesis of the IASC in 1973 and ended in 1988. In this period the IASC published 31 standards, termed 'IAS' (Garrido et al. 2002). Within this early phase, the IASC attempted to proclaim a common set of accounting standards by surveying established accounting practices through the examination and evaluation of treatments for all major accounting problems (Street and Shaughnessy 1998). The approach is labelled as descriptive, as the IASC endorsed a summary of virtually all common accounting methods used in developed countries. Consequently, the endorsed IAS were a hotchpotch of accounting methods that permitted the application of numerous alternatives for the same accounting issues without any precise conceptual basis. This guaranteed a high degree of flexibility and avoided conflicts regarding the content of the standards, but the issued standards provided ultimately no guidance towards standardisation. Nevertheless, this approach was helpful as it allowed for an exchange of ideas between the different constituencies and helped to sensitise them to existing differences between national accounting practices (Thorell and Whittington 1994). However, the flexibility is also due to the fact that the IASC expected a better reception from its members. After all, it had no legal means to enforce its standards (Roberts et al. 1996). One related benefit was that the IASC's standards were useful for countries that did not possess any own set of accounting standards.

*Normative approach towards standard-setting*

After having gained some legitimacy by the descriptive (collecting) method, the IASC moved to a new conceptual stage, which is commonly referred to as the 'normative' phase (Beresford 1992). From 1989 to 1995 the IASC strived for a consolidation of accounting choices: motivated by discussions with the IOSCO in the late 1980s, the IASC embarked on a new strategy by initiating a Comparability and Improvements Project (Botzem and Quack 2005b). The Exposure Draft (ED) 32 on 'The Comparability of Financial

Statements', published in January 1989, proposed a work programme for revising the existing standards and aimed at achieving two goals: first, the range of alternative methods within the standards would be reduced; second, the standards themselves would be made more detailed and prescriptive. Another improvement that followed the ED 32 in April 1989 was the adoption of a 'Framework for the Preparation of Financial Statements' (Thorell and Whittington 1994). The framework would provide the basis for the conceptual restructuring process and facilitate the selection from among the alternative accounting treatments. Since then, the conceptual framework has continued to serve as a guide for the standard-setting process as well as for standard revisions (Street and Shaughnessy 1998). The framework does not contain any detailed accounting rules, but does set out basic principles regarding measurement and recognition.[4]

Concerning the Comparability and Improvements Project, the IASC received approximately 170 letters commenting on the ED. Most of them criticised the lack of rigour and inefficiency of the standards and therefore supported the objective of enhancing comparability, but there was a high degree of diversity regarding the agreement about possible changes (Roberts et al. 1996). For instance, the IOSCO argued that the existing standards were not acceptable for stock market listing requirements. This caused particular concern among accounting professionals outside the Anglo-Saxon countries, who feared that the rise of standards designed for capital market participants might come into conflict with traditional (Continental European) accounting models (Botzem and Quack 2005b). In response to the comments, the 'Statement of Intent: Comparability of Financial Statements' was issued in July 1990, which made detailed proposals for selections and amended three issues in the original ED 32: inventory valuation, development costs and borrowing costs (Thorell and Whittington 1994). The project largely ended in 1993. During its lifetime nearly one-third of the previously existing IAS were truncated as 21 of the proposed 29 accounting choices were eliminated (Hudack and McAllister 1995). Within the revised standards, the distinction between a benchmark method and an allowed alternative – still valid in some of the current standards – was introduced for the first time (Kleekämper 1995). As some of the critics feared, the revisions did indeed eliminate a lot of the accounting choices from the Continental European accounting model, or downgraded them to an 'allowed alternative treatment' subordinate to the Anglo-Saxon methods, considered as the benchmark option. To consider the Anglo-Saxon accounting methods as the preferred option was a logical decision insofar as the IASC aimed at acceptance on global capital markets, which were dominated by the Anglo-Saxon model. The differentiation between a benchmark and an allowed alternative treatment was largely removed in standards revised in or after 2003 (Wagenhofer 2009). The removal eliminated the more Continental approach altogether.

Despite the IASC's efforts to revise its standards, the IOSCO was not willing to recommend the revised IAS to its members (national securities regulators) by 1993, the end of the first improvement phase. The reason for this was that there was dissent among the IOSCO members about the operational readiness of the standards (Botzem and Quack 2005b).

Unlike the European members, the SEC's position was to endorse only a complete set of core standards, of which some still needed to be developed by the IASC. Ultimately the SEC initiated a second wave of revisions (from 1998 to 2000). In them, the IASC pursued an aggressive schedule and issued the core set of standards as early as 1998. The work programme of the 'core standard project' was made up of additional improvements, further reductions of options within the standards and an increase of the overall disclosure level of companies applying the revised standards (Garrido et al. 2002). However, the core set of standards that the IASB presented did not win unconditional endorsement by the IOSCO, as a result of which further revisions were made (Tweedie and Seidenstein 2005). Finally, in May 2000, after a review, the IOSCO completed the assessment of the standards and announced the endorsement of 30 core IAS. The IOSCO recommended its members to allow foreign incoming issuers to apply these standards in financial statements for trans-boundary listings and capital raising instead of requiring them to follow national rules (Radebaugh and Gray 2002). However, the members were allowed to ask for reconciliations of certain items, to demand supplementary information if necessary or to disallow options in standards. Full standardisation had not yet been achieved. Table 2.1 gives an overview of the chronology of the standard-setting activities during the descriptive and normative phase.

Shortly after the IOSCO endorsement, in the course of restructuring the IASC into the IASB, the labelling of the standards changed. Henceforth, standards issued after 2001 are no longer called IAS but are referred to as IFRS,

*Table 2.1* Chronology of standard-setting activities to 2000

| **Descriptive approach (1973–1988)** | **Normative approach (1989–1995)** | **Normative approach (1995–2000)** |
|---|---|---|
| • **IAS 1–26** | • Revised IAS 2, 8, 9, 11, 16, 18, 19, 21, 22, and 23 (in force in 1995). | • Revised IAS 1, 12, 14, 22 (in force in 1998), 16, 17, 19, 28, 31 (in force in 1999), and 32 (in force in 2001). |
| | • IAS 27, 28, 29 (in force in 1990), 31 (in force in 1992), and 32 (in force in 1996). | • IAS 33–39 (in force in 1999). |

*Source*: Garrido et al. (2002).

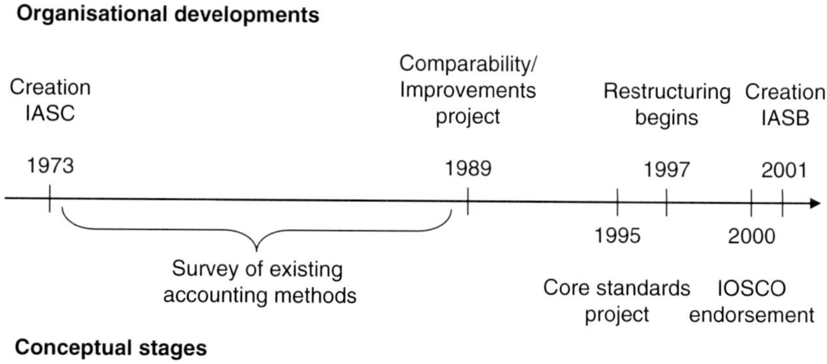


*Figure 2.1* Chronology of the IASB and IFRS history
*Source*: Own contribution.

to emphasise that this marked the beginning of a new era of international accounting standard-setting. Also, shortly after the endorsement of the standards by the IOSCO, the global accounting convergence made huge headway in the early 2000s. The conceptual stages in the evolution of the standards combined with the organisational developments were landmark events that paved the way for the global IFRS revolution. Figure 2.1 lists important milestones and processes in the IASB's history.

## 2.3 The diffusion of IFRS around the globe

### 2.3.1 Growing application of IFRS

In 1976 Sir Henry Benson predicted that IAS would have a dominating influence by about the beginning of the new millennium. Looking at this then daring prediction today, it has to be admitted that Sir Henry was more or less right. Evidently, IFRS dominate the accounting landscape with regard to capital markets, listed firms and multinational companies these days. Ramanna and Sletten (2009) provide data for a sample of 102 countries regarding IFRS adoption status, drawn from information provided by Deloitte's IASplus.com website. We extend the sample by the 30 countries that are members of the EU and EEA, so that we can report on a total of 132 countries.

Table 2.2, which summarises adoption over time, shows that over 50 per cent of the 132 countries adopted IFRS as primary accounting standard for capital-market-oriented companies. Table 2.2 reveals, further, that the 'IFRS revolution' gathered momentum in the years preceding 2002, shortly after the first results concerning the acceptance of the standards by the IOSCO were seen and the restructuring process of the IASB's predecessor began. Since then, IFRS adoption shows continuous growth, with the largest increase coming during 2005. From 2004 to 2005 the non-EU/EEA group

*Table 2.2* Timeline for IFRS-adopting countries

| Year | Number of IFRS-adopting countries | | Number of non-adopting countries |
|---|---|---|---|
| | non-EU/EEA countries | EU/EEA countries | |
| Pre-1998 | –[a] | 1 | 131 |
| 1998 | –[a] | 3 | 129 |
| 1999 | –[a] | – | 129 |
| 2000 | –[a] | – | 129 |
| 2001 | –[a] | 4 | 128 |
| 2002 | 19 | 6 | 107 |
| 2003 | 20 | 10 | 102 |
| 2004 | 24 | 12 | 96 |
| 2005 | 34 | 28 | 70 |
| 2006 | 35 | 28 | 69 |
| 2007 | 39 | 30 | 63 |

*Source*: Ramanna and Sletten (2009); EU (2008).
[a]Data not available.

grew about 42 per cent to 34 adopters, and the EU/EEA group grew 133 per cent to 28 adopters, which exhibit in total a growth rate of 72 per cent. This strong increase among the non-EU/EEA group presumably coincides with the stipulated adoption of IFRS for listed companies in the European member states in 2005, which in turn also explains the growth rate within the EU/EEA group. Adding to the number of adopters those countries from the non-adopter group that only permit but do not require IFRS for listed companies, the total number amounts to 92 countries. Thus, measured by the number of countries in which IFRS are required or permitted, IFRS has a 'global market leader position'. This is also mirrored by the distribution of IFRS application in the Fortune 500: 38 per cent of the Fortune 500 firms apply US GAAP, 36 per cent apply IFRS, and 26 per cent are incorporated in countries that have said they will adopt or converge to IFRS in the next years. IFRS are on par with US GAAP. They deserve to be referred to as an 'international' accounting standard, even though countries with large capital markets have not adopted or converged to IFRS so far. From this group, Canada, in particular, Japan and the US are matters of particular interest for the IASB. However, activities do take place in those countries to make IFRS applicable, whether by means of convergence or adoption; we consider these further in our studies of individual countries below.

### 2.3.2 Switching modes

Countries fall into three different categories: adopters, partial adopters and non-adopters. Adopters are those countries which require IFRS for all listed companies, while partial adopters include those that require IFRS only for

*Table 2.3* Distribution of countries by IFRS adoption status in 2007

| | Full adopters[a] | Partial adopters | Non-adopters | Total |
|---|---|---|---|---|
| Number of countries | 69 | 23 | 40 | 132 |
| (as a percentage) | (52.3) | (17.4) | (30.3) | (100) |

*Source*: Ramanna and Sletten (2009).
[a]Including the 30 EU/EEA countries, but see also Part IV for a more detailed examination.

some listed companies or permit them for listed companies. Non-adopters are those countries that do not permit IFRS for listed companies. Table 2.3 illustrates the distribution of sample countries between the three categories.

In 2007, out of the 132 countries for which information about their accounting requirements was known, 40 countries did not adopt IFRS as reporting standard for listed companies. By contrast, 69 countries adopted IFRS fully as reporting standard for listed companies, and 23 countries limited the adoption of IFRS to some listed companies. Moreover, in some countries IFRS had completely replaced national standards not only for *listed* companies but also for all other companies: for example, in Kuwait, Slovakia and the Ukraine (Wagenhofer 2008). This reveals that there are different scenarios for switching to IFRS. This is because the IASB still lacks the power to enforce their standards at the national level and therefore depends on whether countries opt for IFRS or not. However, if a country decides to turn to IFRS, it can still choose how to implement them. Therefore, the choice between different switching modes is important as they might influence the actual comparability of financial statements. In this context, adoption designates the use of IFRS instead of national accounting rules, whereas convergence depicts the successive alignment of IFRS and national standards. Accordingly, the latter describes a dynamic process, while the former is more or less static. Nobes and Zeff (2008) differentiate both terms by a finer taxonomy, shown in Table 2.4.

*Table 2.4* Scenarios for conversion to IFRS

| | |
|---|---|
| Adoption of IFRS | as an alternative to local GAAP (Scenario 1): e.g., Switzerland.<br>as issued by the IASB (Scenario 2): e.g., Canada, Israel and South Africa.<br>with local amendments (Scenario 3): e.g., Australia, New Zealand and the EU. |
| Convergence achieved by | changes of IFRS (Scenario 4): e.g., first wave of standard improvements by the IASC.<br>moving local GAAP towards IFRS (Scenario 5): e.g., China and Japan.<br>mutual alignment of local GAAP and IFRS (Scenario 6): exists only between the IASB and the US. |

*Source*: According to Nobes and Zeff (2008).

The first scenario is an adoption of IFRS, which depends on the reporting choice that companies make within those countries. The national legislator merely permits them to prepare financial accounts according to IFRS. An example for this scenario is Switzerland, where, in addition to local GAAP, reporting following IFRS or US GAAP is also allowed. The second scenario refers to a mandatory full adoption of IFRS as issued by the IASB, meaning that domestic standards no longer apply. This amounts to a full replacement of the national GAAP by IFRS, with the result that changes of IFRS are immediately effective in those countries. Examples of countries following this scenario include Canada, Israel and South Africa. Both scenarios – although differing in the way IFRS is adopted – describe a dynamic type of 'legislative outsourcing' as legislators refer to IFRS in its respective valid version. Hence, future modifications are *ex ante* anticipated and incorporated in the reference norm (Becker 2005). In contrast to the previous scenarios, the third scenario is a provisional adoption of IFRS. National requirements are substituted by IFRS, but not exactly as issued by the IASB. This allows for local amendments and leads to 'national versions' of IFRS (Wagenhofer 2008). This scenario therefore amounts to an adoption with reservations, which pertain especially to later amendments of the IFRS. In this connection the type of 'legislative outsourcing' is static. Legislators incorporate the IFRS in this way (i.e., amended and promulgated on date of adoption). Changes to IFRS do not pass seamlessly into national law but are incorporated once in a while by changes of the reference norm (Becker 2005). This switching mode is prevalent in most countries, and a famous example of this scenario, to which we will refer later in more detail, is the EU.

Convergence compared to adoption means that national GAAP remain in force, but that national GAAP are aligned with IFRS in an either unilateral or a reciprocal way. The first convergence scenario in which convergence is achieved by changes to IFRS is now almost unthinkable. It happened in the first wave of improvements, when IFRS strongly moved towards US GAAP. The two other options of convergence are in this context more realistic and also observable in the regulatory practice. Japan is a good example of one-sided convergence and the US of reciprocal alignment. From the perspective of regulatory implementation, scenarios three, five and six of Table 2.4 are the interesting ones, as in such cases controversial issues may arise. These may be issues concerning the content of standards, the (bilateral) relationships between related parties and the comparability of financial accounts.

Thus, in the following we will examine the cases of the EU, the US and Japan more closely as role models for the three differing switching modes. Additionally, the case of Canada will be considered, although it belongs to the second scenario category. Canada is of interest as it intends to adopt IFRS in 2011, despite the relevance of the US capital market for Canadian companies.

### 2.3.3 Switching modes: Country cases

*The EU as catalyst for the IFRS revolution*

The EU has adopted IFRS with local amendments. The endorsement of IFRS in January 2005 by the EU and other countries around the world was dubbed 'the greatest revolution in financial reporting for a generation' by the financial press. Even more emphatic, Brackney and Witmer (2005) refer to the EU's decision as 'the largest and most complex accounting conversion in history'. More than 7,000 listed companies had to prepare group accounts according to IFRS, which made the EU the largest user of IFRS (Perry and Nöelke 2005). By adopting IFRS, the EU pursued the goal of integrating the EU financial markets fully (Van Hulle 2003).

The idea of harmonising accounting in Europe has been discussed since the Community's early beginnings. Major steps towards Europeanised accounting regulation were taken in 1978 and 1983, when two important European Council Directives on Company Law were passed to achieve the goal of fully integrated financial markets. The Fourth Directive, of 1978, established minimum requirements for company accounts with respect to contents and presentation (78/660/EEC). The Seventh Directive, of 1983, adopted rules for group accounts, aiming 'to achieve the objectives of comparability and equivalence in the information which companies must publish within the Community' (83/349/EEC). As the EC tried to harmonise accounting through the vehicle of company law, the directives applied to all firms operating in the member states. To illustrate the size of the endeavour, Table 2.5 contrasts the total number of firms with the number of listed ones in France, Germany and the UK for the year 2004 – a year before switching to IFRS.

Table 2.5 highlights the fact that there are only a marginal number of companies within the member states that would benefit from an integrated financial market; most firms do not depend on such an integrated market. It is therefore understandable that ultimate decisions on the most contentious issues in European accounting were left to national legislators. A popular example of national peculiarities prevailing in the case of

*Table 2.5* Structural company data for 2004

| Country | All forms of legal companies | | Of which: private and listed stock corporations | | Of which: listed companies | |
|---|---|---|---|---|---|---|
| | Absolute | Relative | Absolute | Relative | Absolute | Relative |
| Germany | 2,765,168 | 100.00% | 513,341 | 18.56% | 660 | 0.13% |
| France | 2,183,226 | 100.00% | 911,783 | 41.76% | 663 | 0.07% |
| UK | 1,921,860 | 100.00% | 1,091,825 | 56.81% | 2,486 | 0.23% |

*Source*: Eurostat, Euronext and World Federation of Stock Exchanges.

directives is the acceptance of the 'true and fair view' concept as general standard for financial reporting. Most European countries were unfamiliar with the stipulation, and the European legislator had not provided a definition that could have helped in understanding it (Dragneva and Millan 2002). As a consequence, member states used their administrative discretion to implement the 'true and fair view' concept. Hence, substantial differences in accounting remained; the goals of achieving comparative statements and complete integration of European financial markets were thus not fully achieved.

In the early 1990s the changing environment in terms of how business was done propelled the European authorities into rethinking its accounting policy and striving for harmonisation of accounting. Major European companies began to use either IAS or US GAAP in order to have a better benchmark basis to their international competitors, but also in order to raise capital on foreign capital markets (Haller 2002). The US market, in particular, increasingly attracted European companies, starting with Daimler Benz in 1993. This required, however, the application of US GAAP. In the course of events US GAAP gained not only global importance but also the status of internationally accepted standards. These developments forced the EU's hand, particularly in view of the risk of large European companies increasingly adopting US GAAP, which were pronounced beyond the influence of the European legislator. Moreover, compliance with US GAAP was regarded as a competitive disadvantage to US companies, which were usually exempt from the need to reconcile their financial reports when using the European capital market. This manoeuvred the EU legislator into a decision dilemma with five possible solutions (Flower 2004):

(1) Do nothing and accept that globally acting European companies had to prepare two sets of financial statements;
(2) No longer require European preparers of US GAAP financial statements to comply with the EU directives;
(3) Reach mutual recognition between US GAAP and EU rules;
(4) Develop European GAAP; or
(5) Adopt IFRS.

The first two solutions were effectively blocked because of the high political costs for the EU. The next two options were rejected because negotiations with the US about mutual recognition had failed and the expenditure and time needed to develop European GAAP were considered too high. Instead, in 1995, the EU decided to support and cooperate with the IASC in order to achieve convergence of European accounting rules, but also to have influence on future international developments (Haller 2002). After several initiatives, the EU finally came up with the so-called 'IAS Regulation'

(Regulation (EC) No. 1606/2002), which required listed groups to publish financial reports in accordance with IFRS from 2005 onwards. With this regulation, the EU explicitly dismissed the objective of a fully harmonised accounting system in Europe in favour of a partial harmonisation for a subset of companies (Zimmermann 2010b) (Box 2.2).

### Box 2.2 Adoption patterns of internationally accepted accounting standards by listed companies

The 'IAS Regulation' was not the first decision in the EU in favour of an internationally accepted set of accounting standards. Prior to the regulation at the supranational level, some member states provided listed companies with the opportunity to choose between local GAAP and internationally accepted accounting standards (generally, IFRS or US GAAP). This option was mostly given to listed companies and for the preparation of consolidated accounts. Local regulators gave listed companies the chance to choose the appropriate accounting standards for their purposes (ccf. Scenario 1, Table 2.4). The decision of the regulators to give listed companies leeway presumably did not happen voluntarily but as a result of political pressure within the countries concerned. To illustrate the domestic demand for IAS, the adoption patterns of French and German listed companies are shown as examples in Figures 2.2 and 2.3. Both tables encompass a period of 12 years, starting in 1998, the year Germany and France decided to open up the 'market' for accounting standards.

Figure 2.2 shows the adoption pattern for companies listed in the French CAC-40 index at the beginning of 2010. The sample consists of 39 firms, as full data were not provided for all 40 companies in the CAC-40 index. The figure illustrates that there was a basic demand for IAS partly suppressing French GAAP. IFRS and US GAAP were applied by a roughly equal proportion of companies from 1998 to 2004. However, the use of IFRS and US GAAP became rather static. A growing demand for IAS cannot be detected until 2004. The dramatic increase of IFRS adoption in 2005, which relates to the 'IAS Regulation' prescribing the mandatory application of IFRS for consolidated accounts of most companies from 2005 onwards. What is remarkable is that the use of IFRS did not take off after the announcement of the 'IAS Regulation' in 2002. This may be an indication of the limited need for IFRS, US GAAP or information accounting in general for French listed companies. In 2007, the year the special transition period to IFRS for some companies ended and IFRS nearly completely replaced all other GAAPs. Only a small share of US GAAP users remained which disappeared in 2008.

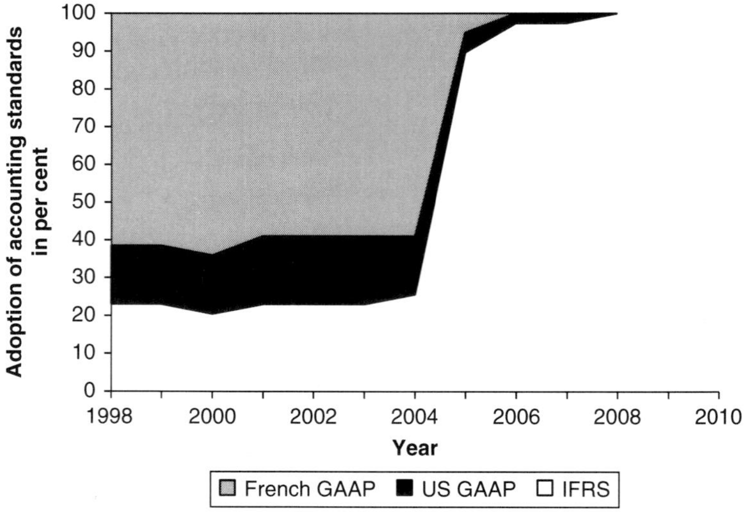


*Figure 2.2* Adoption pattern of CAC-40 companies, 1998–2010
*Source*: CompuStat Globalvantage.

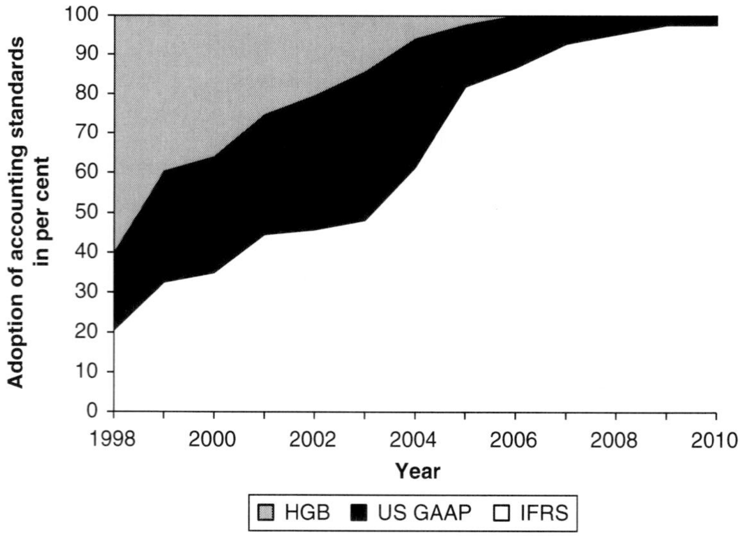


*Figure 2.3* Adoption pattern of HDAX companies, 1998–2010
*Source*: CompuStat Globalvantage.

Figure 2.3 shows the adoption pattern for companies listed in the German HDAX index at the beginning of 2010. The sample consists of 83 firms, as full data were not provided for all 100 companies. Unlike in the French case, Figure 2.3 shows a steadily growing demand for

IAS. This increasing demand went hand in hand with a suppression of the German GAAP and indicates that the necessity for information accounting of HDAX companies was greater than that for CAC-40 companies. The share of IFRS as well as US GAAP adopters was roughly equal in 1998. During this period the IFRS share grew slightly more strongly than the share of US GAAP adopters, which can be explained by the negotiation about the 'accounting strategy' within the EU and the greater likelihood of adopting IFRS. After a short period of stagnation from 2001 to 2003, the adoption of IFRS took off in 2004, accompanied by companies switching not only from local GAAP to IFRS but also from US GAAP to IFRS. This effect follows the same legislative-driven reasoning as in France. The share of US GAAP users after 2007 consists of companies thus applying US GAAP but additionally reconciling their consolidated accounts to IFRS.

Together, the two figures show a pent-up demand on the part of French and German listed companies that existed before 1998 for greater information-oriented accounting standards. This demand has put pressure on political actors in both countries to open up a market for accounting standards and to leave the decision about which set of standards serves them best to individual companies. The two figures, however, show differences in the saturation of demand. While demand is steadily increasing in Germany, the market in France was fully saturated shortly after it opened. Moreover, the saturation level in France remains lower than the ongoing demand for IAS in Germany.

The EU decided not to accept IFRS unconditionally but to install safeguards. Only standards that had previously been adopted and endorsed by the EU now had to be applied by listed companies. For this purpose, the European Financial Reporting Advisory Group (EFRAG) was established in 2001. The institution has an important function in the endorsement process of IFRS in EU law. Its main task is to serve as a connector between the EU as a public standard-setter and the IASB as a private standard-setter, where it represents the European interests (Haller 2002). Although the objectives of the IASB and the EU regarding accounting policy are very similar in general, the EU wants to ensure that the privately set standards are not in conflict with the European public interest (Whittington 2005). Furthermore, the endorsement procedure also serves as a means to exert a sufficiently threatening influence (Wagenhofer 2008). The most prominent case is that of IAS 39, which was initially not adopted owing to opposition from the European banking industry and thereafter only in a modified form, with two carve-outs of the original standard. As a consequence, the IASB revised IAS 39 and limited the use of the so-called 'fair value' option as proposed by the EU (Perry and Nöelke 2006). Another example is the interpretation of the reporting of emission rights, which was not endorsed by EFRAG, and eventually retracted by the IASB. The exercising of influence by the EU became most obvious in light of the financial crisis. The IASB softened the fair value provisions under IAS 39 by introducing the possibility of reclassifying certain financial instruments and, at the EU's request, cushioned accounting consequences in rare circumstances: for example, the financial crisis. The concern expressed by the EU arose from the possible disadvantages that European financial institutions could have suffered in comparison with US competitors as US GAAP allowed for flexibility regarding the reclassification of financial instruments. The IASB responded at short notice and outside the normal working procedures to political pressure articulated by EU leaders and finance ministers.

The adoption of IFRS by the EU is a good example of countries being able to tailor IFRS-based standards to their own requirements by selective adoption. This may lead to different 'flavours' of IFRS – such as, in the European case, 'EU-branded IFRS'. However, it should be borne in mind that the EU is an exceptionally large adopter, with sufficient muscle, and thus a threat to the IASB's independence. The lobbying power is substantial as the adoption by the EU also promoted the international standing of the IASB and increased the pressure on other countries to consider either the adoption of IFRS or the convergence of their national GAAP with IFRS. The EU even intensified the pressure on other countries to intensify their efforts by extending the IFRS requirement to third-country issuers listed on a European regulated market from January 2009 onwards (Regulation (EC) No. 1289/2008 and Decision 2008/961/EC).

### *The US: Cooperation of equals between FASB and IASB*

With more than 15,000 SEC-registered listed companies that have to prepare financial accounts according to US GAAP, the US plays a significant role in the quest for global accounting convergence. Soon after the release of the IAS Regulation by the EU, the FASB and the IASB signed a Memorandum of Understanding called 'The Norwalk Agreement' (FASB and IASB 2002). In this memorandum the two accounting bodies underlined their commitment to achieving convergence between their respective accounting standards. The principal objective is not to create a single set of standards by identifying the best standards or rather to make the two sets of standards equal in every respect. Instead, the independence of the two sets was accepted, although differences should be narrowed down so that the two sets of standards are recognised as equivalent (Gornik-Tomaszewski 2005). Consequently, the proceedings between the two standard-setters are one (and probably the only) example of a two-sided convergence process. It is important to acknowledge that the cooperation between the IASB and the FASB does not indicate a unilateral move by IFRS towards US GAAP. In fact, the FASB realised soon after some of the financial reporting scandals in the US (such as Enron and WorldCom) that it does not have the answer to every accounting problem (De Lange and Howieson 2006). In particular, the rules-based approach of its standards was criticised for its inflexibility. Accompanying this criticism, it has been suggested that US GAAP could be improved, at least in some areas, by using the more principle-based approach of IFRS. For the IASB, equivalence between US GAAP and IFRS would soften the existing reconciliation requirements for IFRS companies listed in the US and simultaneously enhance their global acceptance (Cascini 2008). Furthermore, the prospect of the US optionally allowing IFRS in the US would be an even bigger success for the IASB than the adoption of IFRS in the EU, owing to the higher number of listed companies. To facilitate the flow of information and cooperation between the two standard-setting bodies, the FASB allowed for a full-time representative of the IASB at the FASB office (Gornik-Tomaszewski 2005); the liaison membership of the FASB at the IASB was not expanded. The Norwalk Agreement also started a short-term convergence project aimed at eliminating a variety of narrow differences (Herz and Petrone 2005). For instance, the FASB focused on issues such as balance sheet classification or inventory costs, while the IASB concurrently reviewed the standards related to issues such as discontinued activities or post-employment benefits. In 2004 most differences within the scope of the short-term project were eliminated, but differences beyond the scope of the short-term project were also tackled (Gornik-Tomaszewski 2005). For instance, the FASB issued a standard on share-based payments in December 2004 that took a similar approach to the standard issued by the IASB in February 2004. Similarly, the IASB released a standard in March 2004 that narrowed the differences between US GAAP and IFRS in accounting for business combinations. In the same year the FASB and IASB also agreed to coordinate their technical agendas and to develop a shared conceptual framework. To strengthen their commitment, the two accounting bodies agreed in April 2007 that all future major projects will be carried out together (Street 2008).

The convergence endeavours were additionally supported by bilateral agreements between the US and the EU. In June 2005 the US and the EU expressed their commitment to enhancing transatlantic economic integration and growth, which also included the promotion of convergence between accounting standards (Gornik-Tomaszewski 2005). In April 2007 both parties signed an agreement explicitly stating that they would promote the conditions for US GAAP and IFRS 'to be recognised in both jurisdictions without the need for reconciliation by 2009 or possibly sooner' (Bush et al. 2007). Shortly afterwards, the SEC asked for public comments on the elimination of the reconciliation requirement for foreign listed companies reporting under IFRS (SEC 2007b). In November 2007 the SEC Commissioners voted accordingly to remove the reconciliation requirement for companies that adopted IFRS 'as issued by the IASB'. The SEC release (Nos. 33–8879) approving the vote was issued in December 2007. Despite political influence, the removal can be interpreted as success of the Norwalk Agreement and also as a signal that the US supports the ongoing acceptance of IFRS. However, this rapid development was somewhat astonishing as Christopher Cox, chairman of the SEC, had announced in a press release earlier that year that the SEC 'remains on track to eliminate reconciliation by 2009' (SEC 2007b). By virtue of this decision, foreign private issuers were relieved from the imposed reconciliation costs between US GAAP and IFRS-compliant financial accounts. For example, for European SEC registrants there were approximately 426 reconciliation requirements in 2005 and 2006, most of them attributable to the treatment of tax, pensions, goodwill and intangible assets (Jetuah 2007). All of them disappeared.

Notwithstanding the rapid developments and the progress made in the close collaboration between the FASB and IASB, the decision of adopting IFRS for US-headquartered listed companies remains contingent. In August 2007 the SEC issued a concept release that proposed to treat US and non-US issuers similarly by allowing US-registrants to use IFRS in financial reports for fiscal years from 2014 (SEC 2007a). The concept release followed a heated debate about the merits and disadvantages of IFRS. While some argued that IFRS adoption is necessary for companies, at least in certain industries, to enhance comparability with foreign competitors, to prevent competitive disadvantages or to benefit from the opportunities IFRS offers (Street 2008), others argued that there are still too many differences between US GAAP and IFRS, and that comparability will not be achieved. There was also uncertainty about how the IFRS transition would affect auditing firms and auditing standards (even though the BIG-4 auditing firms unanimously advocate the adoption of IFRS in the US).[5] Eventually, the International Standards on Auditing (ISA), which are set by the International Auditing and Assurance Standards Board (IAASB), became the prevalent standard for financial auditing firms (Loft and Humphrey 2011).

Another strong point of criticism was that, in the past, different 'versions' of IFRS emerged owing to local adjustments, above all by the European endorsement process, which could hamper the bi-lateral convergence process (Street and Linthicum 2007). At the end of the discussion phase on the concept release, the SEC held three public round tables to receive further input concerning the adoption of IFRS. After the last round table, in August 2008, the SEC released a proposed road map for the potential use of IFRS by US issuers (SEC release Nos. 33–8982). The road map scheduled a switch to IFRS in 2014 if the SEC believes that the incorporation of IFRS in the US public reporting structure is in the public interest. The SEC planned to make a decision on this issue at the end of 2011. However, in the meantime the support for IFRS had dwindled. It now seems increasingly unlikely that IFRS will become authoritative accounting standards in the US.

*Japanese and Canadian ambitions*

Japan and Canada can be described as late adopters of IAS. While both countries accept IFRS financial statements of foreign listed companies, they differ in their respective movements to IFRS for domestic listed companies. While Japan strives for mutual recognition through convergence of Japanese GAAP with IFRS, the Canadian Accounting Standards Board (AcSB) replaced Canadian GAAP (for listed companies) fully by IFRS in 2011.

The Japanese decision to strive for mutual recognition was motivated by the fear that Japanese GAAP would not be regarded as equivalent to the EU regulation. This could severely affect the financing activities of Japanese firms in the EU and would burden them with costly adjustments to their financial statements. Moreover, Japan feared negative effects on its own capital market, one of the biggest in the world. In August 2007 the Accounting Standards Board of Japan (ASBJ) and the IASB reached an agreement, known as the 'Tokyo Agreement', to accelerate convergence between the Japanese GAAP and IFRS, a process that had started in 2005 (IASB 2007). Similar to the EU, Japan decided to adopt a national 'version' of IFRS, with carve-outs already announced. Recently, convergence activities have been pursued less vigorously, and it seems unlikely that an IFRS adoption is going to happen in the near future.

Contrarily to Japan, Canada adopted IFRS with almost no carve-outs: it adopted IFRS as issued by the IASB. There were several reasons for this. First, Canada's capital market has less than a 4 per cent share of the global capital market (Cherry 2008a), and Canada considers the adoption of IFRS as a cost-effective method to boost investments in its own capital market (AcSB 2006a). Second, a continued strategy of harmonisation with US GAAP was supposed to impose higher costs of compliance on Canadian firms than IFRS (AcSB 2006b) and, in addition, Canadian GAAP is regarded as fairly similar to IFRS, which reduces switching costs. The various attempts to minimise differences between Canadian accounting standards and US GAAP did not prove successful. Table 2.6 summarises the different modes of switching to IFRS and the use of IFRS for consolidated accounts in the considered countries.

## 2.4 Conclusion

The proliferation of IFRS since the 1990s marks an accounting revolution, at least in relation to the financial reports of listed companies. As a consequence, many listed companies are now able to raise capital in other

*Table 2.6* IFRS requirements and switching modes

| Use of IFRS for | Domestic listed companies | | | Foreign listed companies | Switching mode |
|---|---|---|---|---|---|
| | Not permitted | Permitted | Required | | |
| US | X | | | Permitted without reconciliation | Two-sided convergence |
| EU | | | | Required since 2009[a] | IFRS 'as endorsed by the EU' |
| Germany | | 1998–2004 | Since 2005 | | |
| France | | 1998–2004 | Since 2005 | | |
| UK | | | Since 2005 | | |
| Japan | X | | | Permitted without reconciliation | One-sided convergence |
| Canada | | Since 2008 | Since 2011 | Required since 2011[b] | IFRS 'as issued by IASB' |

*Source*: Own contribution.
[a]Reconciliation not necessary if foreign GAAP is seen as equivalent to IFRS by the EU. This applies, for instance, to Japanese GAAP and US GAAP.
[b]US GAAP continues to be acceptable for US-listed issuers.

countries without having to use foreign accounting standards. Moreover, investors and companies can rely on comparable financial data, enhancing investment decisions. In 2005, around 15,000 listed companies around the world started preparing their financial accounts in compliance with a single set of international rules. Differences between IFRS and US GAAP or Japanese GAAP are diminishing, albeit at a decreasing speed. Discussions around IFRS adoptions in Japan and the US have highlighted substantial differences in use and functions of accounts. The next chapter will discuss these issues in greater detail.

# 3
# Variations in Function: A Barrier to Harmonisation

## 3.1 Introduction

The rapid diffusion of IFRS across the globe seems to indicate a wholesale harmonisation in accounting worldwide. Since IFRS have investor information as their primary objective, this would also suggest that investor information has become the main function of accounting. This is unlikely. Accounting is a versatile tool that is being used to fulfil many more functions. To appreciate the true extent of worldwide accounting harmonisation, one needs to consider the entire accounting landscape, including all other functions. If the maxim 'form follows function'[1] holds true also for accounting systems, and if other functions of accounting still exist, then investor information by means of IFRS reports will not be the only form in which accounting appears. Other forms apart from IFRS accounting are therefore likely to be found.

Accounting can fulfil three primary functions in society: it can help to mitigate conflicts between constituencies of a business organisation by defining and settling claims; it can foster the efficiency of capital markets by conveying and verifying information; and it can assist in determining the share of businesses' profits that the state takes in by means of taxation. These functions are closely related to three legal fields: company law, securities law and tax law. Although the degree of reliance on legal coordination varies from country to country, the three fields exist in every jurisdiction and form the basis for society's coordinative efforts. All of them can tie legal consequences to accounting outcomes and therefore influence the formation of accounting rules. Company law, for example, might use information presented in the annual financial statement to restrict corporate dividends. If this is the case, the law ascribes a payout function to financial accounts. Securities law can rely on financial reports to supply market participants with information on the relevant economic entity, creating the information function of accounting. Finally, tax law may resort to financial accounts to define the tax base. This, again, results in a situation where financial reports determine corporate payouts, in this case through taxes.

Accounting functions are not uniformly distributed between countries, and their distribution makes country-specific divergence between accounting systems likely. An obvious example is the degree to which financial reporting assists in determining corporate payouts: accounting rules are crucial in some countries but are virtually unknown in others. Variations in accounting functions thus form barriers to harmonisation. They can only be overcome when alternative instruments are developed that complement the harmonised IFRS rules. It is the aim of this chapter to show how the use of accounting determines the shape of the national accounting landscape, and we demonstrate how the resulting variations limit efforts at international harmonisation. To achieve this, we distinguish two elements – preconception and focus – that form the basis of every accounting system. We then set out how these relate to the legal framework in which accounting is embedded. For this purpose, the primary task of each legal code, its possible relations to financial information and the resulting consequences in the form of the accounting system are analysed.

## 3.2 Elements of accounting

### 3.2.1 Preconception

In every type of account the process of accounting refers to the representation of company activity in accrual numbers. When all company activity is terminated, results can be shown in cash, and accrual accounting is no longer necessary. However, if an activity straddles more than one reporting period – which is normally the case – the accountant needs to make decisions about how past investments and future cash flows should be represented in present and future periods. Two guiding ideas, which we refer to as 'preconceptions', have emerged in the accounting profession: unbiased representation and prudence. The two forms of preconception process future risks and rewards in different ways. This can be illustrated by the following examples. A profitable contract has been secured, but it will be only fulfilled in the next reporting period. Should the profits from the contract be shown now? Or imagine that contractual obligations have been fulfilled but payment has not been received. Should the risk of counterparty default be reflected in taking profits? Should the risks of re-works or costs of potential guarantees be reported, and what would be a good estimate of these future risks? Accountants who lean towards unbiased representation will give different answers from those who emphasise prudence. Both will argue that their approach will protect the interest of the addressees. We will discuss the two arguments in turn.

Under the preconception of unbiased representation the accountant intends to show the firm's economic resources and performance in an unbiased, or rather, neutral, way. This neutrality is based on the symmetrical treatment of gains and losses arising from business transactions and the full disclosure of all available information. The idea is to present stakeholders with a picture of the firm's economic situation which can be referred to as a 'true and fair view' (Christensen and Demski 2003). Unbiased presentation facilitates the prediction, evaluation and comparison of amounts, timing and uncertainty of future cash flows, and financial accounts become more useful for these purposes. As all stakeholder groups base their information processing on the same neutral information, no group is systematically preferred by accounting rules that display these characteristics. To capture the 'true' economic situation of the firm, all risks and rewards immanent in a transaction are recognised in financial statements. They are valued symmetrically, and the same valuation principles apply for wealth-increasing (rewards) and wealth-decreasing (risk) incidents. Under unbiased representation, all risks (e.g., counterparty default or reworking) are recognised as liabilities. The same accounting principles apply to possible future rewards (such as lower production costs owing to a probable decline in input prices), which will be shown as assets.

Under this preconception, assets and liabilities should be shown at their economic value. In reality, where there is uncertainty about the future, economic value cannot be observed but only be estimated. Existing theory supports the view that a good approximation for economic value can be found in current market prices (Hitz 2007). Accountants leaning towards unbiased representation therefore tend to support current-value accounting. The theoretical underpinning for the pricing accuracy of the market is the theory of (information-) efficient markets, which assumes that all publicly known information is transferred into a fair market price (Beaver 1973).

Starting with an initial expectation of the amount of profit associated with an asset, economic agents estimate its value. This estimation becomes more precise as any additional information is received (Scott 2009). Theory assumes that the sum of all constantly updated expectations reveals the fundamental value of the asset. The efficiency of this transformation process is significantly affected by the quality of information available. The market will not reach its first best equilibrium if information is held back, distorted or biased. In this context unbiased representation offers two major benefits: first, all stakeholders' interests are equally protected by information; and second, it secures efficient allocation of financial resources throughout the economy. Stakeholder interests' are protected by timely and complete information on the economic situation of the firm, and they can react to new signals. Shareholders, for example, can sell their shares when learning about bad news, and creditors may raise the rate of interest or demand further collateral. In other words, accounts with the characteristics of unbiased representation not only further the efficient allocation of financial resources but also strengthen the financial system (Hail and Leuz 2006). From this perspective, accounting standards that reveal complete, timely and unbiased information contribute to social welfare.

The concept of unbiased representation is the favourite of pure (orthodox) economic theory, as unbiased representation aims at approximating a firm's wealth by technically advanced means. But in socio-economic reality it may clash with other political ideas about how to organise a society's welfare production and distribution. Its underlying idea of informational protection of stakeholders relies strongly on the market, which in turn has to be in equilibrium. When there is strong societal doubt about the extent to which the equilibrium solution occurs, market solutions may not be given preference. Further, information protection requires stakeholders to act if they wish to benefit. However, not all stakeholder groups possess the same ability to respond to new information. A share, for example, is easily sold, but conditions of long-term credit lending are adjusted with more difficulty. *A fortiori*, labour is traded with high transaction costs and cannot respond to bad news as quickly as finance. Accounts may therefore be tweaked to protect these weaker stakeholders. Such considerations give rise to the second preconception: prudent accounting.

In prudent accounting the accountant intends to depict the financial situation of the firm in a long-term-oriented way. Prudent accounting centres on two aspects: conservatism and reliable measurement. While the latter aims at making accounting information verifiable and objective (Moxter 1984), the first introduces a systemic bias to financial accounts. The idea behind prudent accounting is to support the going concern of the firm by limiting short-term-motivated actions based on over-optimistic or manipulated accounting data and to mitigate agency problems between stakeholders of the firm (Basu 1997).

Prudent accounting becomes manifest in a number of ways. First, there exist principles that limit the amount of information recognised in financial statements. Under prudent accounting, assets and liabilities need to fulfil some criteria of reliability before they are recognised in financial statements. This excludes the kind of information that is considered too uncertain and prone to manipulation by management. Good examples are in-house-generated intangible assets. In many accounting systems they cannot be capitalised as their longer-term contribution to value creation is considered doubtful. Second, there exist conservatism principles that emphasise the reporting of negative over positive economic effects. These principles introduce asymmetry into various aspects of accounting, such as recognition, measurement and timeliness (see also Box 3.1 The attribute of conservatism). A prudent accounting system recognises expected losses, for instance, in provisions, while expected gains are not capitalised. Assets may be systematically understated, for instance by applying the lower of cost or market rule; liabilities are overstated, for instance by not discounting long-term liabilities. Other examples include asset write-downs, which are recognised immediately, whereas write-ups are deferred over the assets' lifetime. The measurement concept of historical costs harmonises with prudent accounting. Under historical-cost accounting, expenses represent the limit to asset measurement, hindering at least in non-deflationary economies asset overstatement. Further, accounting entries are verifiable and objective as they are backed by previous market transactions.

**Box 3.1 The attribute of conservatism**

The attribute of conservatism has a long-standing tradition in accounting. Asymmetric write-downs were already common in Italian accounting in the early 1400s (Basu 2005). The 'lower of cost or market' principle, contained in the French Commercial Code from 1673, is a further early example for conservatism in accounting (Littleton 1941). However, there is no general definition of conservatism or prudence (Devine 1963). From a valuation perspective, conservative accounting measurements are a systematic bias introduced into accounting, potentially leading to an undervaluation of assets and causing lower book values than their actual market values (Feltham and Ohlson 1995). The core question is whether this bias reduces or increases the information content of financial reports. Accordingly, two types of conservatism are distinguished in the literature: unconditional and conditional conservatism. The unconditional type of conservatism can be described as a systematic undervaluation of book compared to market values, independent from experiencing economic losses in the reporting period. In the conditional type, conservative accounting only applies when economic losses are experienced: on bad news, book values are reduced to reflect the worsened economic conditions. Book values will not be reduced when economic conditions do not change (Ball and Shivakumar 2005). However, the two types of conservatism share some common features, such as capturing investors' perceived asymmetric loss functions, minimising firms' regulatory costs (litigation, tax) and enabling regulators to minimise economic instability and avoid criticism (Beaver and Ryan 2005).

Various studies on conservatism inquire into the degree of unconditional and conditional conservatism in different countries (Ball et al. 2000; Giner and Rees 2001; Garcia Lara and Mora 2004). There is some evidence that unconditional conservatism is more pronounced in Continental European countries while conditional conservatism is more common in Anglo-American countries. There is also evidence that the existence of unconditional conservatism is due to tax and regulatory incentives. A common example is the introduction of conservative depreciation methods. Further, unconditional conservatism might contribute to minimising the risk of over-distribution (Maltby

2000). However, high degrees of unconditional conservatism are seen by some as harming the usefulness of financial reports in decision-making as they go hand in hand with the emergence of hidden reserves, which will only be recognised when assets are sold. Unconditional conservatism thus can be used for earnings management (Healy and Wahlen 1999).

The recent literature associates conditional (but not unconditional) conservatism with contracting efficiency. Contracting parties demand timely information about the companies' assets. Owing to the debtors' compensation scheme – bearing the full risk without receiving additional compensation – they demand timely bad news recognition (Watts 2003). However, it is not clear whether conditional conservatism is mainly driven by the demands of debt holders or shareholders (Ball and Shivakumar 2005; Hammermeister and Werner 2010).

Many of the techniques mentioned for prudent accounting have the effect that book value deviates from economic value and they create hidden reserves (Moxter 1984). Prudence in accounting therefore comes at the cost of a blurred representation of underlying economic value. Still, major accounting systems list both the quest for a 'true and fair view' and the application of 'prudence' among their guiding principles (e.g., IFRS Framework and US GAAP). Accounting systems contain elements supporting either characteristic and can thus only be located on a scale somewhere between prudent and unbiased representation rather than at one end or the other.

The exact location of a system on this scale is largely influenced by the role accounting has to fulfil in society. An institutional setting in which accounting primarily serves as a tool to inform investors will be less conservative than a system in which accounting is used to calculate taxes and other corporate payouts. The choice of accounting elements, such as preconception, will be discussed in detail at the end of this chapter.

### 3.2.2 Focus

When preparing financial reports, the accountant applies a certain preconception of how to allocate cash flows between current and future accounting periods. She also applies judgement where the business that she accounts for ends, which is a value judgement about the boundaries of the firm. In the basic case, accounts are prepared to track the development of an entrepreneur's wealth. But what happens if personal and business property is separated by the creation of a legal entity with limited liability? How does the focus of accounting change once the legal entity takes a share in other businesses? Again, this depends on the context in which accounting is used. To determine the tax burden of a single businessperson, accountants will choose a different focus from informing investors about the financial situation of a multinational business group. Historically, two major types of accounts have evolved in this context: single and group accounts.

Until the 19th century, when the concept of limited liability first came into use, personal wealth and business wealth were not separated in legal terms (Maltby 2000), and early accounting thus focused on a natural person's wealth. The introduction of companies with limited liability made it possible to shelter private wealth by restricting the possible loss to the amount of means invested (Easterbrook and Fischel 1989). The resulting pooling of investment favoured large ventures that a single person could not have undertaken (Manne 1967). Famous early examples for such investments include the railway companies that established the train lines between all major British cities in the Victorian era. A consequence of the pooled investments was the investors' need to track the development of their share in the company. Accounting moved away from determining personal wealth, and the legal entity became the focus of accounting; its accounts could be used for the calculation of payouts as well as for information purposes. Ongoing industrialisation and the first wave of globalisation in the 1920s again changed the nature of business and, with it, the nature of accounting. As companies grew, and as they became more international, they created subsidiaries in the form of separate legal entities, often under foreign jurisdiction. The corporate group with a number of associated companies, both national and international, was born. Associated companies carried out various activities and were tied to the corporate group by differing degrees of financial interrelation. An accounting technology that focused solely on the legal entity no longer provided sufficient information to investors, as only a fraction of a subsidiaries' economic activity was disclosed in the traditional account of the parent company. A detailed view of the economic situation of the associated companies was walled in by an accounting technique that only provided insight into the cost of the investment and its payout in the form of annual dividends (Taylor 1996). Accounting practitioners reacted with the preparation of group accounts which displayed the economic rather than the legal situation of the parent company. These accounts tried to consolidate the group's assets and liabilities as if they belonged to one hypothetical economic entity. This new technique, which is referred to as 'consolidation', enhanced the information about the economic situation of corporate groups. Consolidation techniques date back to the 1890s but became more common in the 1930s. The first legal obligation to prepare group accounts was established in Australia in 1938 (Taylor 1996). Since then, group accounts have become known to most financial reporting systems of the world. Depending on national accounting regulation, consolidated accounts replaced, eclipsed or accompanied the traditional company accounts. Before their different interrelations are discussed, some technical characteristics need to be set out.

Company (or single, unconsolidated) accounts refer to the business as a legal entity. They depict a legal person's financial situation by listing the pertinent assets and liabilities. Single accounts are of juridical use, as a company is typically held responsible for its own legal actions but not those of affiliates and subsidiaries. Examples for juridical uses of accounting are the determination of the taxable income or the liquidation of assets in the case of a bankruptcy. From an informational perspective, the parent company results are potentially informative, as they represent the basis for dividend payments to the parent company shareholders (Niskanen et al. 1998). However, the limitations of single accounts become apparent when looking at a company that has control over a subsidiary through its voting power. In its (parent-only) single account, the holding company shows the investments in its subsidiary as a financial asset. The annual dividend it receives from the subsidiary is recognised as investment income. However, the assets and liabilities controlled by the parent company are not shown. The shareholder therefore cannot evaluate their possible future returns, or any risk related to the investment in these assets. The business as an economic entity is thus eclipsed by the legal form. Consolidated accounts pierce the legal veil and show all controlled assets.

Consolidated (or group) accounts refer to the business as an economic entity. They thus summarise, from a parent company's perspective, the assets, liabilities and activities of the holding company and all subsidiaries in one financial statement. Not all subsidiaries have the same degree of integration in the parent company owing to the different modes of financial involvement. Financial investments, joint ventures and partly or completely owned subsidiaries serve as examples. To display the group's activities, the consolidated balance sheet has to list assets and liabilities of the associated companies only as far as they belong to the group in an economic sense. A number of consolidation techniques have evolved to separate group and non-group activities (see Box 3.2, Consolidation techniques).

**Box 3.2 Consolidation techniques**

Consolidated accounts integrate the economic activities of a number of legal entities into the balance sheet of a single economic entity. A key aspect in the preparation of such financial statements is the delimitation of activities that belong to the economic unit. Once identified, these activities can be aggregated, excluding inter-group activities and transactions out of the group's range. The existence of various participation structures, each reflecting different amounts of capital invested, complicates this process. Therefore consolidation techniques that discriminate between core group and non-core group activities have evolved. The book-value, the full-goodwill, the revaluation, the proportional consolidation and the equity methods are common techniques. These methods fall into two classes, of either partial or full consolidation. Where full consolidation applies, all assets and liabilities of the subsidiary are included into the consolidated financial statement of the parent company. Partial consolidation only includes parts of the assets and liabilities of the associated company. Whether partial or full consolidation is carried out is determined by the degree of control that the parent company has over the subsidiary. Control is constituted when the parent company can exercise dominant influence: that is, with the actual majority of voting rights in the company or the ability to staff management or supervisory bodies. This is often associated with the parent possessing a majority of shares. If a parent has established control, the concept of full consolidation applies. A holding of 100 per cent of a company's shares yields full inclusion of all assets, liabilities, hidden assets or liabilities and goodwill. If a parent company has control, but a rate of participation less than a 100 per cent, full consolidation is still carried out, but minority interests are accounted for in equity. Again, there are several methods of how to include minority interests. The three consolidation methods named – book value, revaluation and full goodwill – result. The book-value method only includes the parent company's associated hidden assets and liabilities; the revaluation method additionally covers the hidden assets and liabilities of the minority shareholders; and the full goodwill method additionally incorporates the goodwill attributable to the minority. The book-value method only includes hidden assets and liabilities up to their initial costs, so that minority interests are only included with their book value. In contrast, the revaluation method captures hidden assets and liabilities of both the parent company and the minority shareholder; they are shown in the group account at fair value. A resulting goodwill is applied proportionally to the amount of participation. The full goodwill method, finally, constitutes the strongest form of consolidation as it additionally includes the appropriate goodwill of minority shareholders.

If the parent entity has no control over the associated company, the investment is only partially consolidated. Two methods, the equity method and proportional consolidation, are typically used. Associated companies, which are characterised by interest between 20 and 50 per cent, have to be consolidated using the equity method. In this case, the shares are valued, starting from their initial value, simultaneously to the value of the equity of the consolidated company. This implies that no assets and liabilities are consolidated into the group account. It only discloses the participation in form of a financial instrument. Gains and losses will also not be included in the group income statement, but rather have an effect on the accounted equity. Changes in the value of equity-consolidated companies cause gains or losses in the consolidated income statement, which are disclosed separately. The equity method is thus the weakest form of consolidation. The proportional consolidation method is applied for joint ventures, which are characterised by a joint leadership of two or more equally inclined companies. The aim of this method is to include assets, liabilities and gains or losses proportionally in the group account. Hidden assets and liabilities are also accounted for proportionally. Minority interests of other shareholders, both in the proportional consolidation and the consolidation at equity, are not taken into consideration. In effect, the two methods entail the same values and differ only in methodology. Over time, a number of consolidation techniques have been developed that have now become defunct. The most common one was the pooling-of-interest method that consolidates subsidiary companies with their book value minus the proportionate equity of other investors. This method does not consider hidden assets, liabilities or goodwill. Recently, proportional consolidation has also been phased out by the new IFRS 11. The standard is mandatory for reporting periods after 1 January 2013.

Existing accounting systems differ in respect to the preconception they apply and to the sets of accounts they provide. Comparative accounting research often focuses on the former, investigating whether a country's accounting system tends towards prudent accounting or unbiased representation (Jaafar and McLeay 2007). The latter is largely ignored. Although modern accounting systems in most cases provide group accounts as well as some sort of legal-entity-focused accounting, the interrelation, legal status and importance of these sets of accounts are distinct, and even within a single country the emphasis will vary from one set of accounts to another (Goncharov et al. 2009). An overview of the different sets of accounts is displayed in Figure 3.1.

## 3.3 Accounting functions

The primary function that accounting plays within society influences the operational characteristics of the ensuing reporting systems. Which of the functions of accounting has primacy depends technically on the legal

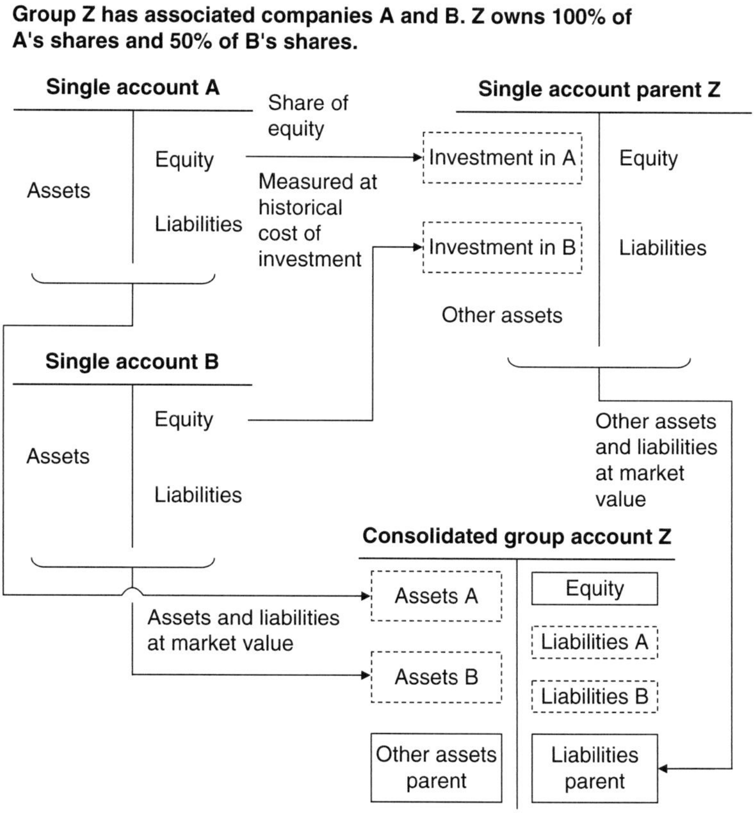


*Figure 3.1* Different sets of accounts
*Source*: Authors' own.

framework, as the law assigns functions to financial accounts. In the following section we introduce the legal framework by discussing the three fields of law that are relevant to accounting regulation: company law, securities law and tax law. Each of them attends to core conflicts in business relationships. Company law addresses the regulation of conflicts arising from the creation and operation of a business organisation (Davies 2002). By mitigating possible conflicts between various stakeholder groups and by providing protection mechanisms for some of them, company law sets the playing field for business conduct and guarantees the functioning of the business sector. Securities law assures the supply of capital by fostering efficient capital markets (Goshen 2003). Tax law, finally, determines a firm's sustainable tax contribution to society by defining taxable income and tax rates in such a way that they do not erode the firm's substance.

### 3.3.1 Mitigating conflicts: Company law

Companies are institutions that transform a number of inputs into marketable goods. Even in the most basic case of buying a good on one market and vending it with arbitrage profits on another, a number of tasks have to be assumed by economic agents to make this happen. First there is the task of financing the operation. The financier has to be compensated for the risk she incurs and the time-value of the money she contributes. Then there is the task of operating the business. This includes all the activities that are related to obtaining the input, transforming it and the act of selling the final good. The person administrating this process has to be compensated for the effort and time she puts into the operation. On a small scale, one natural person can assume all these functions. But as the business process becomes more complex, they will be separated and performed by different functional groups. Financiers appear as owners and creditors. Owners carry the major part of the business risk, as their investment is not secured. They are rewarded for this with the right to obtain all residual cash flows that the business generates. Creditors, in contrast, have a fixed claim against the company. As they also carry a relevant part of the business risk, they will seek ways to secure the invested means. This is done by credit contracts, which regulate the relationship between creditors and the business organisation. Further, as the owners do not run all the operations themselves, they will delegate parts of the operational activities to employees, who receive remuneration for their efforts. Employment contracts will result.

The aim of the contracts is to balance the conflicting interests of the different constituencies of the company, by establishing rights and conditions for their contractual relationship. In this sense, a business organisation can only exist due to the contractual alignment of otherwise conflicting interests. That is why companies are also defined by some authors as a 'nexus of contracts' (Easterbrook and Fischel 1998). In theory, all these contracts are privately negotiable between the concerned parties. In reality, though, the state interferes by providing a standard set of contracts for common situations by means of company law.[2] These standard rules lower transaction costs and help efficient contracting in the economy (Jensen and Meckling 1976). Company law can be designed in a flexible way, so that it provides a number of possible standard clauses that can individually be chosen between contractual parties (default rules). It may also provide binding clauses that apply under certain circumstances (mandatory rules). Both approaches exist in reality and within one legal code (Cheffins 2006). With the introduction of mandatory rules company law moves beyond the mere support of contractual efficiency, as it then limits private choice in favour of a specific type of contract. This modifies the balancing of structural conflicts to achieve certain political goals and to foster preferred social values, and adds a normative component to corporate law.

Seen from the process level, company law defines the contractual relationships of a business organisation and addresses their immanent conflicts for the duration of the business's lifetime from creation to liquidation (Hansmann and Kraakman 2001). Upon creation, it provides different legal forms under which the business organisation may operate. A fundamental distinction can be made in regard to setting up the business either as an independent legal vehicle (incorporation) or as legal status of a natural person (partnership). In a non-incorporated partnership, partners are privately liable for all the business's obligations. Here the company possesses no separate legal identity and can only act on markets through its owners. As partners are privately liable, their private wealth serves to secure creditor interests. Private liability also makes business activities highly risky for owners, as they cannot limit the amount of capital they invest, nor can they diversify their risk. This restricts the ability of partnerships to raise capital. A common legal form of larger business organisations, therefore, is the incorporation with limited liability. Under this form, the business organisation possesses an individual legal identity. It is able to perform legal actions independently from its owners: that is, it can enter into contractual relationships, sue other parties or be sued. Owners of incorporations can only be held liable for the amount of capital they have invested. Limited liability companies can be further divided into private and public incorporations. While public incorporations are anonymously traded on capital markets, private incorporations are only traded directly between individuals.

In the case of a non-incorporated firm, the potential number of conflicts during the course of business is limited owing to the restricted number of owners, the likely overlap between owning and running the company and the private liability of the owners. For incorporated firms, the number of potential conflicts increases with the marketability of corporate shares, with the separation of the private personality of owners and the legal personality of firms and with the concept of limited liability. Three main areas of conflict arise from these characteristics. First, the possible marketability of shares leads to different motivations, time horizons and amounts invested by shareholders. These differences may lead to conflicts within the group of shareholders, as different motives, for example, may result in each group preferring a different business strategy (Burkart and Panunzi 2006). Second, as investors cannot be held privately responsible for liabilities of the business, creditors (and other stakeholders) can only assert claims against the corporation. Owners may harm creditors by transferring resources from the firm to their private wealth. In the case of bankruptcy, liabilities remain unsettled, which constitutes a conflict between creditors and owners (Fama and Miller 1972). Third, the concept of limited liability and the resulting pooling of investments favour large business ventures which a single investor can no longer oversee. This encourages the separation of ownership and management (Bryer 1998). As employees may not always act in the best interest of owners, another possible conflict arises between these two groups.

Company law helps to mitigate these conflicts by assigning decision and profit participation rights to stakeholder groups. The rules that allocate decision rights form the part of corporate governance regulations in corporate law. They focus on the distribution of control and mainly address conflicts within the group of owners and between owners and employees. In general, these corporate governance regulations have little to do with accounting.[3] The rules that establish profit participation rules focus more closely on conflicts between owners and creditors and owners and employees. They often refer to accounting information, as the starting point for all profit allocation is the systematic recognition of economic transactions provided by financial accounts (Zimmermann et al. 2008a). During the lifespan of a business organisation there exist a number of conflicts in profit allocation that might be regulated in company law under reference to accounting information.

When setting up the business, the choice of legal form straight away determines possible cash participation conflicts. Incorporated companies and partnerships are structurally different with respect to the way in which creditors can secure their fixed claim. While claims against liable partners outlive the business and can be settled from the person's private wealth, in the contrary case of an incorporated company these claims perish with the liquidation of the organisation. A need for mechanisms to protect creditor and other constituencies' interests thus arises for incorporated companies. In a liberal approach, the legislator can leave this conflict unregulated and to private negotiations. In a more interventionist approach, a safeguarding mechanism can be established via company law. A very common method is the legal requirement to provide a minimum amount of capital by owners upon incorporation. This capital belongs to the legal entity and serves as security for claims against it.

Accounting rules have relevance both in the more liberal setting of default regulation as well as in the more interventionist setting of mandatory rules. In the former case financial accounts provide the information upon which credit partners negotiate their conditions. Depending on the initial balance sheet and the amount of equity transferred to the legal entity, creditors will set up the terms of credit. A strong equity position will result in lower rates of interest as creditors can satisfy their claims against this capital. In the latter case, company law requires a certain capital to be supplied before gaining legal capacity. In either regulation, the accounting rules that calculate the future changes from business transaction define its capacity as security for creditor claims. Accounting rules, for example, that allow the use of vague immaterial assets can overstate equity as those assets may turn out to have little value once they are to be individually liquidated. The shape of accounting rules therefore has important effects on the quality of capital.

During the course of business, capital continues to play a vital role, as it is an indicator of the stability of the business. Most stakeholder groups have a strong interest in the going concern of the company, as its bankruptcy would cause them a loss of financial means (creditors) or at least an increase in transaction costs (suppliers, employees). In most countries the nation state assumes some residual responsibility for its citizens and will bear part of bankruptcy costs, for instance by providing benefits or continuing pension arrangements. The state therefore also has an interest in the survival of the company. The general objective of supporting the going concern of the company can, in accounting terms, also be described as capital maintenance. Capital can be harmed if dividends are paid above earnings: that is, when capital is transferred to the owners at the cost of other constituencies, including creditors and the state. Capital maintenance thus centres on activities hindering excessive distributions to owners. The systematic recognition of business transactions provided by financial accounts helps to track the development of this capital even in the absence of further legal requirements (El-Gazzar and Pastena 1990). In most countries, though, company law defines mandatory rules that restrict payouts as an instrument to maintain capital. In this case dividend payments are prohibited once they affect the legally required capital.

There exist two ways to organise payout restrictions. They can be based either on case-by-case calculations or on financial accounts. In the first setting, they take the form of solvency tests, where accounting data are adapted in order to assess the ability of a company to distribute dividends. In this sense companies, for example, might only be allowed to distribute dividends as long as liquid funds equal short-term liabilities (Leuz 1998). In the second setting, there may be a prohibition on dividend payments that exceed annual earnings or the capital that has been accumulated through earnings. Whether payouts are possible depends on the way in which earnings and capital are calculated by the applicable accounting rules.

In the case of a company not being able to continue as a going concern, insolvency is triggered, and the firm will disappear from the market. Conflicts between stakeholder groups arise in respect to the settlement of their remaining claims. In the theoretical example of a business continuing to operate until all of its assets are completely exhausted, the claims of lenders, suppliers and employees will remain unsettled. In reality this will not occur, as the business process will collapse long before all the assets are used up. However, defining the moment of bankruptcy is crucial to the settlement of remaining claims and therefore lies within the scope of company law. The legislation has to balance different interests in this context. The earlier bankruptcy is declared, the more claims will be settled, which protects creditors. At the same time it harms shareholders, as the risk of erroneously terminating a business that would have survived increases, and it may harm employees, who are forced into redundancy, with possibly doubtful job prospects. Different versions of company law give different definitions of bankruptcy, but they generally determine bankruptcy on the basis of accounting information. Again it is possible for insolvency to be triggered by events that are directly observable in annual accounts (e.g., percentage of equity falling below a certain level), or accounting aggregates may be adjusted to suit the purpose (e.g., balance sheet tests, where assets have to exceed liabilities while both are measured at market values). The shape of the accounting rules again has an effect on the outcome of both these instruments.

In all business organisations conflicts arise over the distribution of profits. Even where the state does not interfere in the business process via company law, accounting will still be a crucial instrument for profit allocation. Commonly, though, company legislation provides a set of standard contracts that include the provision of capital, its maintenance and distribution in case of bankruptcy. The mechanisms for maintaining capital – and with it the company – are of major importance in the company-law perspective on accounting. Here the shape of accounting rules will directly influence the allocation of profit rights such as dividend payments.

Requirements on accounting rules from company law are ambiguous. In most cases, prudent accounting figures help in writing standard contracts. Unbiased information will, in some cases, support the writing of efficient contracts.

### 3.3.2 Promoting capital market efficiency: Securities law

While company law addresses internal aspects typical of all business organisations, securities law governs the external trading of ownership rights and debt titles of large incorporations. In the literature, the contribution of capital markets to economic growth and social welfare is widely recognised (Levine and Zervos 1998). Among the functions the capital market assumes in society, the efficient allocation of financial resources plays an outstanding role.

Securities markets contribute to efficient capital allocation by enabling investors to diversify risk and to create an investment portfolio that suits their individual risk profile. If risk and return are both observable on the market, rational investors will always choose the highest possible return for the amount of risk incurred. Consequently the market mechanism will allocate all financial means to their most productive use; companies will find finance at the lowest possible cost, and investors will earn the highest possible compensation for their risk. To make this work, prices need to be accurate and markets need to be liquid. Price accuracy depends on the information processing capacity of the market. Under the theory of (information-) efficient markets, the market consensus is able to transfer all available information quickly into market prices. If this is the case, securities markets are efficient and investors are price-protected, as no asset trades above or below its fundamental value (Scott 2009). Liquidity refers to the possibility of selling or buying any listed asset immediately at the given price. It complements efficient pricing, as fair pricing can only lead to efficient allocation if the information is actionable.

All markets are subject to market failure, and financial markets are no exception. Information asymmetries, in particular, can harm the functioning of the market. This is the case when some market participants have access to private information. On the basis of their superior knowledge, they are able to outperform other market participants. In the extreme case, which almost never occurs, this situation would lead to the collapse of the securities market. The general argument has been put forward by Akerlof (1970); normally skewed information only leads to windfall profits, representing a lack of efficiency, and lower trading volumes, representing a lack of liquidity (Abée 2012). To guarantee the allocative function of capital markets, securities law has the objective of minimising the risk of market failure by reducing information asymmetries.

The problems resulting from informational asymmetries can be tackled from two sides. A first solution focuses on their emergence; it minimises the amount of private information by enforcing the dissemination of information. A second solution focuses on the negative results of information asymmetries by prohibiting people with private information from trading. In existing securities regulation these two lines of action often complement each other. The insider trading rules that prevent trades on the basis of private information have little to do with accounting regulation.[4] Minimising the risks from the use of private information can also take the form of making that information public, which refers directly to corporate disclosures and financial reports.

Similar to contractual relationships in company law, corporate disclosures can either be left unregulated or be subject to mandatory rules. The rationale behind the approach of voluntary disclosures relies on market-induced incentives for companies to disclose inside information. These incentives exist because of the pricing mechanism of the market, where companies with few or poor-quality disclosures have to pay a premium when raising capital (Easterbrook and Fishel 1982). The regulatory approach of mandatory disclosures is based on the idea that the level and quality of disclosures provided by the market are not perfect, and that state intervention is therefore necessary (Grundfest 1998). During the course of a public listing of shares, a number of mandatory or voluntary disclosures might support information processing. Upon the initial public offering (IPO) a prospectus and, later, annual and quarterly reports are published. Occasional ad-hoc reports give immediate information about important corporate events.

Financial accounts provide the core element in all these corporate disclosures. They provide systematic and quantitative information about the past, present and future financial situation of the company and establish the basis for the pricing mechanism of the market. As prices are only accurate in respect to the amount and quality of publicly known information, the way in which accounting standards are designed is crucial to the quality of corporate disclosures and their ability to reduce information asymmetries. The accounting requirements from the securities-law perspective therefore are clear-cut. In this perspective, the ability to reveal as much inside-information as possible to the public represents the main qualitative characteristic of accounting. Rules will therefore largely rely on concepts of unbiased representation.

### 3.3.3 Collecting the state's share: Tax law

Like a natural person, legal entities are often obliged to help finance state activities through tax payments. Collecting taxes represents a sovereign act and is therefore codified by law (Brennan and Buchanan 1980). National tax legislation establishes the basis for organising the taxation process. This process can be shaped in a number of ways and is subject to fiscal, ethical, political and technical considerations (Rosen and Gayer 2008). Most of these considerations are interrelated: already the underlying concept of tax equity influences the technical determination of the taxable base and vice versa. These considerations have consequences for the state budget and affect political goals, which again influences their formulation. Taxation principles that influence these considerations have therefore been a matter of debate since the very beginning of the modern scientific discourse in economics (Smith 1776). The question of how to organise a fair and just distribution of the tax burden is foremost among these principles. Here, the ability-to-pay principle has emerged; it can be seen in a broadly similar form in every modern economy. Following this principle, every taxpayer is charged according to his economic ability.

The ability-to-pay principle has two forms. In its horizontal specification it states that identical economic capability will lead to equal tax charges. In the vertical specification the principle claims, further, that a stronger economic ability will result in a higher tax burden. While the first specification formulates horizontal equality as a necessary condition for tax justice, the second adds vertical difference as a sufficient condition for it. Unlike the horizontal specification, the vertical gives room for discretion, as the amount in which taxes increase with an increase in economic ability is not specified. A number of mathematical relations (proportionate, disproportionate, etc.) result. Another crucial component for the implementation of the ability-to-pay principle is the underlying concept of economic ability and how it is measured. Three aggregates are commonly used: wealth, income and consumption. While the last is directly observable from market transactions, the first two are provided by accounting information.

When accounting information is used to determine the tax base, the ability-to-pay principle has implications for the formulation of accounting standards. Horizontal comparability in performance implies that the same economic transactions lead to an identical representation in annual accounts. Freedom from bias and manipulation can be regarded as technical requirements for accounting that follows horizontal tax equity. Vertical comparability in performance further means that a higher ability to pay results in higher tax payments. If this is achieved in all cases, tax payments do not affect competition between firms. In this sense, tax payments are to collect a share of profits that does not harm the future ability to compete on markets (i.e., the substance of the company).

From a tax-law perspective, accounting rules serve to calculate the taxable base of a company. Tax calculations are required to be justly distributed and comprehensively determined. In addition, they are meant not to harm the capital of the firm and thereby to ensure its future ability to pay. This results in a situation where the ability of accounting standards to provide an unbiased picture of the firm is in competition with the ability to foster objectiveness and limit the risk of excessive tax payments. From the tax-law perspective regulators will have to combine these two aspects or decide which one is given preference.

## 3.4 Form follows function: The choice of accounting elements

Accounting systems combine the 'preconception' and 'focus' elements so that accounting's social utility is best achieved. If there is one single objective that accounting systems have to achieve, its design is relatively simple. The situation becomes more complex when different objectives are simultaneously pursued. In this case, the different objectives can only be completely achieved if there is one specific instrument – one specific accounting system – addressing each one of them (Tinbergen 1956). This means that ideally there would be a separate set of accounts that fulfils company-, securities- and tax-law needs. In practice, though, a smaller number of accounts is used. There might even be a situation in which one set of accounts is used as single 'one size fits all' solution. In such cases when the number of accounts in use is smaller than the number of objectives, the different objectives will compete with each other. A situation of compromise and domination of one function over the other will result. This adds complexity to the accounting process and can favour country-specific solutions that cannot easily be reconciled.

In the following, the likely design of a set of accounts is discussed depending on the context for which it is used. The most basic case, in which a singular set of accounts corresponds with each of the three major accounting functions, serves as a starting point, as it outlines an ideal form of accounting that corresponds to every function.

### 3.4.1 Three independent accounts

Accounts that are exclusively used to mitigate conflicts by allocating profit rights to different constituencies of the firm have a clear focus on the legal entity. As any claim held against the business organisation results from an underlying legal contract, only accounts taking the same focus can be helpful to settle legal cases. Consider, for example, rights after a company is unable to repay its debt. The creditor can only settle claims against assets that legally belong to the entity. Only single accounts that focus on the legal entity display these assets. With regard to which preconception to apply, the company-law perspective generally corresponds to a prudent representation of firm value. The objectivity criterion for company outflows and the concept of capital maintenance are two major reasons for this correspondence.

Whenever profit rights are allocated, objectivity in the way they are determined is a major concern. Due payments should be calculated in such a manner that other actors can reconstruct them later, to guarantee that they can be tried in court. Second, uncertain events should not lead to payments which cannot be reversed. The reliability criteria introduced by prudent accounting chime with the company-law perspective's requirement of objective accounting data.

To fortify capital maintenance as a major instrument in securing the interests of long-term stakeholders in company law, accounting standards will build on the asymmetric representation of prudent accounting to minimise the risk of exaggerated distributions (Maltby 2000). Not over-estimating the amount of funds that can be withdrawn from the company is particularly important for creditors and employees, since they are particularly interested in maintaining the company as a permanent institution. The position of these two groups worsens if the company distributes not only money from earnings but also from capital, as this jeopardises its existence. Prudent accounting rules help to calculate earnings useful for capital maintenance by understating or deferring profits ('understating' refers to unconditional and 'deferring' to conditional conservatism) and thereby limiting the possibility of dividend payments. The rationale for this lies in a political judgement, where the benefits related to hindering excessive payouts are valued higher than the costs resulting from deferring dividends.

The configuration just laid out corresponds to a concept of company law that largely builds on mandatory rules. These result in fixed conditions for individual contract situations that are mostly inflexible when circumstances change. In such a setting implicit protection mechanisms are indispensable, as stakeholders cannot directly react to relevant events. The accounting-coordinated concepts of capital maintenance or the creation of hidden reserves are expressions of this type of company law. In the contrary case of a more flexible company law, private arrangements that complement the mandatory legal rules may rely more strongly on information protection. An example for such mechanisms could be the private negotiation of credit terms (debt covenants). Accounting rules in this setting need not be as prudent, since explicit protection mechanisms exist that allow stakeholders to react to information. The degree of conformity between the company-law perspective and prudent accounting rules therefore also depends on the degree of flexibility in company law.

Accounts that are exclusively used to foster capital market efficiency by supplying market participants with information have a clear but distinct focus on the economic entity. Accounting information affects the quality of the market mechanism with information on firm performance released in a timely and completely manner. Single accounts only display the book value and dividend payments of associated companies. Transactions of associated companies are therefore only displayed in single accounts with a time lag until dividends are distributed, and they only come in a summarised form. This allows for little investigation into future prospects of the economic entity. Group accounts in turn allow a complete assessment of the performance of the economic entity and therefore support the securities market perspective on accounting. The preconception of accounts to be applied from this perspective is unbiased representation, as rules set out in this way do not withhold or distort any information. Prudent accounting may reduce market efficiency as (in particular good) news is deferred, and hidden reserves may also arise. Both theses aspects influence the market price if no other source reveals the information.

Accounts that are exclusively used to determine tax payments focus on the taxable entity. Taxable entities are those legal and natural persons that by law are subject to taxation. Commonly, this applies for any corporation. The focus of taxation-oriented accounts therefore generally coincides with the focus on the legal entity. The preconception that best corresponds to the taxation perspective on accounting is not so straightforward. Taking the ability-to-pay principle as a starting point, economic income represents the superior measure for the taxable base, as it best reflects an organisation's ability to pay (Coenenberg 2005). The concept of unbiased representation, which aims at approximating the economic income, corresponds with this view. Still, economic income can only be estimated, introducing discretion and the possibility of misrepresentation under real-world conditions. A conflict with the ability-to-pay principle arises, as these defects can lead to exaggerated tax payments, which will harm the future ability to pay. Even in the unlikely event of accounting profit and economic income coinciding, profit and cash realisation can still differ. In the extreme case, when all profit is unrealised and does not show in cash, the payment of taxes will necessitate the liquidation of productive assets. Economic income will in turn be lower. This effect may be exacerbated if accounting profit and economic income diverge. The ability-to-pay principle can therefore be achieved best if accounting standards show little room for discretion and calculate profits close to cash realisation. These characteristics relate to prudent accounting, which therefore dominates the preconception of unbiased representation from a tax-law perspective.

### 3.4.2 Two functions included

Every type of account applies the same basic technique of double-entry bookkeeping to aggregate information on the balance sheet. Even though realisation principles and valuation methods differ in relation to the transaction at hand, all accounts still have a lot in common. Regulatory solutions may build on these similarities by including two accounting functions in one set of accounts to reduce regulatory costs. Three combinations are possible in this context. First, the company- and tax-law perspectives can be combined, leaving accounting for capital markets apart. Second, accounts for company- and securities-law purposes can be prepared jointly, while tax accounts are prepared individually. Third, company-law-oriented accounts can represent an individual set of accounts, while the remaining securities market and tax accounts are integrated. The three combinations do not all have the same practical value.

The integrated response to company- and tax-law requirements in a single set of accounts seems convenient, as both apply a similar focus and are used to determine corporate payouts. Normally the legal and taxable entity coincides so that legal-entity-focused accounts also serve the purpose of determining taxable income. The determination of payouts holds general implications for the shaping of accounting standards that are identical under both perspectives. These include objectivity and conservatism. All payouts have to be calculated in a comprehensive manner, to guarantee their comparability in time and between issues. The reliability criterion of prudent accounting goes hand in hand with this requirement. Capital outflows cannot be reversed so that an over-optimistic income calculation will debase the substance of the firm. Conservative accounting standards limit this risk. Prudent representation combining these two requirements and legal-entity-focused single accounts that are based on this preconception can similarly be used for both payout-oriented accounting functions.

A conflict can arise when tax legislation interferes in accounting regulations beyond the basic idea of determining the tax base in a fair and reliable fashion. With fiscal policy being a major instrument of national economic policy, nation states often create tax rules to achieve specific political goals. These rules have repercussions for accounting if they apply at the level of calculating taxable income. The case of a government wanting to stimulate investments in productive assets can serve as an example. This can be achieved, among other ways, by allowing for special depreciations that lower tax payments in years of investment. From a company-law perspective, these fiscally motivated rules distort income calculation and limit the ability to allocate profits. This competition between fiscal and accounting motives sets the limits of the integration of dividend and tax calculation in one set of accounts.

The inclusion of accounts that serve a company- and securities-law perspective is even more complex. Already with regard to the focus they apply, the two perspectives differ. Market participants are interested in the development of an economic unit that will pay dividends, while other stakeholders are interested in the situation of the legal unit to which they are contractually bound. To solve this problem, information can be disclosed in a way that allows for a distinction between parent and other activities. This would imply displaying the more extensive picture of the economic unit and making it possible to identify parent-only activities. In respect to the preconception, information- and payout-oriented accounting also vary. The concept of unbiased representation, which best suits information needs, will not fulfil the reliability and conservatism principles necessary for payout determination. In a case where mandatory company-law rules require implicit protection, both concepts can hardly be followed in one set of accounts. On the contrary, in a setting where company law is designed in a more flexible way, explicit protection mechanisms fit to the concept of information accounting. In this case the integration of the two accounting functions seems more likely.

The third case of including the securities- and tax-law perspective in one set of accounts presents most difficulties. The two concepts vary in their focus. They have different requirements in regard to preconception, with the one aiming at payout calculation and the other at information provision. While this challenge can be solved for company laws, which rely to a large extent on information, it cannot do so for taxation, which is always payout-oriented. Furthermore, fiscally driven effects in profit calculation run counter to the purpose of showing a true and fair view of the company. The integration of tax- and securities-law purposes in one set of accounts therefore has little relevance for the configurations of accounting systems.

### 3.4.3 One global account

A regulatory solution that stipulates a single set of accounts will face all conflicts between accounting objectives at once. The shaping of accounting rules will then depend on prioritisation between the three functions. Again three general cases of domination of one function over the other two are theoretically possible.[5] Whenever the securities-law perspective dominates all other functions, the risk of over-distribution exists, and we can observe a conflict with the company- and tax-law perspective. Whenever any of the two payout-oriented functions dominates the accounting process, accounting information is likely to supply the market with information at a less than optimal level. A conflict with the securities-law perspective of accounting arises. These conflicts will pertain in any setting that relies on a single set of accounts.

Nevertheless, the factor that finally determines the number of accounting instruments is whether the cost resulting from sub-optimal representation is higher than the cost related to the preparation of an additional reporting instrument. If this is the case, the preparation of different accounts for different purposes will be reasonable in an economic sense. This possibility will be more likely with an increase in size of the organisation. A set of accounts is used more extensively in a large company, which reduces its marginal cost of production. Turning this argument around, the benefits of a differentiated reporting system diminish for small corporations. In business reality, only a small part of the overall company population has access to capital markets (see data in Chapter 2). For all other organisations only the taxation- and company-law perspective applies. In this context the idea of a single set of accounts is more likely to be achievable. With a manageable number of specific tax regulations, accounts can be integrated from this perspective. The situation where only one set of accounts exists is indeed very common for non-capital-market-oriented companies.

## 3.5 Conclusion

Accounting is a flexible instrument that can be used in multiple situations. Owing to possible variations in the design of accounting rules, they can be shaped in whatever way best suits the social task in question. Common tasks are the allocation of profit rights from a company-law perspective, the provision of information to foster securities market efficiency and the determination of the taxable base to collect the state's share in business success. Accounting rules from the company- and tax-law perspective determine corporate payouts. They will probably be calculated differently from rules based on a securities-law perspective that results in providing information. These functions conflict, as the principles on which they are based are distinct and different. Information-oriented accounts focus on unbiased representation for the economic entity, while payout-oriented accounts aim to depict the economic situation of a legal entity in a prudent way. Harmonisation efforts therefore have to overcome this first barrier if they straddle different accounting functions. But accounting rules do not only reflect the task they are assigned with; they are also designed in relation to the institutional setting in which they are embedded. Accounts that have direct payout consequences will be shaped differently from accounts that build the basis for further processing and only possess indirect payout relevance. These two cases can be observed, for example, in the protection mechanisms laid out by company law. Depending on the legal structure, these are either organised implicitly, drawing on accounting related concepts (e.g., capital maintenance) or they are organised explicitly and function on basis of information (e.g., debt covenants). Harmonising accounting rules becomes more difficult the more deeply an accounting system is integrated with other social functions. Here a complete and comprehensive accounting harmonisation will imply additional changes in the complete institutional system. The degree of integration into the institutional setting of a country thus creates a second barrier to harmonisation. Finally, as nation states are interested in maintaining control over some core aspects of business conduct, harmonisation is limited where national sovereignty over corporate payouts is affected. National interest in payout determination thus forms a third barrier to harmonisation.

# 4
# The Transformation of Accounting Regimes: Six National Case Studies

IAS have been developed and are increasingly being applied in the EU and around the world (Tweedie and Seidenstein 2005). Many more states also mimic the new system in their national settings as they adapt, without fully subscribing, to the international setting. Chapter 2 has painted the picture with a broad brush; the aim of this chapter is to assess in detail whether and to what extent accounting regulation has actually converged over the last decades. For this purpose we compare regulatory developments in six countries.

The country sample consists of three EU member states – France, Germany and the UK – and three non-EU member states – Canada, the US and Japan. All these countries have large economies and are thus important country cases in their own right. Moreover, the six countries have traditionally displayed different business and legal systems: insider (code law) systems in France, Germany and Japan, and outsider (common law) systems in Canada, the UK and the US (La Porta et al. 1998; Hall and Soskice 2001). Accordingly, the countries began with diverging institutional set-ups in financial reporting. While in the latter three countries there has been a long-standing tradition of self-regulation by the accounting profession, the former three have relied on a more legalistic approach. In fact, the national configurations represent different paths of accountancy, with distinct formative institutional developments. Thus, convergence in these traditionally different regimes would point to a possible global harmonisation of the regulatory landscape.

To analyse different regulatory solutions and to assess changes over time, we analyse accounting regulation within each country in terms of four criteria: the predominant uses of accounting; the legal backing of financial reporting; the extent of professional self-regulation; and the degree of internationalisation. The criteria are briefly described in the following.

'Predominant uses of accounting' refers to the primary function that accounting has in the respective country. We distinguish between the securities market perspective of accounting, to provide useful information for decisions of capital market participants (Demski and Christensen 2003), and a tax- and company-law perspective, which seeks to determine distributable income and payable taxes. This first criterion is informative about the roles financial accounting has to fulfil within each country, and therefore considers the influence of legal rules and the resulting attributes of the accounting system (Haller 1992). The securities-market perspective emphasises group accounts for the economic entity; the tax- and company-law perspective stresses single accounts for the legal entity. Accounting rules for decisions on contracting with the economic entity rely on timely and unbiased information and a material true and fair view concept; conservative accounting rules serve the company law and taxation function, and 'true and fair view' is interpreted as fulfilling formal requirements. The detailed argument for this was made in Chapter 3.

'Legal backing' denotes the degree to which the public sector intervenes in accounting regulation. It provides information about how accounting practices relate to the law. Different forms of legal backing exist. The nation state may prescribe formal and material accounting regulations directly by law, or it can delegate parts of this task by making legal reference to other sources of regulation. Legal backing can, however, also be achieved by strong state agencies, or it can be furthered through a strong role of courts setting 'accounting case law'. The state's incentive to intervene in accounting regulation depends on the dominant forms of social coordination and on the functions accounting has to fulfil in society.

'Extent of professional self-regulation' is a criterion because in many countries accounting has been self-regulated by those directly concerned with preparing or attesting accounts. However, as there is also a social function of accounting, the question may arise whether society can rely on professional self-regulation when the public interest is at stake. According to the extent to which state intervention may be necessary to secure the public interest, private actors will typically retain some function or role in accounting regulation (Olivier 2001). This criterion, together with legal backing, is informative about the public–private mix in accounting regulation (Puxty et al. 1987).

'Degree of internationalisation' refers to reliance on international rules and actors. While accounting has traditionally been regulated at the national level, in the last decades international elements of regulation appeared. Some of these regulatory elements are rooted in the private sector, others in the public. Most remarkably, privately organised international standard-setters such as the IASB have gained increasing relevance. Its predecessor was founded by a number of countries, among them the six country cases in question. However, each country participated for its own reasons and with its own degree of vigour. The EU, obviously belonging to the public sector, is also increasingly engaged in regulating financial reporting for its member states (Brackney and Witmer 2005). Standard-setting and self-regulation as well as public intervention into accounting regulation may thus become internationalised (Decker 2002; Benner et al. 2004).

## 4.1 European case studies

Recent developments in accounting regulation of European countries are largely influenced by EU legislation. Accounting-related company law was harmonised via European Council Directives, which led to a certain degree of formal convergence in the EU (Zimmermann et al. 2010). Two EC Directives are of outstanding importance in this context: the Fourth Directive, of 1978, which recognised minimum requirements for single accounts with respect to contents and presentation (78/660/EEC), and the Seventh Directive of 1983, which formulated rules for group accounts with the aim of achieving comparability and equivalence in the reports of the corporate group (83/349/EEC, 2). As these harmonisation efforts took place in company law, they applied to all firms operating in the member states. It is hardly surprising, therefore, that controversial issues were not regulated in full detail and that final decisions on these issues were left to national parliaments. Substantial differences in accounting remained.

A further integration of European group accounting occurred with the requirement for listed groups to publish financial reports in accordance with IFRS from 2005 onwards. This was introduced by the so-called IAS Regulation (EC No. 1606/2002). However, the mandatory switch to IFRS in the EU is restricted to consolidated accounts of listed firms. Accordingly, a variety of national standards remain relevant for all other types of company accounts. The consequences for convergence will become apparent when looking at the country cases of Germany, France and the UK.

### 4.1.1 Germany: Advancing the role of information accounting

*The predominant use of accounting*

In the traditional German business system accounting played a major role in calculating corporate payouts and payable taxes. This was due to the strong connection between financial accounting and company law and taxation. German company law is largely based on rules that refer directly to financial accounts in determining dividends and other payouts. Moreover, financial reports traditionally provided the basis for calculating taxable income, as financial accounting choices also affected tax accounts. This connection, in fact, worked in both directions, which led to the reverse authoritative principle, where tax legislation had an effect on financial reports. Both tax- and company-law orientations are centred on payouts of the legal entity. Accordingly, single accounts formed the dominant set of accounts in Germany. The legal orientation was also reflected in the characteristics of accounting rules, which applied a concept of unconditional conservatism. Accounting information was therefore of limited use from a securities-market perspective and for efficient individual contracting.

While it would, in theory, have been possible to develop separate accounting rules for group reporting to remedy adverse effects on financial reporting from tax and company laws, this did not happen for a long time. In fact, accounting rules for single and group accounts remained fairly similar. A possible explanation for this may be found in the German business system – often referred to as 'Deutschland AG' – where accounting information had little relevance for the decision-making process (Busse von Colbe 1996; Ali and Hwang 2000). Consolidated accounts, more or less dispensable in this system, were first introduced in Germany as a mandatory element of financial reporting with the Stock Corporation Act (the *Aktiengesetz*, or AktG) in 1965. Even then they remained relatively unimportant until the 1990s (Nobes and Parker 1991), when capital markets gained more weight with changes in the German business system. Large listed companies began to express concerns that German (group) accounting rules were not informative for investors and hence prevented them from raising capital abroad (Thiele and Tschesche 1997; Schildbach 2002). The legislator responded to this change in the use of accounting information with a number of pieces of modernising legislation and the creation of a private standard-setting institution. These developments were completed with the EU's switch to IFRS in 2005, when information-oriented financial statements became mandatory for all listed firms in Germany at the group account level.

### *The legal backing of financial reporting*

Accounting regulation in Germany is commonly associated with a high degree of state intervention, as parliamentary rule-setting is a long-standing tradition: the relevant law on accounting is put forward by the respective ministries and has to be approved by the parliament. Traditionally, the German Commercial Code (*Handelsgesetzbuch*, or HGB) at least technically constituted the primary source of accounting regulation. However, the HGB did not contain many detailed rules on financial reporting, and Generally Accepted Accounting Practices (GAAP) in Germany consisted of further sources. They comprised common and legal practice, as well as academic inputs and professional judgements. Lobbyists frequently intervened into parliamentary rule-making, and the final law can be considered as a consensual solution (Ordelheide 1999). Legal practice was of major importance in this context, as court decisions finally determined what was acceptable as GAAP.

Even though these different influences on standard-setting existed, formulating accounting rules ultimately remained the responsibility of the public sector. Accordingly, German accounting rules strongly reflected the needs of the payout-oriented company- and tax-law perspective. The first changes to this institutional setting occurred in the mid-1980s, when the legislator integrated EU requirements into national law and initiated reforms to improve the legal framework for investors. The Fourth and Seventh European Council Directives were simultaneously integrated into German law with the Accounting Directives Act (BiRiLiG) in 1985. This strengthened the role of consolidated accounts and introduced more detailed rules on financial reporting as well as the 'true-and-fair-view principle' to the HGB.[1]

An important step towards a more investor-oriented accounting framework came with the Securities Trading Act of 1994 (*Wertpapierhandelsgesetz,* or WpHG), which introduced additional disclosure rules for listed companies and improved the information basis for security trading. In 1998 the Capital Raising Facilitation Act (*Kapitalaufnahmeerleichterungsgesetz,* or KapAEG) allowed listed (parent) companies to publish their consolidated financial statements following accepted IAS. This also aimed at advancing the securities market perspective on financial accounting. Another major change happened the same year, when the Corporate Sector Supervision and Transparency Act (*Gesetz zur Kontrolle und Transparenz im Unternehmensbereich,* or KonTraG) was passed. It authorised the Federal Ministry of Justice (MOJ) to accredit a private standard-setting institution. In the same year the German Accounting Standards Committee (*Deutsches Rechnungslegungs Standards Committee,* or GASC) was appointed. Complementing these developments in group accounting, the Accounting Law Modernisation Act (BilMoG) of 2009, in particular, aligned German accounting laws with international practice. The law intended to establish a cost-efficient alternative to IFRS for small and medium-size companies without giving up the traditional function of calculating the distributable income (Hoffmann 2009; Zimmermann 2009).

### *The extent of professional self-regulation*

The profession in Germany is organised into two institutions: the older Institute of Auditors (*Institut der Wirtschaftsprüfer,* or IDW) and the Chamber of Public Accountants (*Wirtschaftsprüferkammer,* or WPK). Membership of the IDW, founded in the 1930s, is not mandatory, but only auditors qualify for membership. Its role is mainly to lobby for the interest of the accountants and give advice in accounting-related policy issues. The Public Accountant Act (*Wirtschaftsprüferordnung,* or WPO) stipulated the creation of the WPK in 1961 and made membership mandatory for every auditor. The WPK is an organisation under public law and mainly responsible for the supervision and admission of its members, quality control of audits and the development of auditing standards.

With the state assuming a dominant role, German accounting traditionally relied little on the forces of self-regulation. Nevertheless, the profession did play a role in finding the consensual solution that finally formed German

*Table 4.1* Major developments in German accounting regulation

| Year | Law | Reform |
|---|---|---|
| 1961 | Public Accountant Act (*Gesetz über eine Berufsordnung der Wirtschaftsprüfer*, or WPO) | Foundation and mandatory membership of auditors in the WPK |
| 1965 | Stock Corporations Act (*Aktiengesetz*, or AktG) | Mandatory consolidated accounts for certain capital-market-oriented companies |
| 1985 | Accounting Directives Act (*Bilanzrichtliniengesetz*, or BiRiLiG) | Transformation of the Fourth and Seventh European Council directive into German law |
| 1994 | Securities Trading Act (*Wertpapierhandelsgesetz*, or WpHG) | Introduction of additional disclosure rules for listed companies |
| 1998 | Corporate Sector Supervision and Transparency Act (*Gesetz zur Kontrolle und Transparenz im Unternehmensbereich*, or KonTraG) | Creation of the GASC |
| 1998 | Capital Raising Facilitation Act (*Kapitalaufnahmeerleichterungs-Gesetz*, or KapAEG) | Option for listed companies to publish consolidated financial statements according to IAS or US GAAP |
| 2002 | EC Regulation Nr 1606/2002 | Requirement for capital-market-oriented companies to apply IFRS from 2005 |
| 2009 | Accounting Law Modernisation Act (*Bilanzrechtsmodernisierungsgesetz*, or BilMoG) | Strengthening of informational content of German GAAP financial statements alignment with IFRS |

GAAP. The profession contributed, for example, by giving advice during the law-making process or by exerting indirect influence on standard-setting via the pronouncement of auditing standards (Marten et al. 2003). These standards not only affected the quality of corporate audits but were also informative for balance sheet preparers and relevant in court decisions (Schruff 2006).

A stronger incorporation of private actors into the standard-setting process came with the creation of the ASCG (before 2012 known as GASC). The standard-setter is organised as an incorporated association under private law, membership of which is open to companies and bodies that are involved with accounting issues. The Administrative Board appoints two committees, the IFRS committee and the German GAAP committee. The tasks of the ASCG include advising the MOJ in accounting legislation proposals, representing Germany in international standardisation bodies and, most importantly, developing independently accounting standards for consolidated financial statements, the German Financial Reporting Standards (*Deutsche Rechnungslegungs Standards*, or DRS). The ASCG is privately financed, and the state has no influence on its staffing. Its standards, though, are not immediately binding but must be approved by parliament. Like all national bodies in Europe, the board lost its competencies in setting accounting rules for listed groups with the EU-wide solution of uniform IFRS application. Today the ASCG focuses on developing group accounting standards for non-listed companies and on participating in the IASB's deliberations (Zimmermann 2010a).

*The degree of internationalisation*

International developments in accounting regulation have been influenced by the German accounting profession ever since the foundation of the IASC, as both professional institutes could be found among the founder members. The first international developments affecting German accounting regulation came with the transformation of the relevant EC regulation into German law. Qualitatively, however, even after that transformation the accounting system remained broadly unchanged owing to the wide scope for choice within the accounting directives and their Continental European imprint. Internationalisation of accounting rules was advanced with the issuance of the KapAEG and the possibility of preparing group accounts according to IAS. The act was not only intended to strengthen the German capital market by introducing investor-oriented financial reports but also to enhance the ability of German firms to access foreign capital markets. As US GAAP statements of US firms were accepted for listing on Germany's stock exchanges already, the legislator saw its act as abolishing discrimination in favour of domestic companies. Retrospectively, the intention to encourage cross-listings of German firms turned out to be less important, as only a small number of firms found these new rules attractive enough to list in the US. The motive of advancing information accounting in fact was more relevant, as a large number of companies used the opportunity that they had lobbied for (Born 2002) and applied IFRS or US GAAP after the new law had been passed. With the switch to IFRS in 2005, standards for group accounting were mainly outside the jurisdiction of German authorities and became a matter of EU regulation.

*Summary*

The German accounting system emerged in connection with tax and company legislation. The primary use of financial reports lay in the determination of distributable income, serving as an instrument to hinder excessive payouts and support the going concern of the company. In this institutional system accounting regulation was dominated by state activities, as parliamentary rule-setting seemed best suited to achieving the goals set by the state. The legal backing for German accounting rules, therefore, was traditionally high, while the information function of accounting, which is geared towards securities markets, was almost neglected. The accounting landscape started to change with the increased use of capital markets as a source of finance and the internationalisation efforts brought forward by EU legislation in the late 1980s. To strengthen the information function, separate group accounts were introduced to German law and the profession became more involved in the standard-setting process, especially through the private standard-setter ASCG. The current accounting system consequently is a hybrid, with the traditional rules remaining the basis for payout-oriented single accounts and information-oriented accounting rules determining the content of consolidated accounts. The movement towards more information-oriented accounting standards finally spilled over into HGB regulation. To sum up, German regulation shows a clear tendency towards more information-oriented accounting, although some national preferences remain in the area of single accounting. Table 4.1 displays major developments in German accounting regulation.

### 4.1.2 France: Arranging national institutions for supranational regulation

*The predominant use of accounting*

In France the accounting system evolved under the dominant influence of the state, which linked financial reporting with tax calculation and promoted its usefulness for creditor relations. In the traditional accounting model the main users of financial statements were consequently long-term financiers and fiscal authorities. In this payout-oriented system consolidated accounts were of minor importance and single accounts represented the common set of accounts. Qualitatively they were designed according to the preconception of depicting company value in a prudent way. Even though company law reform introduced some regulation on group accounting in 1966, only a few companies started to publish consolidated accounts (Nobes and Parker 2010). Comprehensive regulation on group accounting was not introduced until the Seventh European Council Directive was integrated into national law (National decree 85–11) in 1985.

The functions that accounting had to fulfil in the French business system changed in the 1990s as a result of altered capital needs of French companies. After two waves of privatising public enterprises, in order to increase the competitiveness of the business sector, companies started to raise funds on international capital markets (Rutz 1998). This forced them to prepare more information-oriented financial reports. With the EU's broad move towards IFRS for group accounts in 2005, information-focused financial reports became a mandatory element for capital-market-oriented companies in France.

### *The legal backing of financial reporting*

Two major sources of accounting regulations existed in the traditional French accounting system, both controlled by the state: the legal accounting statutes and the National Accounting Code (*Plan Comptable Général,* or PCG) (Hoarau 2009). The accounting statutes comprised the laws of the Commercial Code, the relevant tax legislation and other decrees and ministerial orders put forward by the state. These accounting statutes mainly set out formal accounting requirements, which were detailed by the PCG (Hoarau 2000). The code contained a detailed chart of accounts, requirements for the annual presentation of balance sheets and profit-and-loss accounts, and general accounting principles and valuation regulations (Flower and Ebbers 2002). The legal status of the PCG was merely that of an appendix to a ministerial approval order and, as such, it had little formal coercive power even though it was typically observed (Colasse and Pochet 2009). It was maintained and amended by the National Accounting Council (*Conseil National de la Comptabilité,* or CNC), which was set up simultaneously with the enactment of the PCG in 1957. Its opinions had the status of recommendations until a ministerial order made them binding (Colasse and Standish 2001). The Ministry therefore had the ultimate authority to change the PCG. Nevertheless, the code had broad acceptance in the accounting community, as its users were involved in the process of drawing up the regulation (Colasse and Pochet 2009). In 1965 the PCG also became the basis for tax accounting (Decree of 28 October 1965), and in 1982 its (then reformed) regulations became compulsory for all companies subject to the Commercial Code through a ministerial order (Decree of 27 April 1982). In 1985 rules concerning the preparation of consolidated accounts were introduced to the PCG with National Decree 85–11.

Major changes to the French accounting institutions were initiated in 1996, when the structure of the CNC was changed (National Decree 96–746). With this reform the number of members of the CNC was heavily reduced and the participation of the profession was increased in order to make the decision process more efficient (Hoarau 2009). These changes were complemented by the creation of the Accounting Regulation Committee (Comité de la Réglementation Comptable, or CRC), which was created as a public body under the control of the Ministry of Finance (MOF). It gained formal standard-setting competency for all bookkeeping entities in France in 1998 with Law 98–261. The CRC was established to simplify the standard-setting process by creating a single body with the ability to set mandatory standards for all bookkeeping entities (Hoarau 2009). All rules of the PCG were rewritten into CRC regulations. However, the committee was mainly designed to adopt accounting standards following CNC recommendations, with the latter continuing to be the most important actor in standard-setting (OEC/CNCC 1999).[2] Legal backing in this setting remained high, as all accounting regulations of the CRC had to be transposed into national law and the state sector still controlled the two major accounting institutions.

In 2007 the legislator again modified the accounting institutions (National Decree 2007–629). In particular, the structure of the CNC was modified in preparation for the setting up of the National Standards Authority (*Autorité des Normes Comptables*, or ANC) with Law 2009–79 in 2009. This institution now combines the tasks of the CNC and CRC in a single standard-setter (Hoarau 2009). The creation of the ANC is part of a major reform to modernise the legal framework of the French financial market. Its decision-making body will be much smaller and rely even more on accounting professionals.[3] The ANC fulfils two major roles: it develops the standards that become binding regulation once the Ministry has integrated them into national law, and it responds to international developments by taking part in work groups (working parties on accounting regulation and standard setting) and publishing statements in regards to current IASB projects. It is co-financed by private actors and the state, and its decision-making body consists of representatives of the private and public sector, but the Ministry of Economy chooses the members of the executive board, and its chairman is even designated by the President of the Republic.

### *Professional self-regulation*

Owing to the potent French nation state, the influence of the private sector on accounting regulation in the traditional French accounting model has been restricted to its role as deliberative partner. The accounting profession had little formal competence, but was present in the consensus model (Hoarau 2009). Two professional bodies exist: the National Institute of Statutory Auditors (*Compagnie Nationale des Commissaires aux Comptes*, or CNCC) and the Institute of Public Accountants (*Ordre des Experts Comptables*, or OEC). Both institutions are privately incorporated, but they are under the supervision of the MOJ and the MOF respectively. The OEC was founded back in 1942 as the association of certified accountants. Its purpose was to secure the independence and good name of the accounting profession and to publish recommendations concerning auditing procedures and standard interpretations (Hoarau 1998). The CNCC was created and legally acknowledged in the Commercial Code of 1969. Its main tasks were to develop and issue new auditing standards, to supervise the statutory audits and to publish technical guidelines for the application of the standards (OEC/CNCC 1999). Since then, membership of the National Institute has been mandatory for all certified statutory auditors, and the organisation has been responsible for ensuring the reputation and independence of its members.

Both bodies have sent delegates to the respective accounting bodies of every institutional phase and have therefore always influenced the development of accounting standards. While they played a minor role – and occupied fewer seats – in the CNC when it was founded, their influence grew steadily with every reform of the council. In the ANC the profession now represents an important group (8 out of 16 people) of the decision-making body (Hoarau 2009).

*The degree of internationalisation*

The harmonisation of accounting standards in Europe via the implementation of the Fourth (78/660/EEC) and Seventh (83/394/EEC, 2) EC Directives brought several changes to the French accounting regime that aligned it with international developments. Most notably, the requirement to prepare consolidated accounts in 1985 was due to the adoption of European regulation into French law. Previously, some companies published group accounts on the basis of international rules (Touron 2005). In the 1990s the use of foreign capital markets became a common source of finance also for French companies. They had a strong interest in allowing consolidated accounts according to international rules also for national use to minimise reporting costs. The accounting profession, which participated in the foundation of the IASC with the OEC, also lobbied for such practice. But the French state had difficulties in allowing foreign standards because it was afraid of a significant loss of influence. In the end, EU politics rendered this discussion meaningless with the mandatory introduction of IFRS for the consolidated accounts of all capital-market-oriented companies in 2002 (EC Regulation 1606/2002). The creation of a committee that deals with international accounting issues shows that the ANC has developed the capacity to take a proactive part in IASB developments (Hoarau 2009).

*Summary*

Accounting regulation in France has traditionally been dominated by the state. In particular, the rules in the National Accounting Plan, which formed the main source of accounting regulation, used to be released and amended via ministerial orders (Colasse and Standish 2001). However, professional bodies also affected the standard-setting process through their presence and influence in the debates of the standard-setting institutions. Since the 1980s, the French accounting system has found itself at odds with financial globalisation and the EU harmonisation process. However, accounting regulation did not change significantly until 1998. With the establishment of the CRC a single body responsible for developing accounting standards was created to simplify the standard-setting process. The usefulness of accounting information for investment decisions remained limited, as companies in France were not allowed to opt out of local accounting standards. This changed when the EU introduced IFRS as the only applicable standards for group accounting. In consequence, a hybridisation of the accounting landscape, similar to Germany, occurred: single accounts remain dominated by

*Table 4.2* Major developments in French accounting regulation

| Year | Law | Reform |
|---|---|---|
| 1957 | | Foundation of CNC |
| 1965 | Decree 28 October | The PCG becomes the basis for tax accounting |
| 1969 | Amendment to the commercial code 12 August | Foundation of CNCC |
| 1982 | Arrêté 27 April | The PCG becomes applicable to all companies subject to the commercial code |
| 1985 | National decree 85–11 | Implementation of the Fourth and Seventh EU Directives: Consolidated accounts become mandatory |
| 1996 | National decree 96–746 | Reorganisation of the CNC |
| 1998 | Law 98–261 | Foundation of CRC to complement the role of the CNC with regulatory powers |
| 2002 | EC Regulation Nr 1606/2002 | Requirement for capital-market-oriented companies to apply IFRS – from 2005 |
| 2007 | Decree 2007–629 | Restructuring of the CNC |
| 2009 | Law 2009–79 | Creation of the ANC, taking over and combining the tasks of CRC and CNC |

a prudent set of national accounting rules, whereas group accounts follow international standards. However, the national perception of these similar developments differs in the two neighbouring countries. While the German regulator welcomes information-oriented accounting elements into national legislation, the French accounting system organises national institutions to form a stronghold against supra-national regulation, of which the recent reforms that created the ANC is a further example. Table 4.2 displays major developments in French accounting regulation.

### 4.1.3 UK: Boosting state influence

*The predominant use of accounting*

In the UK financial statements are predominantly used to provide useful information for financial market participants seeking to make decisions. Traditionally, financial reporting was seen as a matter between the stakeholders in the firm, and its regulation was largely left to private arrangements. The overriding principle for the preparation of accounts was to give a fair presentation of the company's prospects (Walton 1993; Flower 2004). This principle was applied for single accounts as well as for group accounts, which became mandatory in the UK in the first half of the 20th century (Companies Act of 1948). Financial statements have a clear information perspective and mostly follow the concept of unbiased representation. Nevertheless, single accounts are also used for the calculation of distributable income to pay dividends. Company law here distinguishes between accounting profit and realised profit, which is the basis for distributions. Accounting profit is the starting point for determining the realised profit, which requires some adjustments in accounting figures. Although a matter of company law, the determination of these adjustments lies within the competence of the accounting profession (KPMG 2008). Some authors (Nobes 2006) see a marginal influence of taxation on financial reporting while others deny this relation completely (Lamb 1996; Eberhartinger 1999). Being a EU member state, consolidated accounts in the UK have had to be prepared according to IFRS for listed firms since 2005. Unlike most other EU members, British regulation also allows companies to prepare single accounts according to IFRS.

### *The legal backing of financial reporting*

In the British model the legal backing for accounting practices was rather weak. In traditional corporate law only the formal requirement to disclose an audited balance sheet and profit-and-loss account were laid out. With regard to material regulation, the law merely required a true and fair view to be given to a skilled addressee, especially an investor (Walton 1993; Flower 2004). Beyond this, company law also introduced some basic accounting rules, such as the distinction between reserves and provisions, in order to make the creation of hidden reserves more difficult (Nobes 2006). Generally, laws remained relatively unimportant, and the legislator avoided interfering with questions of recognition and measurement, and determining rules was delegated to professional self-regulation (Flower 2004).

The period of *laissez-faire* lasted about until British accession to the European Community. As a consequence of harmonisation efforts, the Companies Act of 1989 introduced major changes into the accounting regulations in company law. The act implemented the requirements of the Seventh EC Directive and consolidated the changes already made in the previous Act of 1981, including the execution of the Fourth EC Directive. Unlike in France and Germany, requirements such as the 'true-and-fair-view' override and the mandatory preparation of group accounts had already been common features of British accounting. In contrast, the requirement to recognise accounting standards in company law represented a novelty for British regulation. Also the Companies Act of 1989 required accounts to be prepared according to 'applicable accounting standards' for the first time. The accounting standards that were published by the Accounting Standards Committee (ASC) from 1970 were considered as such standards and thus gained legal backing through the act. This blanket reference made newly released standards instantly applicable without further endorsement.

In November 1987 an expert group (the 'Dearing Committee') was appointed to propose changes for the standard-setting process (Eccles and Holt 2005). Following the recommendations contained in the report of this group, the Accounting Standards Board (ASB) took over responsibility from the ASC in 1990. Although privately organised, the creation of the ASB represents an increase in state intervention, as it is partly funded and staffed by the Department of Trade and Industry (DTI).

*The extent of professional self-regulation*

Professional self-regulation has been a long-standing tradition in the UK. British literature rightly claims the emergence of the 'accounting profession' as one of the nation's contributions to accountancy (Flower 2004). It is therefore hardly surprising that Britain has the oldest and largest organised accounting profession in the world (Nobes 2004). In the UK and Ireland there are six institutions representing the profession. The Institute of Chartered Accountants in England and Wales (ICAEW) and the Association of Chartered Certified Accountants (ACCA) stand out, as these two bodies represent the majority of all certified accountants.[4] Unlike other countries, Britain saw professional bodies emerge by a process of self-regulation, and there was no need to establish them by law (Puxty et al. 1987). The task of the six professional institutes was to control the admission of members, to supervise their practice and give guidance for practical accounting questions. In absence of legal stipulations these professional bodies also dominated standard-setting in the UK for a long time. The guiding principles and recommended accounting practices that the institutes issued for their members formed the basis for GAAP for a long time. Guiding principles could vary between the different professional bodies (Walton 1993). This left the market to operate freely, and as a result accounting practice varied considerably over time and from industry to industry (Lee 1984).

In the early 1970s, impending EC-membership made the diversity of accounting rules within the UK seem arcane. Hence, the professional bodies started to harmonise rules among the institutes and created the ASC as standard-setting institution. Three major professional bodies sponsored the initial enterprise, and others joined later that decade (Defliese 1981). This group of professional bodies became known as the Consultative Committee of Accountancy Bodies (CCAB) (Pong and Whittington 1996). The accountancy bodies jointly financed the ASC, and each retained the power of veto over any standard. In consequence, the ASC had little authority of its own. Very often, the final standards were based on compromise (Choi and Meek 2008). With the creation of the ASB in 1990 a new standard-setting institution was set up, which also comprised actors from the public sector. The ASB is incorporated as a subsidiary of the Financial Reporting Council (FRC), which is a non-profit organisation financed by the state, the profession and the companies to which its standards apply. The FRC is a limited liability company with state guarantee, whose directors are mostly drawn from the business world but are appointed by the state.

As a consequence of the reforms, the role of the respective professional bodies has been much reduced, providing the standard-setter with the now customary independence from the profession. In acknowledging the wide array of interests in financial reporting, the ASB now also has a membership with a corporate and investment background. Although the state intervenes more strongly in accounting regulation in this new model, it has taken on only a coordinating role: a closer look into the membership of the council bodies reveals some distance from the state and political decision-making.

*The degree of internationalisation*

International developments did not influence UK accounting significantly until the early 1980s, when EC directives were adopted into national law. Once internationalisation became increasingly relevant through the rise of European harmonisation and the search for a global set of accounting standards, the UK took on a leading role. London, in particular, as the financial heart of Europe, played a major part in the international regulatory expansion. Allowing international disclosures on the London Stock Exchange (LSE) broadened the market for foreign listings and fostered the internationalisation of capital markets. The involvement of the UK in the creation and operation of the IASC – and later the IASB – also relate to this motive of internationalisation. With the ICAEW, the British accounting profession has been among the leading proponents of the establishment of an international standard-setter. Its president became the first chairman of the IASC, and its headquarters are still located in London. As British accounting rules emerge from the tradition of financial reporting serving security markets, they also formed an important input for the development of the IASB standards.

The UK has also been a front-runner in the assimilation of international accounting regulation. As early as the late 1990s the ASB began to harmonise accounting standards in the UK with existing IFRS. For consolidated accounts these efforts became irrelevant with the switch to IFRS at the European level in 2002 (EC Regulation 1606/2002). But for single accounts this process has continued. It has also become possible to choose to prepare single accounts according to IFRS instead of UK GAAP with the implementation of the IAS regulation.

*Summary*

Accounting in the UK looks back on a long-standing tradition of private responsibility. In the old model all material accounting regulation was formulated by the professional bodies, the accounting institutes. Since the 1970s the British financial reporting system has adopted some new

*Table 4.3* Major developments in UK accounting regulation

| Year | Law | Reform |
|---|---|---|
| 1948 | Companies Act of 1948 | Requirement to prepare consolidated accounts |
| 1973 | | Establishment of the ASC |
| 1981 | Companies Act of 1981 | Adoption of the Fourth EC Council Directive into national law |
| 1989 | Companies Act of 1989 | Adoption of the Seventh Council Directive into national law, requirement to refer to 'applicable accounting standards' |
| 1990 | | Creation of the FRC; replacement of the ASC by the ASB |
| 2002 | EC Regulation Nr 1606/2002 | Requirement for capital-market-oriented companies to apply IFRS from 2005 |
| 2009 | | ASB discussion paper: Replacement of UK GAAP with IFRS for Small and Medium-Sized Entities (SME) |

features. Changes were triggered to a large extent by EU harmonisation, leading to more detailed stipulations in company law. Accounting rules were harmonised among the different institutes, and an independent standard-setting institution was created. In contrast to the traditional approach of self-regulation, this body is officially acknowledged and at least indirectly monitored by the government. State influence in the UK has constantly increased over the last decades, but the state has abstained from explicitly formulating accounting standards. Being one of the world's most important financial centres, the UK has always been a promoter of international accounting regulations. The ability to prepare all financial accounts according to international rules can be seen as an expression of this leading role in internationalisation. Table 4.3 displays major developments in UK accounting regulation.

## 4.2 Non-European case studies

The European case studies have shown common patterns of change. The information function of financial reporting, at least for consolidated accounts, has become a predominant aspect throughout. There is an increasing balance between state and self-regulation: the UK, with its reliance on the private sector, shows a stronger involvement of the state, while France and Germany embrace more private involvement. Over all, there is a tendency to replace national by international solutions at least for listed firms. To assess whether convergence in accounting regulation truly represents an international and not merely a regulatory European phenomenon, country cases outside the EU need to be considered. In the following chapters, the changes in accounting regulation in the US, Canada and Japan are discussed.

### 4.2.1 The US: Adjusting the public–private mix

*The predominant use of accounting*

In the US one set of financial accounts dominates, which is designed for information purposes. The calculation of amounts distributable to shareholders may be linked to accounting figures prepared in accordance with GAAP, but in general this is not the case, and dividend distribution is left to private arrangements with financiers. Moreover, financial statements are not used for the calculation of taxable income. Accounting rules and fiscal rules are strictly independent, as tax reports are generated outside of the accounting framework (Lamb et al. 1998). National securities law has assigned the SEC the competency to set the financial reporting standards for listed firms; to all others individual state regulations apply. With this clear securities-law focus, informing investors constitutes the primary objective of most financial reporting. This is reflected in the shape and focus of US accounting rules. Corresponding to the informational needs of capital market participants, they favour the concept of unbiased representation and emphasise group accounting. Although group accounts used to be common practice, the first accounting standard on consolidation appeared only in 1959 (Taylor 1996). In the one-statement approach of the US, where consolidation is seen as a qualitative characteristic rather than an individual category of accounts, consolidated accounts virtually substitute companies' parent-only statements.

*The legal backing of financial reporting*

In line with the information orientation of financial reporting, accounting in the US first emerged as a matter of private arrangements. This changed with the stock market crash of 1929, when the federal government decided to intervene substantially in financial reporting (Morgan and Previts 1984). As a consequence, accounting regulation was ushered in with the Securities Act (SA) of 1933 and the Securities Exchange Act (SEA) of 1934, most visibly with the creation of the SEC. The road to accounting intervention taken by the US government was different from that taken by most other countries, as it did regulate accounting via securities law and by delegating regulatory competency to a state agency. Owing to the federal character of the US, where company law is not a federal responsibility, only securities law allowed for uniform intervention into corporate disclosures. Nevertheless, the amendments to the securities law did not formulate detailed accounting requirements but transferred the ultimate responsibility for accounting regulation to the SEC. This state agency is responsible to the US Congress and is endowed with the power to prescribe the formal and material content of financial reports. The SEC remained in line with the liberal approach, restricting its role to the supervision and encouragement of standard-setting in the private sector (Nobes and Parker 2010).

In the years following its creation, the SEC loosely cooperated with a sequence of different standard-setters. None of them met the regulator's expectations, as they were perceived to lack either independence or efficiency.[5] In 1973 the Financial Accounting Standards Board (FASB) was created in an attempt to make good these shortcomings. It was explicitly and for the first time recognised as the institution to set binding accounting standards in the US with the SEC's Financial Reporting Release No. 1, Section 101 (Morgan and Previts 1984). Practically, the role of the SEC since then has rested on its powers of veto and its participation in the FASB's deliberations (Newman 1981). The Commission primarily participates in the standard-setting process through comments on draft regulations, although it always made clear that it would step in and set standards itself if the private-sector standard setter failed to meet the regulator's expectations (Hendriksen 1977).

*The extent of professional self-regulation*

The accounting profession has always been a major actor in US accounting regulation. First, the accounting profession solely determined accounting practices, and later the SEC officially incorporated them into the standard-setting process. In the US there exists one body representing the accounting profession and another private organisation representing the realm of accounting academe. The profession is organised in the AICPA, the academe in the American Accounting Association (AAA). The AICPA was founded in 1887 as the American Association of Public Accountants and was renamed in 1957. It sets auditing standards and represents the profession in the regulatory discourse. Unlike most other countries, membership in the professional body is not obligatory in order to practice as a certified accountant in the US, as regulation of the profession is a matter of the individual states. The AAA was established in 1916 as the American Association of University Instructors in Accounting and was renamed in 1935. Its objectives are to enhance accounting education and to advance accounting-related knowledge, but also to perform a service to society in the form of expertise. Both organisations have had a significant influence on accounting practices as well as on the institutional shape of the regulatory system in the US.

Following its creation, the SEC transferred the standard-setting responsibility to the AICPA. Two efforts by the Institute to formulate accounting standards failed[6] because of their complicated standard-setting process, their lack of independence and legitimacy (Roberts et al. 2005). In 1971 the AAA proposed appointing an interdisciplinary commission to consider how

*Table 4.4* Major developments in US accounting regulation

| Year | Law | Reform |
|---|---|---|
| 1933/1934 | Securities and Exchange Act 1933/1934 | Creation of the SEC; federal regulation of accounting rules for listed companies |
| 1973 | Financial Reporting Release No. 1, Section 101 | Establishment of the FASB as primary authority setting financial reporting standards in the US |
| 2002 | 'Norwalk Agreement' | Formalisation of the intend to harmonise IFRS and US GAAP |
| 2007 | SEC Release nos. 33–8879 | Permission for foreign companies registered at US stock markets to use IFRS |

accounting standards should be developed in future. The AICPA reacted by setting up a study group, known as the Wheat Committee. Its recommendations included the creation of a standard-setting institution separate from the accounting profession. The almost immediate adoption of the Wheat Committee's recommendations resulted in the creation of the FASB, which ended the AICPA's standard-setting role.

The new standard-setter was, and has continued to be, administered by the Financial Accounting Foundation (FAF). Ownership of the foundation rests with the trustees, who are appointed by the FAF's constituent organisations. They reflect the wider accounting community, including the AICPA, the AAA and other groups of users, preparers and interested parties. The foundation is set up in such a way that no constituent group is able to dominate it. The FAF appoints the members of the FASB, who are drawn from the accounting community as well as from the corporate and investment world. The board is officially charged with the task of establishing and maintaining binding accounting standards for all entities registered with the SEC. Initially it was financed by voluntary contributions; now independence is further guaranteed with a fee-based financing system introduced in 2004.

### *The degree of internationalisation*

US accounting standards have been adopted by many other countries, but the regulator's gaze remained solely on the development of accounting standards relevant for the national financial system. Although the AICPA was among the founding members of the IASC, international developments were largely neglected in the US. Only when international harmonisation in accounting became more relevant regulators got more closely involved in the internationalisation activities of the IASB. In this regard, the FASB and IASB published a memorandum of understanding (the 'Norwalk Agreement') in October 2002 formalising their commitment to the convergence of US GAAP and IAS. In 2007 the SEC decided that foreign companies registered at US stock markets and classified as foreign private issues were no longer required to prepare a reconciliation of IRFS accountings to US GAAP (SEC Release nos. 33–8879). Further changes to group accounting in the USA are included in the road map proposed by the SEC in 2008 and reaffirmed in 2010 for the full adoption of IFRS for US issuers beginning in 2014, but this has become increasingly unlikely. Although the SEC published a staff paper in May 2011 suggesting one possible approach to incorporate IFRS into the financial reporting system, no clear progress has been made. The final IFRS work plan report of the SEC neither provides any final policy decisions nor suggestions when an incorporation of IFRS should occur (SEC 2012).

However, compared with most other OECD countries the US represent a rare example where the financial reporting system has not been influenced by international developments until very recently, and where the influence has not been deep.

*Summary*

Accounting regulation in the US is built on a unique mixture of a state (government) engagement and private-sector activity. Originating in the British tradition of self-regulation, professional bodies have traditionally been strong and played a decisive role in the development of the US accounting landscape. Unlike the UK as a European outsider system, the state intervened fairly early in the accounting regulation for listed groups. Here securities laws and the SEC guarantee that the federal state has a strong influence. The FASB, as the most important standard-setter, belongs to the private sector: organisationally independent, it balances interests, receiving input from the profession and other lobbying groups. Tax regulation has no influence on accounting regulation in the US, and the use of single accounts is left to private arrangements beyond the regulatory scope of the state. Internationalisation has not been an issue in the US for a long time, as US GAAP were often used as international accounting rules and broadly accepted by foreign states. With the increased relevance of IFRS, the US is engaging more strongly in international cooperation in the field of accounting regulation. Table 4.4 displays major developments in US accounting regulation.

### 4.2.2 Canada: Strengthening local markets with international accounting

*The predominant use of accounting*

Financial reporting in Canada is also in the Anglo-Saxon accounting tradition. Similarities to the US are due partly to the two countries sharing the same British legal ancestry but partly also to their deep economic connections, which have led to similar developments in the two neighbouring countries (Nobes and Parker 2010). In consequence, a clear orientation towards the information function of financial reports exists in Canada. It is reflected in the 'true-and-fair-view' concept and in the dominance of consolidated accounts.

The payout function of accounting has no relevance for financial reporting in Canada. It is separated from financial accounting and performed by additional regulatory instruments, such as insolvency and liquidity tests. With these legally relevant functions being performed outside the scope of accounting regulation, the Canadian legislator has had few incentives to intervene in accounting regulation and has left this policy field to the concern of private actors. Canada continued to represent a regulatory model where the state completely delegates responsibility for developing accounting standards.

Not only has the source of accounting standards remained – with a few organisational modifications – unaltered, but also the predominant use of accounting has not changed significantly. Accounting in Canada mainly serves as an instrument to inform capital markets. The limited size of the national capital market makes it necessary for Canadian companies to find sources of finance abroad. A major concern of recent accounting regulation in Canada is therefore the international acceptance and comparability of Canadian financial reports.

### *The legal backing of financial reporting*

As is typical of a country in the Anglo-Saxon tradition, the state has tended to interfere very little in accounting regulation, and accounting rules were formulated by the profession. At the beginning of the 20th century material accounting regulation by the legislator did not exist, and securities law merely required the provision of audited annual accounts in some Canadian provinces. This period of extreme self-regulation lasted until the 1970s, when concerns arose about the adequacy of existing accounting and disclosure standards in response to repeated financial scandals. As a consequence, in 1972 the securities commissions published National Policy Instrument No. 27, which required all listed companies to report in accordance with the instructions set out in the CICA Handbook. This requirement was reinforced at the federal level with the Business Corporations Act of 1975. The act widened the application of the standards to all companies incorporated under the Act and represented the first legal intervention into material accounting regulation in Canada, as the privately set accounting standards of the CICA Handbook became Canadian GAAP. Securities regulation first introduced the handbook as a common basis for accounting, but company law made it legally binding for all Canadian incorporations. Encompassing both legal dimensions, the CICA standards consequently formed the uniform basis for all accounting in Canada (Rennie and Senkow 2009).

In the following years the state did not interfere with standard-setting beyond the delegation of the regulatory competency to the CICA. To maintain and amend the accounting standards remained a task of the accounting profession. A string of private standard-setting institutions has been created since the 1970s to fulfil this task.[7] Currently, this task is performed by the AcSB, set up by the profession in 1991. The AcSB is indirectly backed by federal legislation through the Act 'Governing the Canadian Institute of Chartered Accountants' of 1990, which provides the CICA with the authority to develop and establish accounting standards in Canada.

*The extent of professional self-regulation*

Being a federal state, Canada can look back on strong regional forms of coordination. In the accounting profession this led to a number of independent provincial institutes, each carrying out the examination and supervision of its members as well as determining accepted accounting practices. To coordinate activities among these institutes and to harmonise education and examination of chartered accountants, the CICA was incorporated early in the 20th century under a Special Act of the Canadian Parliament.[8] Membership of the CICA is associated with membership of one of the provincial institutes. In the early days of Canadian accounting, professional practices as conducted by the members of the different institutes formed the basis for preparing financial accounts. The CICA undertook an attempt to harmonise these practices by issuing bulletins on accounting and auditing practices through the associated Accounting and Auditing Research Committee (AARC). These bulletins represented an initial step towards a common Canadian set of accounting rules, as they codified for the first time existing principles of practice for all member institutes similar to common law (Baylin et al. 1996). In the 1960s, the structure of the standard-setting process was altered when the existing bulletins were reorganised and aggregated into the CICA Handbook. Once the handbook was legally enacted as the only source of Canadian GAAP in 1975, the profession was confronted with the task of finding an organisational structure to maintain these standards efficiently. The early Accounting Standards Committee (AcSC) was replaced by the smaller AcSB in 1990, which continues to develop and enact accounting standards today. Currently, the board draws its members from the wider accounting profession. The AcSB is incorporated under the umbrella of the Accounting Standards Oversight Council (AcSOC), which was established in 2000 by the CICA. Its mission is to oversee the AcSB and to appoint its members. All of these bodies are solely financed by the CICA.

*The degree of internationalisation*

The Canadian accounting system evolved with the limited nature of local sources of finance in mind. Adapting accounting standards to access foreign capital markets has therefore always been an issue in Canadian accounting regulation. One expression of this is the CICA's membership of the IASC's predecessor, the AISG. Several cooperative arrangements, such as the North

American Security Administrators Association and the Multi Jurisdictional Disclosure System (MJDS), are also relevant to this move towards internationalisation. The latter came into force in 1991 with National Policy Instrument 71–101 and had a major influence on the common evolvement of both countries. The objective of the agreement was to make access to US capital markets more efficient and less costly for Canadian companies and vice versa. Under the MJDS, foreign private companies are granted access to the national capital markets without additional registration and reporting requirements once they are registered with a securities authority in a country participating in the MJDS agreement. The adoption of the MJDS was applauded by large Canadian issuers but has been used much less by US issuers to access Canadian markets.

The similarities and joint agreements with the US did not prevent the AcSB deciding in 2006 to require listed companies to report in accordance with IFRS from 2011 on (Amendment to NI 52–107). With this decision Canada became one of the first major OECD countries to replace national reporting standards completely with IFRS. Three main factors made Canada decide to adopt IFRS. First, Canada's capital market has less than a 4 per cent share of the global capital market (Cherry 2008b). Therefore, Canada considers the adoption of IFRS as a cost-effective method to boost investments in Canadian capital markets (AcSB 2006b). Second, a continued strategy of harmonisation with US GAAP would impose increased costs of compliance compared to IFRS on Canadian firms, since Canadian GAAP is regarded as relatively similar to IFRS (AcSB 2006b). Third, considerations of the SEC to remove reconciliation requirements of cross-listed companies preparing financial statements according to IFRS contributed to the Canadian decision. As this requirement has already been dropped, Canadian companies listed in the US will not face any additional costs as a result of a mandatory switch to IFRS.

In order to prevent difficulties at the switching date, the adoption strategy is supported by a comprehensive implementation plan issued by the AcSB in 2006 (Cherry 2008a). The plan outlines key activities that should facilitate adoption in 2011. Among other things, the AcSB started to make changes to the Canadian GAAP to reduce differences from IFRS. The EU already recognises the Canadian GAAP as equivalent to IFRS as adopted by the EU. Additionally, since 2008, the AcSB has begun periodically to issue the entire body of IFRS and amendments as omnibus ED to incorporate them as benchmarks into the existing standards, and moreover to allow early adoptions.

### *Summary*

Canadian accounting regulation has traditionally been characterised by professional self-regulation. The provincial accounting institutes were united at the national level with the creation of the CICA, which gained

*Table 4.5* Major developments in Canadian accounting regulation

| Year | Law | Reform |
|---|---|---|
| 1972 | National Policy Instrument No. 27 | Requirement for all listed companies to report in accordance with the CICA Handbook |
| 1975 | Canadian Business Corporation Act 1975 | Requirement for all publicly incorporated companies to report in accordance with the CICA Handbook |
| 1990 | Canadian Institute of Chartered Accountants Act | Delegation of the standard-setting competency to the CICA is reinforced |
| 1991 | | Creation of the AcSB |
| 1991 | National Policy Instrument 71–101 | Setting up of the MJDS |
| 2006 | Amendment to NI 52–107 | Decision to replace Canadian GAAP by IFRS for listed companies from 2011 on |

standard-setting competency in 1975. Since then, Canadian companies have been legally required to prepare financial statements in accordance with the accounting standards set out in the CICA Handbook. The standard-setting process has been reorganised a couple of times, but has remained the responsibility of the accounting profession. Neither the governments nor the securities commissions are directly involved in standard-setting. Owing to the limited size of the national securities market, Canada has always supported efforts at internationalisation. The move to replace national GAAP fully with IFRS for listed companies from 2011 on is a further step in strengthening local markets with international accounting. Table 4.5 displays major developments in Canadian accounting regulation.

### 4.2.3 Japan: Bringing together different legacies

*The predominant use of accounting*

Japanese accounting combines a mix of Continental European and Anglo-American elements. The principal objective of Japanese financial reporting has traditionally been to measure distributable and taxable income in a business system characterised by large conglomerates around banks, known as Keiretsu systems (Gordon 1999). Accounting supplied the market with prudent information that focused on the legal entity. Single accounts prepared in accordance with the Japanese Commercial Code (CC) under the supervision of the MOJ were the dominant set of accounts. They also provided the basis for taxation, so that financial and tax accounting were deeply interrelated. In addition to the single accounts according to the CC, publicly traded companies also had to apply to the Securities and Exchange Law

(SEL) under the administrative responsibility of the MOF, which required additional financial statements with a stronger investor orientation (Shiba and Shiba 1997). However, the two sets of accounts differed only in the amount of disclosures; net income was identically calculated in both statements (Nobes and Parker 2010). Consolidated accounts were introduced in 1977 (Ordinance No. 30, October 1977) but remained of minor interest in the old model.

From the late 1990s, the financial system was transformed. The government started to deregulate and liberalise the financial sector, with the aim of strengthening Japanese financial markets (Ito and Melvin 1999). These developments can be seen as a response to the severe financial crisis and corporate scandals that shook the Japanese economy throughout the 1990s. The reforms initiated changes in the legal system, the standard-setting institutions and the material content of Japanese accounting standards and moved Japanese accounting closer towards an internationally accepted information-oriented model. This new model includes, for example, fair-value measurements of financial instruments and strives to produce unbiased rather than prudent information (Benston et al. 2006a).

### *The legal backing of financial reporting*

The main characteristic of the Japanese governance model during the last century was a 'triangular legal system' comprising the Commercial Code, the SEL and the National Tax Legislation (Benston et al. 2006a). The legal backing for accounting regulation in this setting was strong, as formal and material accounting requirements were mostly provided by the state via law. The original Japanese Commercial Code was based on the German Commercial Code and applied traditional concepts of conservatism (Roberts et al. 2005). Tax law had a significant influence on financial reporting since it prescribed measurement rules also for financial statements (Gordon 1999). The information usefulness of financial reports in this setting was limited for anonymous investors, but in line with the bank- and relation-based economic system.

In 1949 the US occupation forces introduced the SEL. This law was a transplant supposed to stipulate an information- and shareholder-oriented accounting system in Japan (Benston et al. 2006a). Further expressions of this intention were the modification of the CC, the foundation of a Securities and Exchange Commission (SEC) and the creation of an independent standard-setting organ, the Investing Committee on Business Accounting Systems (ICBAS). All this can be seen as an attempt to dismantle the old Keiretsu system, of which the US was suspicious. This period of more private solutions ended with the departure of the allied forces in 1952. The SEC, established as an independent agency to administer the SEL, was abolished, and its duties were transferred to the Securities Bureau of the MOF (Cooke

1991). In the same way the ICBAS lost its independence and became a governmental unit under MOF oversight. In 1952 it was renamed the Business Accounting Deliberation Council (BADC). Since then it has served as the public standard-setter for listed firms in Japan. Its 'Business Accounting Principles' were enacted by the MOF and applied to all companies under the regulation of the SEL. The rules differed from those of the commercial code in respect to disclosure requirements (e.g., cash flow statement) and materially in regards to group accounting, which was not addressed in company legislation.

The recent Japanese reforms have reversed this trend and nudged the accounting system towards a securities-market-oriented approach. The reasons for this are the altered financial structure of Japanese companies, many of which started to rely more strongly on equity financing, and a desire to be part of the international harmonisation developments advanced by the IASB. The first changes became apparent in 1997, when the BADC revised a number of crucial accounting standards (e.g., standards for financial statements, post-employment benefits and consolidation) by introducing accounting elements that strengthened the information function of accounting. These developments were completed when the main competency in accounting regulation shifted from company law to securities legislation and the standard-setting competency was transferred from the BADC to a new private standard-setting body – the ASBJ, which will be discussed in the context of self-regulation. Unlike those of its predecessor, the accounting standards of the ASBJ also apply to accounts prepared under the commercial code, as the 2006 revision of the code dropped most material accounting rules in favour of a blanket reference to ASBJ rules (Osugi 2010).

### *The extent of professional self-regulation*

The accounting profession traditionally played a minor role in accounting. It was first organised under US occupation, when the Japanese Institute of Chartered Public Accountants (JICPA) was founded in 1948 (Nobes and Parker 2010). The institute persisted after the occupation ended, and membership even became mandatory for all Certified Public Accountants (CPAs) in 1966. The JICPA releases statements and opinions on accounting issues and sets working rules for their members. It also publishes recommendations on critical aspects, which have quasi-legal status since non-compliance is considered as violating GAAP (Nobes and Parker 2010). However, these recommendations generally address issues of minor relevance.

Two other private associations are important for the development of Japanese accounting regulation: the Japanese Federation of Economic Organisations (Keidanren) and the Corporation Finance Research Institute (COFRI). Keidanren appointed members to the BADC in order to represent business interests in the council (Cooke 1991). Besides this official lobbying, the organisation used its close relationships with the policy and bureaucracy to keep disclosure requirements to a minimum level (Oguri and Hara 1990). COFRI, a private organisation financed by donations from the business sector, undertook research into financial accounting and reporting issues and published opinions and recommendations on accounting.

Self-regulation existed in the system introduced by the occupation forces (Oguri and Hara 1990). ICBAS acted as an independent standard-setting organ with the (eventually failed) purpose of setting generally accepted accounting principles in Japan (Kikuya 2001). After the standard-setter was reorganised as the BADC, self-regulation disappeared and the state assumed control. Only in recent years has professional self-regulation been strengthened once more. As part of the reforms towards a securities-market-driven accounting for listed firms, the Financial Accounting Standards Foundation (FASF) was founded in 2001 (Nobes and Parker 2010). Under its auspices, the ASBJ produces information-oriented accounting standards as a private body (Choi and Meek 2011). The ASBJ consists of a board and several committees that are organised around issues. Its accounting standards enhance and will eventually replace the set of BADC standards that are still in use. The ASBJ is funded and staffed by the FASF, which collects financial means from different companies and the accounting profession (Benston et al. 2006a). Its members are drawn from a variety of interest groups, such as the JICPA, audit firms, financial institutions and other companies, as well as accounting academe.

### *The degree of internationalisation*

Japanese accounting regulation has historically been influenced by different foreign jurisdictions and accounting philosophies. In a first phase the Japanese Commercial Code took the German Commercial Code as a role model (Roberts et al. 2005). During the occupation years the US forces introduced parts of their own regulation model (Benston et al. 2006a). These changes were mostly abolished after the occupation forces left, and an inward-looking business system was re-established as it fitted in better with the corporate context.

A first step towards internationalisation was taken when the JICPA became a founder member of the IASC. Still, significant progress did not take place until 2005, when the ASBJ started to harmonise Japanese accounting rules with IAS to make the Japanese security market more attractive to international investors. Continuing this process, in August 2007 the ASBJ and IASB published the Tokyo Agreement to accelerate convergence between Japanese GAAP and IFRS (ASBJ 2007). The two boards agreed to eliminate major differences between the two standard sets by 2008, with the remaining differences being resolved before June 2011. Recently, the pace of change has slowed down, and full convergence is no longer on the cards. In this regard the

*Table 4.6* Major developments in Japanese accounting regulation

| Year | Law | Reform |
|---|---|---|
| 1948 | | Creation of the Investing Committee on Business Accounting Systems (ICBAS) as private standard-setter |
| 1952 | | Transfer of responsibilities from the ICBAS to the BADC |
| 1966 | Amendment to the CPA Act | Obligation for all CPAs to become members of the Japanese Institute of Chartered Accountants (JICPA) |
| 1977 | Ordinance No. 30, Ministry of Finance October 1976 | Obligation to prepare consolidated accounts |
| 2001 | | Creation of the ASBJ as independent standard-setter |
| 2007 | 'Tokyo Agreement' | Treaty on the convergence of Japanese GAAP and IFRS |
| 2008 | Commission decision 12 December 2008 | Decision by the European Union to consider Japanese GAAP as equivalent to IFRS |

minister for Financial Services in Japan notified in June 2011 that mandatory application of IFRS should not proceed from fiscal year-ending March 2015 (FSA 2011). In December 2008 the EU announced that Japanese GAAP is considered equivalent to IFRS as adopted by the EU, a decision that has allowed Japanese companies to report using their national accounting standards while listing in the EU from January 2009 on. However, it is already possible to foresee that Japan will also adopt a national version of IFRS, as carve-outs have already been announced.

*Summary*

Japan traditionally featured an accounting system that was in large part regulated by law and provided prudent accounting rules that suited the company-law perspective well. Japan followed the approach of the German Commercial Code. This formed the most important source for accounting rules for single accounts in the traditional Japanese accounting model, and group accounts were of minor importance. In the post-war years the occupation forces tried to transform the Japanese business system, which also resulted in severe interventions in accounting regulation. However, attempts to introduce an US-oriented system of accounting regulation came to an end with the departure of the allied forces. The heritage of the occupation forces' reforms persisted in the foundation of the JICPA and the existence of the SEL. This, however, did not undermine the public sector's regulatory responsibility for accounting.

The traditional accounting regulation has been significantly altered by a recent spate of reforms. As a result, private and international institutions have gained importance. Moreover, the Japanese reforms that strengthen private solutions are in line with transformations of accounting systems observable elsewhere. The convergence of Japanese accounting standards with IFRS further illustrates the move towards an international model of accounting regulation. With this move towards more information-oriented accounting the different legacies of Japanese accounting finally come together. Table 4.6 displays major developments in Japanese accounting regulation.

## 4.3 A summary view

Looking at the status quo in accounting regulation around 1970, different approaches become apparent. While some countries – such as France, Germany and Japan – show a tradition of state-dominated accounting regulation, others – such as Canada, the UK and the US – rely more on the self-regulating forces and the expertise of the market. When the nation state dominates, accounting regulation financial accounts tend to be used to calculate corporate payouts. This is the case in France, Germany and Japan, where accounting information determines dividends directly and tax payments indirectly. The opposite case is observable in the Anglo-Saxon countries. Payouts are determined by instruments other than financial accounts. Accounting information has little direct effect on corporate payouts, and virtually none on tax payments (Zimmermann et al. 2008a). The main purpose of financial reports in these countries is to provide information to market participants, who have to respond actively to signals about the economic fundamentals of their contractual relation.

In France, Germany and Japan accounting regulation has a strong legal framework, and private actors play a minor role in accounting regulation. In Canada, the UK and the US professional self-regulation was dominant and the nation state, if it acted at all, enacted regulations developed by the professions. The predominant use of accounting in these countries was from a securities market perspective and therefore focused on group accounts, which applied concepts of unbiased representation more forcefully. In respect to the degree of internationalisation, all six countries solely relied on national solutions in the old model.

Over the last decades the systems have taken a different shape, showing patterns of convergence as well as retaining national peculiarities. A major convergence of national regulation can be observed in the field of securities-market-oriented information accounting. Change encompasses a harmonisation of three areas of accounting: functions, organisation and standards. The first becomes obvious looking at the developments in the predominant use of accounting in the six country cases. Preparation of consolidated accounts has become increasingly important and is now common practice in all the countries examined here. Those which formerly dispensed with economic-entity-focused accounts (France, Germany and Japan) have acknowledged their importance for securities markets and introduced them into their regulatory system. Second, the public–private mix in allocating responsibility for accounting organisation also shows convergence owing to the rise of information accounting. Here the search for high-quality investor-oriented accounting standards has led to the modification of the standard-setting process. Today standard-setting bodies exist in all countries. They belong – or operate in close relation (France) – to the private sector, incorporating the expertise of accounting professionals. Countries that formerly relied on a strong state sector (France, Germany and Japan) show more fundamental changes than the Anglo-Saxon countries. For them self-regulation has always been a prevailing coordination mechanism in accounting regulation. However, liberal accounting systems (Canada, the UK and the US) have strengthened the legal framework for accounting rules to provide them with legitimacy (Luthardt and Zimmermann 2009). The third major area of convergence, accounting standards, can best be observed in the category internationalisation. International harmonisation has been a major catalyst for the turn towards information accounting, as IAS are an expedient way to strengthen the information function and support the creation of efficient securities markets. This has led to convergence of the applicable accounting standards, with the IASB playing a central role. All the countries examined here align their national accounting system with IFRS: Canada most comprehensively, as national accounting standards will be fully replaced by international rules. The UK allows companies to choose to prepare all accounts according to IFRS. In the US, the national standard-setter operates in close relation with the IASB. Germany and France apply IFRS as endorsed by the EU in their consolidated accounts, with Germany adopting similar elements also in national GAAP.

A closer look at these convergence processes also indicates its limits: accounting regulation converges only where accounting is used for information supply; for payout calculation national solutions prevail. This becomes most apparent in the category 'predominant use of accounting'. No relevant changes can be found for the group of liberal countries. Where financial reports had no payout relevance in the traditional accounting model (Canada and the US), the same alternative instruments for determining corporate payouts still apply. In the group of Continental European countries, payout-relevant single accounts remain largely unaffected by the convergence process. This effect can be noted in a similar way in the categories addressing the public–private mix. Privately set standards apply only to group accounts, while rules for single accounts continued to be determined by parliament (e.g., in France and Germany), and the involvement of private actors is limited to information-oriented accounts. The same holds for internationalisation. In this category the different degrees of incorporating international rules into national regulation can be explained by the payout relevance of accounting in the respective country. In France and Germany, where single accounts determine corporate payouts, internationalisation is strictly limited to group accounts. In the UK, in contrast, mechanisms exist that adapt accounting information if used for payout calculation. Here the use of IFRS in single accounts has caused little change in the national system of payout regulation. In Canada and the US accounting does not possess a direct payout function. The shift towards information-oriented international accounting rules for all financial reports does not affect corporate payouts. It is only in Japan that a payout function based previously on conservative accounting rules now refers to information-oriented accounting standards.

In conclusion, the examination of the country cases indicates a two-speed process of international accounting harmonisation: a widespread and steady convergence process in the area of information accounting is accompanied by partial and incremental convergence in the area of payout accounting. In the following chapters, possible explanations for these differences in regulatory dynamics are discussed.

# Part III
# Explaining Global Convergence

OECD accounting systems have undergone significant changes over the last three decades: financial reporting rules for (public) companies have become more similar, and the ways in which rules are set have converged. Accounting scandals, business crises, network effects, cultural reasons and the process of Europeanisation have been advanced as explanations for this development (Zarzeski 1996; Perry and Nöelke 2005; Schipper 2005; van Zandt 2005; Zimmermann 2007).

Part III of this book considers three explanations in greater detail: financial globalisation (Chapter 5), corporate crises (Chapter 6) and social networks (Chapter 7). According to our explanatory framework, isomorphism can explain convergence in accounting, and the following three chapters each capture one facet of isomorphism. It coercive aspect is discussed in Chapter 5, as we argue that competitive pressures contribute to convergence. Learning from others and mimicking their behaviour is the second aspect in isomorphic behaviour. In Chapter 6 we show how corporate crises have led to mimetic isomorphism and convergence. Finally, convergence presupposes shared ideas and beliefs. These come about in a process of normative isomorphism. Chapter 7 therefore looks at international networks in accounting and how they have facilitated learning.

Globalisation has altered the shape of global markets, and curtailed the scope of the nation state for intervention (Posner and Veron 2010). We will look in particular at financial globalisation. Companies and their shareholders have taken the opportunity to do business outside their country of incorporation and have realised economies of scale and positive effects from diversification. This global expansion has led to increased capital needs that can only be met when funds are raised outside the country of incorporation. These economic demands were met by deregulation of capital flow restrictions. Advances in information technology such as the automation of trading processes have facilitated securities trading around the world at high speed and low cost. Chapter 5 looks at the role that globalisation plays as a triggering process for the change of accounting regulation. Some figures set the scene: the turnover of foreign shares increased eightfold in

Germany and fivefold in France within a decade. In the US the NYSE's turnover ratio of foreign shares increased from about 5 per cent in 1990 to about 9 per cent in 2007. Within 20 years, the issuances on foreign markets more than quadrupled. Competition for funds increased the demand for comparable, high-quality, investor-oriented accounting standards. These desirable attributes are mostly associated with accounting standards from outsider economies. Listed companies as competitors for funds lobbied for these standards mainly for two reasons: to reduce their costs of capital and to reduce transaction costs (Jayaraman et al. 1993; Hail and Leuz 2006). Moreover, large stock exchanges began to require companies to prepare financial reports on an international basis, to make their markets more liquid. Companies modelled their accounting systems on those of other companies that were being successful in raising capital. We argue that this can be regarded as a form of coercive isomorphism inducing a process of accounting harmonisation. In this process the role of the state diminished as national (public) regulators increasingly failed to provide the necessary resources and technical expertise for creating accounting standards appropriate to meet global reporting demands. Evidence in Chapter 5 strongly suggests that globalisation should be regarded as an important triggering event for the global convergence of accounting regulation.

Accounting scandals and corporate crises have – more or less frequently – taken place in many countries. As a consequence, national governments have faced uncertainty about the best way to respond to these events. They have responded by introducing reforms both in the country in question and in other countries not directly affected. We consider this as evidence for a process of mimetic isomorphism. Chapter 6 shows how national and international crises have indeed furthered convergence. Consistent with the concept of mimetic isomorphism, nation states have altered their accounting systems by imitating other systems owing to uncertainty about the quality of their own systems.

Normative isomorphism mainly emerges as a result of the similar values and similar educational backgrounds of professionals working as accountants, auditors or standard-setters. Similarity in values and educational backgrounds can be explained by several factors: for example, by globally uniform approaches to accounting education taught in universities, by a uniqueness in vocational training or by parallel gate-keeping mechanisms around the world which regulate the entry to the profession. The similar background *per se* is a driver for emergence of normative isomorphism; the latter, however, is reinforced by influential networks of professionals who articulate professional opinions. As Chapter 7 discusses, networks amplify the use of specific accounting technologies through learning effects, economies of scale or adaptive expectations (Katz and Shapiro 1985).

# 5
# Coercive Isomorphism: Reporting Demands in a Globalised World

## 5.1 Introduction

Scholars often argue that general globalisation developments have had an influence on accounting regulation (Nöelke 2005; Chua and Taylor 2008). This chapter takes up this argument and looks in particular at (financial) globalisation as a driver and explanation for the convergence of financial reporting systems.

Recent scholarly work posits that the financial system of a country is most important for the development of its financial reporting system (Nobes 1998; Ball 2001). Leuz and Wüstemann (2004) even see the accounting system as a subsystem of the financial system. Connecting these theoretical assumptions with our empirical findings, we will argue in the following that the accounting system and the financial system develop in a co-evolutionary process. We measure the globalisation of the financial system according to an index calculated from various macro-economic data such as foreign capital markets usage, foreign direct investments (FDI) or cross-border M&A. A high-growth period of globalisation could be expected to be followed by changes in accounting regulation. Moreover, the accounting systems could be expected to show a tendency to converge owing to the coalescence of financial systems, which leads to a more homogeneous demand structure of stakeholders.

Globalisation has changed the corporate environment in many ways. Not only are corporations now physically operating around the world in widely extended value chains, but they also raise money on foreign markets and shares are traded across borders. Increased demand for financial resources, the liberalisation of capital flows and the ensuing financial globalisation have in general led to outside finance having a stronger role. Globalising firms were simply unable to generate the necessary funds for expansion from internal sources or to raise them from existing owners.

As discussed in Part II, accounting systems are embedded in the legal, financial and cultural systems of nation states, leading to highly diverse country-specific accounting systems (Soderstrom and Sun 2007). In recent years the country-specific national solutions have come under pressure. One important reason is (financial) globalisation: multi- or transnational companies have share- and stakeholders in many countries. Corporate financial reporting needs to respond, as investors with varying backgrounds require intelligible information about the performance of their investments and about further investment opportunities, and they prefer information that is presented in a familiar format. Companies have economic incentives to meet these demands, as this allows them to lower their cost of capital (Hail and Leuz 2006). At a global level, comparable sets of information-accounting rules can thus lead to a more efficient allocation of the world's supply of funds, with lower cost of capital and a higher overall welfare (Ruder et al. 2005). The demand for high-quality standards is articulated not only by investors but also by stock exchanges, which want to increase their liquidity by attracting trade. Therefore, large stock exchanges also ask for reports prepared under comparable information-accounting rules. So do national regulatory authorities, which are interested in the competitiveness and stability of capital markets (Coffee 2002).

This chapter discusses the reasons and presents the evidence for changing reporting demands in a globalised world. We show that internationalisation has led to a higher demand for and supply of comparable, high-quality annual reports, and that this demand has led to a harmonisation of accounting regimes. We argue that larger companies experience pressures to use standardised sets of information-accounting rules and that they accommodate this demand by supplying share- and other stakeholders with financial reports on the basis of IFRS or US GAAP.

In the second section of this chapter we will present evidence for the coalescence of the corporate world by presenting data on globalisation in general and on financial globalisation. The third section deals with the question how globalisation encourages the convergence of accounting systems; and in the fourth section we present evidence for the concurrence of globalisation and accounting harmonisation.

## 5.2 The coalescence of the corporate world

The most apparent reason for accounting harmonisation is the evolvement of MNEs that do business across the borders of their country of incorporation. Globalisation promotes the development of MNEs and is itself amplified by MNEs. Technical innovations such as advanced communication, the possibility of mass production and global trade along with decreasing costs of transport around the world have changed the environment in which companies do business (Levitt 1983; Chandler 1992). This increases the opportunities for MNEs, and their number and size are growing

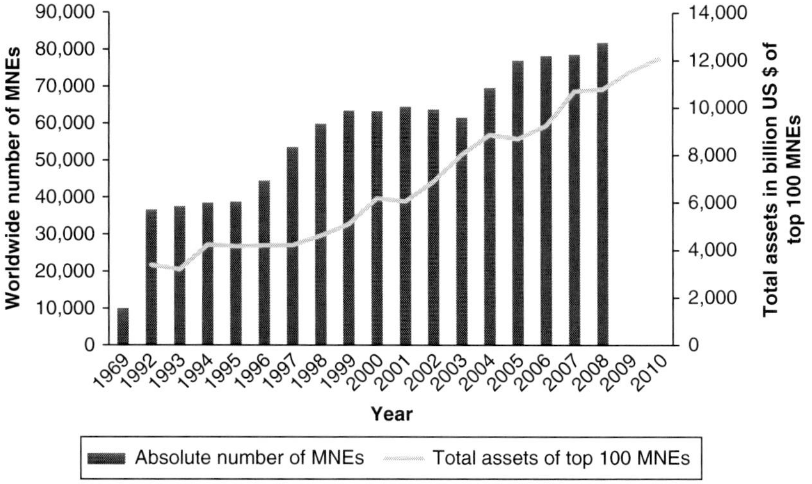


*Figure 5.1* Number and size of MNEs

*Sources*: United Nations Conference on Trade and Development (UNCTAD)[1] World Investment Reports 1993–2011; *Bundeszentrale für politische Bildung*, Value for 1969 approximated by UNCTAD.

further. Figure 5.1 shows the constant growth of the absolute number of MNEs and the size of the 100 biggest MNEs, measured by their total assets.

For a long time economic activity was limited to the regional sphere. There was little manufacturing for export and no competition for global market shares. However, this has changed radically. Developments since the 1980s especially have reshaped the corporate world. Radical shifts in communication and transport technologies as well as the politically achieved possibility of free trade of goods, services and capital have triggered an unprecedented process of internationalisation. Moreover, the use of foreign financial markets has been facilitated by the emergence of electronic trading systems.[2] Automation of trading processes has facilitated security trading around the world at high speed and low cost. Meanwhile, the reasons for companies to internationalise have become more complex than just seeking economies of scale, and organising corporate activity has become more challenging.

The global expansion in trade and production has led to increased capital needs, which could be met neither by capital markets in companies' home countries nor through debt nor by internal financing. Hence, companies started to raise capital on foreign markets and thus supplemented their internationalisation in operations by trade and FDI through international financial activities. To give empirical evidence for the rapid globalisation developments since the 1980s, we look at (former) barriers to worldwide operating activity (data provided in Table 5.1), worldwide investment and

*Table 5.1* Transport and communication costs

| Year | Telecommunication[a] | | Sea freight[a] | | Air freight[a] | |
|---|---|---|---|---|---|---|
| | Index | in US $ | Index | in US $ | Index | in US $ |
| 1930 | 100.00 | 244.65 | 100.00 | 60.00 | 100.00 | 0.68 |
| 1940 | 77.05 | 188.51 | 105.00 | 63.00 | 67.70 | 0.46 |
| 1950 | 21.75 | 53.20 | 56.70 | 34.00 | 44.10 | 0.30 |
| 1960 | 18.75 | 45.86 | 45.00 | 27.00 | 35.30 | 0.24 |
| 1970 | 12.91 | 31.58 | 45.00 | 27.00 | 23.50 | 0.16 |
| 1980 | 1.96 | 4.80 | 40.00 | 24.00 | 14.70 | 0.10 |
| 1990 | 1.36 | 3.32 | 48.30 | 29.00 | 16.20 | 0.11 |
| 2000[b] | 0.35 | 0.86 | 35.00 | 21.00 | 11.80 | 0.08 |

*Sources*: Busse (2001); Bundesverband der deutschen Industrie (2002).
[a]Costs for a three-minute call from New York to London/average costs for sea freight per short ton (907.17 kg and mile)/average air freight turnover per passenger and mile.
[b]Data for sea and air freight from 1998.

organisational restructuring activity (data provided in Figures 5.2 and 5.3) and global financing activity (data provided in Figures 5.4–5.6 and Table 5.2).

Decreasing prices for communication and transportation show that the worldwide operating activity of companies became more feasible and more cost-efficient during the 20th century. Table 5.1 illustrates typical costs for the facilitation of worldwide activity. The costs for sea freight and air freight have fallen by 65 per cent and 88 per cent respectively since the 1930s. The amount of transported goods has risen significantly since the 1970s. For example, the amount of worldwide sea freight doubled between 1970 (10,654 billon ton-miles[3]) and 1995 (20,187 billon ton-miles). Some 27,635 billion ton-miles were shipped across the oceans in 2004. Technical innovations and higher demand have led to a circle of falling prices through economies of scale and even greater technical improvements. Moreover, the liberalisation of markets has had a positive effect on costs. These cost reductions and the development of a global transport and communication network have made the coalescence of the corporate world possible in the first place, and have led to a self-enforcing process of globalisation.

If firms are not only selling products on foreign markets but also investing directly in foreign countries, the term 'FDI' is used. Figure 5.2 shows the FDI flows between OECD countries and the related FDI stock relative to GDP. The flow is the annual amount invested in foreign countries, and the stock shows the total amount invested in foreign countries relative to total GDP. All these indicators have increased significantly since the beginning of the 1970s. In total, since the late 1970s the flow of foreign investments per year increased from about $35 billion to over $1,600 billion in 2007, the year

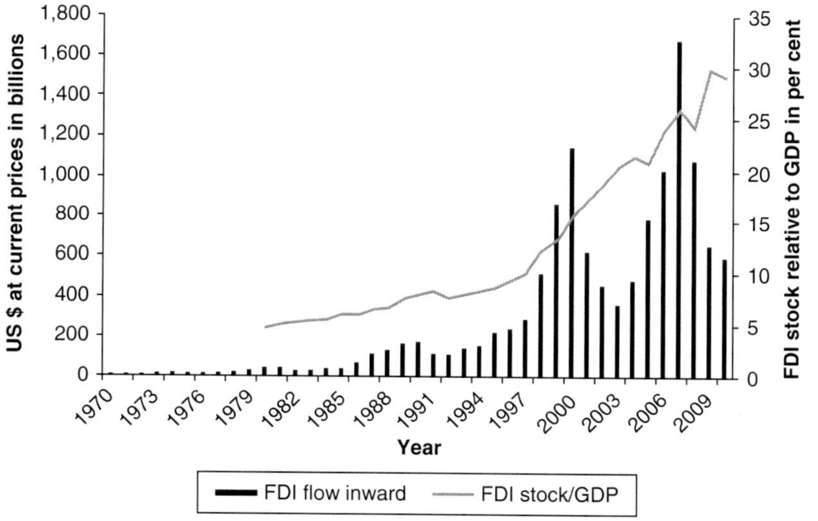


*Figure 5.2* OECD FDI flow (1970–2010) and FDI stock relative to GDP (1980–2010)
*Source*: UNCTAD, database.

before the financial crisis. The FDI stock relative to the GDP rose from about 5 per cent in 1980 to nearly 30 per cent in 2010. This growth was especially pronounced in three periods: at end of the 1970s, between 1985 and 1989 and between 1995 and 2000. This shows that there have been certain periods in particular during which globalisation of the economy has progressed. Globalisation is thus taking place in stages; it is not a continuous process, and there are even some periods of negative growth: after a peak in 2000 the FDI flow was lower in the following three years. In general, periods with low or negative growth are linked to (economic) shocks, such as the collapse of the New Economy around the year 2000, which was exacerbated by the terrorist attacks on the US in late 2001 or the financial crisis beginning in 2007.

Globalisation has not only increased international operational activity but also changed the way business is done. While the previous indicators measure operational and investment activity across the globe, global M&A can show how corporate value chains evolve. Figure 5.3 shows the global cross-border M&A from 1988 to 2010. Again there was a constant increase from the 1990s until 2000, and two periods after the millennium with lower M&A activity (from 2000 to 2003 and since 2009). The collapse of the New Economy, the ensuing depression of world stock markets and the effects of the terrorist attacks on the US in late 2001 and the financial crisis beginning in 2007 dented the growth pattern. Over all, the amount of global cross-border M&A before the financial crisis was over four times the amount in

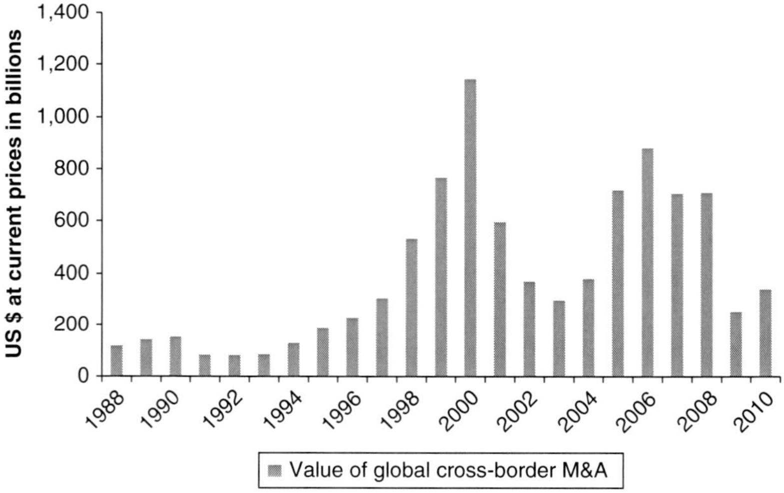


*Figure 5.3* Global cross-border M&A
*Source*: UNCTAD, database.

1995. Rising worldwide investment activity and increasing FDI flows point to a corporate world that is growing closer together.

Even more important than the real economy is the integration of capital markets; investors are the most important group demanding financial reports. The extent of integration becomes apparent from the global financing activities of companies. Figure 5.4 shows the market capitalisation relative to the GDP of the three large outsider (Canada, the UK and the US) and three insider economies (France, Germany and Japan) that we are studying

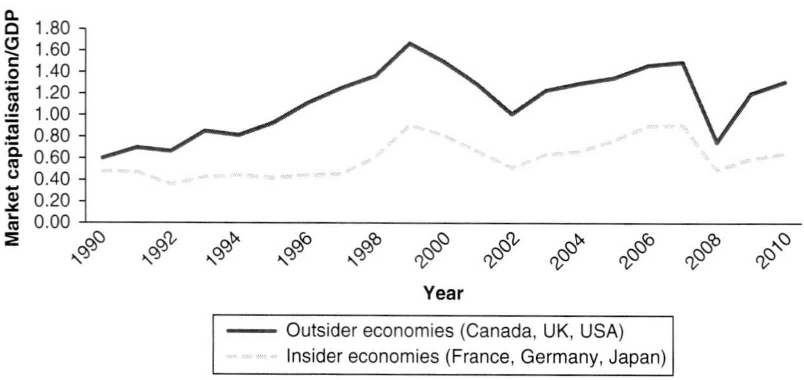


*Figure 5.4* Share of market capitalisation relative to GDP
*Source*: World Bank (World Development Indicators Online 2010).

in detail. The data point to a growing use of capital markets. While the importance of capital markets in each system differs, the example illustrates the general growth of equity markets, at least until the beginning of the last financial crisis. Notably, though, differences between outsider economies and insider economies remain pronounced. As a general tendency, the importance of capital markets has increased significantly over the last 20 years (Obstfeld and Taylor 2004).

Integration of capital markets can be measured by the share of foreign investors, the share of foreign stock turnover or the equity issues on foreign markets. These data allow an analysis of the internationalisation of markets from the perspective of capital providers and capital suppliers. Let us first look at the supply side, the investors.

Figure 5.5 shows the share of foreign equity investors in Germany, Japan, the UK and the US. This is the amount of shares from listed firms incorporated in one country held by foreign investors. In 1995, for instance, about 8 per cent of all shares of German public companies were held by foreign investors. Generally, the capital markets were only slightly internationalised at the beginning of the 1990s. Since then, the share of foreign investors on international markets has increased significantly. Today it is much more common to invest in foreign equity markets. Only the US stands out in this comparison: its international share is relatively small. However, when looking at absolute numbers, the US has by far the largest total amount of international investments: for instance, the total amount of foreign investments in the US in the year 2000 was about three times higher than in the

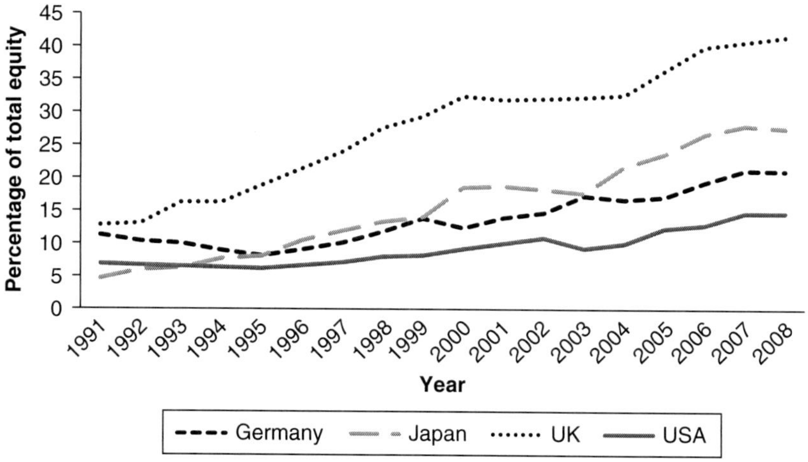


*Figure 5.5* Share of foreign equity investors
*Source*: *Deutsches Aktieninstitut* (DAI)-Factbook 2009, US Federal Reserve Board 'Flow of Funds' March 2010, UK Office for National Statistics, Tokyo Stock Exchange (TSE) Factbook 2009; data for Canada and France not available.

UK, which has the second highest total amount of international investments. The high percentage of foreign equity investments there can be traced to the success of the Alternative Investment Market (AIM), a softly regulated sub-market of the LSE launched in 1995.

*Table 5.2* Turnover of foreign shares in US $ million

| Year | Germany | France (Euronext) | UK | US | Japan |
|---|---|---|---|---|---|
| 1990 | 10,709 | 4,598 | 262,064 | 80,600 | 1,232 |
| 1995 | 13,802 | 3,616 | 626,863 | 341,996 | 1,039 |
| 2000 | 321,323 | 10,390 | 2,669,122 | 1,986,296 | 627 |
| 2007 | 344,170 | 27,136 | 4,277,166 | 4,072,594 | 2,769 |

*Sources*: DAI Factbook 2009; data for Canada not available.

Table 5.2 shows the turnover of foreign shares on the major stock exchanges of the selected countries. This is the turnover of shares at a stock exchange from companies that are not incorporated in the country of the stock exchange. The ratio also reveals a growing integration of markets: in 1990 Germany had just 2 per cent of the total share turnover coming from foreign shares ($10,709,000). A decade later, 15 per cent of share turnover in Germany can be assigned to foreign shares ($321,323,000). In August 2007 the ratio was 13 per cent ($344,170,000). The LSE already had a very high turnover of foreign shares in the 1990s. In 1990 about 45 per cent ($262,064,000) of LSE total turnover came from trades with foreign shares. However, the ratio increased to about 60 per cent ($2,669,122,000) in 2000 but went back down to 41 per cent ($4,277,166,000) in 2007. NYSE's turnover ratio of foreign shares increased from about 5 per cent ($80,600,000) in 1990 to about 9 per cent in 2007 ($4,277,166,000). The relative values for France stay rather constant, at around 3 per cent, as do the absolute and relative values for Japan. However, the absolute trading volume of foreign shares increased considerably at the OECD's largest stock exchanges.

Company-level data yields further insights. The growing use of foreign markets by companies can be shown by looking at primary markets. Figure 5.6 depicts the equity issues of companies outside their country of incorporation: for example, a company incorporated in France issuing equity on the US market. The chart shows the total amount of equity issues and the percentage of equity issues relative to GDP from Canadian, French, German, Japanese, UK and US companies on foreign markets between 1975 and 2007 (main and parallel markets are included).

The data shown in Figure 5.6 also point to an increasing use of foreign markets: in the mid-1970s companies only took limited advantage of foreign capital markets. Significant equity issues did not exist until the mid-1980s. The total amount of equity issued from companies out of the six countries

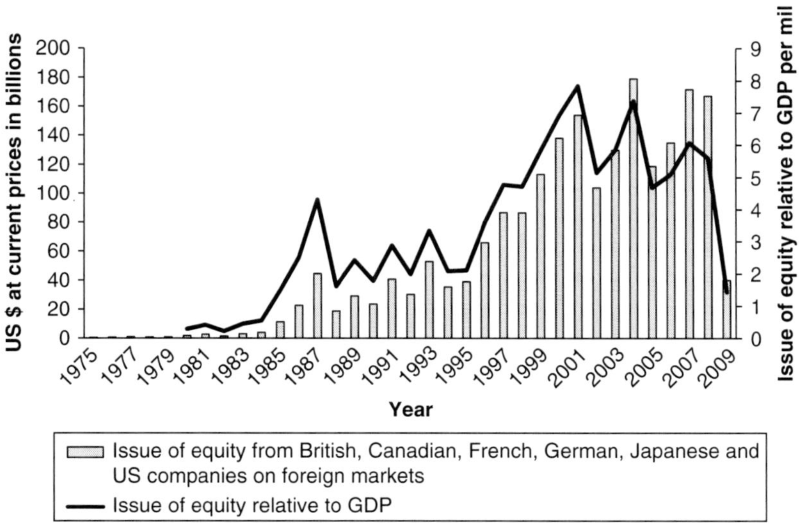


*Figure 5.6* Issue of equity on foreign capital markets
*Source*: Thomson One Deals, International Monetary Fund (IMF) World Economic Outlook Database.

on other markets than their home markets was $1,781 million in 1980. In 1990 the total amount issued was $23,592 million (about 2 per mil relative to GDP of all six countries), and in 2008 the companies from the six sample countries raised $167,462 million (about 6 per mil relative to GDP) outside their country of incorporation. The aftermath of the financial crisis only becomes apparent in the year 2009, when the amount of equity raised on foreign markets dropped dramatically to 1.4 per mil relative to GDP.

The illustrated data reveal that financial markets have undergone a substantial internationalisation process during the last two decades. Companies increasingly use international markets to raise capital. Moreover, investors have started to hold shares from companies all over the world. This means that share- and stakeholders interested in financial data are now distributed all around the world – the financing and investment business today is global for many firms. The more globalised the markets, the higher the demand for globally comparable rules (Tweedie and Seidenstein 2005). This development is an important trigger for the convergence of accounting rules and is discussed in the next section.

## 5.3 Comparable accounting rules: Supply, demand and regulation in globalised financial markets

This section links the increasing transnational economic activities, the integration of capital markets and the harmonisation of accounting regulation.

The main argument is that the increasing use of international capital markets has had a significant influence on the demand for and supply of financial reports: investors demand comparable financial reports, with a focus on providing useful information for making financial decisions, and companies face the challenge of participating in various institutional settings with the aim of having a competitive, cost-effective and reliable reporting system in a cross-border trading environment (Ruder et al. 2005). Nevertheless, companies are still subject to the authority of nation states, which are – despite the process of Europeanisation and internationalisation – able to take autonomous decisions. However, the globalisation developments exert pressure on national regulators (Flower 2004; van Zandt 2005). In particular, the institutional arrangements in insider countries no longer match the new demand from companies and investors for information-accounting rule sets. This leads to inefficiency within the regulatory environment, and national governments need to take action. They have an interest in providing a regulatory framework that strengthens the national capital market to increase countries' welfare. Moreover, they respond to the lobbying of companies, investors and stock exchanges (Zeff 2002). At least for listed companies' group accounts, a similar demand for and supply of financial information is evolving worldwide.[4] In what follows we look more closely at the economics that govern the behaviour of the stipulated actors in a globalised world: investors, companies and regulatory actors.

### 5.3.1 The viewpoint of investors and companies

Outsider investors need decision-relevant information to be able to devise entry and exit investment strategies. Financial reports are an important element in the provision of such information: decisions should be facilitated with the ability to predict future cash flows by analysing financial reports. Hence, (outside) investors demand information-accounting rule sets, which are supposed to have a higher (earnings) quality than most local GAAPs (Barth et al. 2008). IFRS are supposed to deliver more 'accurate, comprehensive and timely financial statement information', leading to a more precise valuation in capital markets and a reduction of information risk for investors (Ball 2006). Referring to the data presented in Section 2, the share of outside investors rose considerably during the last decades. Hence, the general demand for information-accounting rule sets – such as IFRS – increased.

This development is amplified by the integration of capital markets. Investors are able to reduce their financial risk by holding a more diversified investment portfolio through international investment activity (Ball 2006). Hence, investors demand transparency and standardisation in financial reports to lower analysis costs. This is achieved through an enhanced comparability of available investments, lower costs for investors collecting information and a greater degree of reliability in the presented financial data (Zimmermann and Abée 2006). In general, lower information costs are expected if a shared set of accounting standards is used (Barth 2007). International investors do not have to convert financial numbers and are thus able to analyse more quickly financial reports from firms located in foreign countries; information asymmetries among investors are lowered, and the estimation risk is reduced (Daske et al. 2008). Moreover, worldwide investors understand financial reports better and are aware of possibilities for companies to window-dress the data. Hence, all investors are able to process the reported figures in a proper way and to identify the expected return on their investment. This is different from reports on the basis of local GAAP. Foreign investors might have difficulties understanding the prospectus of a company and thus insist on a higher risk premium or not invest at all in these markets (Nicolaisen 2005). They may also not be able to disentangle figures that are possibly dressed up. Local investors are favoured if companies only use local GAAP.

MNEs have several economic incentives to apply international accepted accounting standards. A major argument is closely linked to the investor side; companies have to take the claims of investors into account if they want to be successful in raising capital (Shleifer and Vishny 1986; Sikka 2001). As argued above, the number of potential investors will be enlarged by the use of comparable information-accounting rule sets. The worldwide attractiveness of a company's shares increases, inducing a higher share price and a lower cost of equity capital for the listed entity. The cost of equity capital is composed of several factors, such as agency costs and the cost of adverse selection (Jensen and Meckling 1976; Healy and Palepu 2001). One important component is the required return of investors, which includes a risk premium resulting from agency, adverse selection and monitoring costs (Perridon and Steiner 2009). If this risk premium can be reduced, the cost of capital can be lowered. This, again, can be achieved by lowering information asymmetries between the company and worldwide investors, for example, by providing internationally comparable financial reports. Another factor reducing the premium is extending the investor base and increasing the liquidity of capital markets. Higher market liquidity reduces the transaction costs investors expect when selling their shares (Engel et al. 2007).

Transaction costs for companies which have to prepare several sets of consolidated accounts (for example, based on local GAAP and international standards) create a demand for a single set of accounting standards. In broader terms, transaction costs arise in economic exchanges between different actors and contain bargaining, policing and enforcement costs (see in greater detail Coase 1937 as well as Williamson 1975). Here, costs arise because of higher bargaining costs arising from differing financial numbers presented in the two reports. Therefore, MNE have a strong interest in applying only one set of accounting rules to access markets worldwide without being obliged to create separate financial reports.

Besides arguments based on transaction costs, institutional theory offers further explanations of why a single set of accounts may be desirable. The adoption of a foreign institutional setting can be explained by the neo-institutional concept of coercive isomorphism (DiMaggio and Powell 1983): organisations absorb the structures of other organisations that are in a leading position. In our context the role models are listed companies with high market capitalisation and international activity. Companies experience coercive pressure from 'other organisations on which they depend and [from] the society in which the company works' (DiMaggio and Powell 1983). Based on arguments of bounded rationality, firms mimic other successful ones, and so they may model their accounting system on the accounting system of other companies that are (more) successful in raising capital (Coffee 2002). Companies may also gain legitimacy on regional and global markets by applying internationally accepted accounting standards (Chua and Taylor 2008).

### 5.3.2 Responses of national regulators

The pressure to accept or prepare financial reports with a focus on decision usefulness (information accounting) extends not only to companies but also to regulatory authorities. The most important regulatory authorities are agents in the nation states, but supra-national organisations, such as the EU, and large stock exchanges also play a crucial role in the harmonisation process. Especially in Continental European countries, a pressure on national regulators to accept IAS has emerged during the last few decades. This pressure applies not only to the rules but also to the institutional setting of accounting systems. Investors and companies have expressed more confidence in rules set by private, professional bodies, giving these bodies the highest legitimacy (Rodrigues and Craig 2007). Private standard-setters, such as the IASB, are supposed to set more efficient, higher-quality accounting rules. This constitutes a second dimension of the harmonisation process. Not only the sets of rules but also the organisation of accounting systems – that is, their institutional set-up – experience pressure to harmonise.

One can differentiate between two triggers for governments to change their accounting regulations: on the one hand, lobbying from firms, investors and stock exchanges; on the other, self-interest on the part of the nation states in changing the regulatory set-up, with the aim of strengthening the national capital market and firms in the international competition to increase countries' welfare. The first trigger is obvious, given the outlined demands of firms and investors. Since the flow of capital has been liberalised, transnational actors, in particular, have put pressure on national regulators to accept or enact information-accounting rule sets.

The second trigger warrants more attention. National governments may want to adjust accounting regulation not only for companies that look for cheap capital. States and stock exchanges compete for companies and (international) investors as customers and taxpayers. Efficient, strong and liquid capital markets are the fuel for economic growth (Bekaert and Harvey 1998). Nation states in the OECD experience pressure to keep up with the prevailing developments in accounting practice. National politicians and regulatory authorities, especially from countries with a previously underdeveloped capital market, are under pressure to enhance the comparability of financial reports. This supposedly increases investor protection and improves the allocation of capital on global markets (Zarzeski 1996). Thus, accounting harmonisation takes on a general welfare aspect for national regulators.

Stock exchanges compete for market share and for investors, as they tend to invest where the best products and the lowest transaction costs are offered (Domowitz et al. 1998). The larger the number of companies listed at an exchange, the greater the economies of scale that can be achieved. To remain in a leading position, the world's largest exchanges permanently set up innovative financial products to satisfy investor and company needs (Zimmermann et al. 2008a). Stock exchanges also demand investor-oriented accounting standards and make high disclosure requirements, and they are important actors in the process of accounting harmonisation. The Deutsche Börse AG, for example, demanded financial reporting according to internationally accepted accounting standards for the segment *Neuer Markt* as early as 1997. The LSE allowed the issuing of annual reports on the basis of IFRS for the AIM as early as 1995 (Fisher and Bewsey 2003). Also in 1995 the IOSCO and the IASC (the precursor of the IASB) envisaged that IASC standards would be accepted by the stock exchanges for accounts of foreign companies. Today this is the case for all major stock exchanges in our six sample countries.

## 5.4 Concurrence of globalisation and accounting harmonisation

Theory suggests that the coalescence of the corporate world will result in harmonised accounting systems. We will now present some empirical evidence for a concurrence of financial globalisation and accounting harmonisation. We will look both at the use of IFRS and US GAAP and at institutional changes in the accounting systems in the OECD. The increasing use of IFRS and US GAAP in the OECD since the beginning of the 1990s will be considered first. We capture this phenomenon by comparing total assets of listed firms that use international reporting standards with total assets of firms that use local GAAP.

Companies outside the US started to prepare financial reports on the basis of internationally accepted reporting standards at the beginning of the 1970s. The pioneers in this process were Saint-Gobain from France (already 1970), Glaxo Wellcome (1995) from the UK and Daimler-Benz from

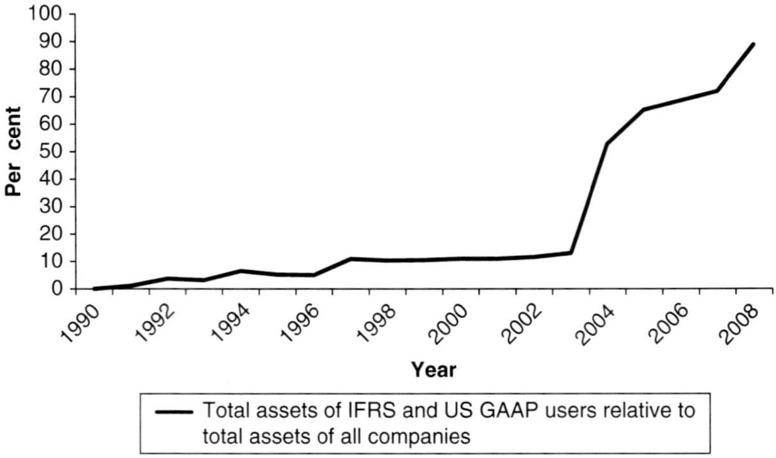


*Figure 5.7* Total assets of IFRS and US GAAP users relative to total assets of all listed companies in the OECD; US firms excluded
*Source*: Osiris.

Germany (1996). All of them presented additional consolidated accounts on the basis of US GAAP. However, a significant increase of published financial statements prepared in accordance with IFRS or US GAAP can only be observed since the 1990s. Figure 5.7 depicts the ratio of total assets from users of IFRS and US GAAP relative to total assets of all listed companies in the OECD (US firms are excluded because the usage of US GAAP is mandatory for all publicly listed companies in the US).

Before 1990, voluntarily issued financial reports on the basis of US GAAP or IFRS cannot be measured; the above-mentioned companies had not yet set a trend. The importance of internationally accepted accounting standards rose continuously from 1990 to 2003. Because of the legal prescription for listed companies in the EU to prepare consolidated accounts on the basis of IFRS from 2005 on, the ratio substantially increased since 2004. The implementation of the IAS regulation had various political and economical reasons (Zimmermann et al. 2008a), but one of the most important triggers was certainly financial globalisation. As Chapter 2 has shown, many firms stopped hesitating to switch to IFRS after the issuing of Regulation 1606/2002, as switching costs were no longer avoidable and could thus be seen as decision-irrelevant.

More and more firms from outside the EU have switched voluntarily to international reporting standards in recent years. Today the majority of listed firms throughout the OECD prepare their financial reports on the basis of international reporting standards.

Next we look at the concurrence of globalisation and institutional changes. A high growth period of globalisation should be followed by changes in accounting regulation. Moreover, the accounting systems should show a tendency to converge owing to the integration of capital markets, as the demands of stakeholders become more homogeneous. The influence of globalisation on the organisation of accounting regimes began as early as the 1970s, when the first changes in the organisation of accounting regimes were observable. Our analysis accordingly begins in 1970.

To show the connection of globalisation and accounting systems, a newly developed financial globalisation index and changes in accounting regulation are jointly analysed. We measure the globalisation with an index calculated out of the data presented in Section 2 of this chapter. The data on the institutional changes in accounting regulation are taken from (our) previous work. Most institutional changes and changes in laws and regulations are described in Part II, and we do not describe the country cases here again in greater detail (see also Gadinis and Jackson 2007 as well as Hammermeister and Zimmermann 2010).

To inquire into the concurrence of globalisation and accounting harmonisation we use the following approach: we first calculate annual globalisation growth values for each of the six sample countries (Canada, France, Germany, Japan, the UK and the US) and for the six countries in total from 1970 to 2007. The globalisation growth value is determined by calculating the unweighted average of the annual percentage changes in the FDI flows and – where available – the value of cross-border M&A, the share of market capitalisation to GDP, the stock market value traded to GDP and the share of foreign equity investors.[5] We then calculate the geometric means of the growth rates (GR) for periods of five years (the last period comprises only three years, from 2005 to 2007). The resulting average growth value for five-year periods allows us to identify the speed of globalisation. We generated four different growth clusters for the five-year time periods: no or negative growth ($GR \leq 1$), moderate growth ($1 < GR \leq 1.1$), high growth ($1.1 < GR \leq 1.25$) and very high growth ($GR > 1.25$). Table 5.3 shows the calculation of the US globalisation growth rate exemplarily for the period 1995 to 1999.

We observe the highest growth rates for the periods 1985–1989, 1995–1999 and 2005–2007, while the highest average annual growth rate is 39 per cent, in the period 1985–1989 (comparable results can be found in Werner 2008). The mean growth rate for the six sample countries from 1970 to 2007 was about 13 per cent. The variance is relatively high with 8.4 per cent. This shows that there are years with low or negative growth and years with high growth rates. Comparing the countries, the US has the highest average growth rate with 16 per cent while Germany has the lowest with 9 per cent.

*Table 5.3* Globalisation index calculation for the US (1995–1999)

| **Annual Growth Rates (1.00 = no change in growth)** | **1995** | **1996** | **1997** | **1998** | **1999** |
|---|---|---|---|---|---|
| FDI flow | 1.30 | 1.44 | 1.22 | 1.69 | 1.63 |
| Global cross-border M&A | 1.19 | 1.28 | 1.20 | 2.56 | 1.20 |
| Market capitalisation relative to GDP | 1.12 | 1.22 | 1.21 | 1.19 | 1.15 |
| Share of foreign equity investors | n.a. | n.a. | n.a. | 1.12 | 1.03 |
| Stock market total value traded relative to GDP | 1.37 | 1.32 | 1.35 | 1.22 | 1.33 |
| Globalisation growth (unweighted average) | 1.25 | 1.31 | 1.25 | 1.56 | 1.27 |
| Geometric mean of globalisation growth | | | **1.32** | | |

*Note*: n.a., not applicable.
*Source*: Own calculations.

To show the concurrence of financial globalisation and accounting harmonisation we illustrate the growth speeds and milestones in accounting harmonisation for the specified periods in Table 5.4. Developments at the international level are given in the first column, together with the aggregated growth rates from all six sample countries. Major events in the development of accounting harmonisation are displayed in bold letters (concerning the importance of reforms see Part II). We identified 46 events in total between 1970 and 2007, of which 12 were at the international or transnational level. Moreover, 16 events are classified as of particular importance. Countries with an accounting system that can be classified as investor-oriented (Canada, the UK and the US) had fewer changes in their standard-setting processes, disclosure laws and organisational structures over the previous 40 years. The US accounting system, in particular, has been relatively stable during the last decades.

The changes in laws and regulation are incremental. As the index shows, the financial globalisation is incremental as well. We also see a time lag between the coalescence of the corporate world and the harmonisation of accounting systems. Changes in (or the enactment of new) laws seem to follow globalisation developments with a delay. Over all, 26 events follow periods of high or very high growth. Moreover, the overall level of globalisation seems to be important. In the 1970s and 1980s developments were fewer and mostly not incisive. However, these changes laid the basis for developments since the middle of the 1990s, in particular the harmonisation of accounting at the international level. Major developments took place after periods of (very) high growth rates. In the periods between 1990 and 1994 and between 2000 and 2004, respectively, important events can be observed in the development of the leading role that IFRS have today. Looking at

*Table 5.4* Concurrence of globalisation and harmonisation of accounting

| Periods | Aggregate of sample | | US | | Canada | | UK | | Germany | | France | | Japan | |
|---|---|---|---|---|---|---|---|---|---|---|---|---|---|---|
| | Glob. | Acc. Harmonisation | Glob. | Acc. Harmonisation | Glob. | Acc. Harmonisation | Glob. | Acc. Harmonisation | Glob. | Acc. Harmonisation | Glob. | Acc. Harmonisation | Glob. | Acc. Harmonisation |
| 1970–1974 | +++ | – First draft of Fourth EC Directive (1971)<br>– Foundation IASC (1973) | +++ | – Foundation FASB (1973) | + + | | +++ | – ASC (1970) | +++ | | +++ | | ++ | – Commercial Code requires external audits (1974) |
| 1975–1979 | + | – **Fourth EC Directive (1978)** | ++ | | + | – Canadian Business Corporations Act (1975) | + | | o | | + | | + | |
| 1980–1984 | + | – **Seventh EC Directive (1983)** | ++ | | o | | o | – **Companies Act: Implementation Fourth EC Directive (1981)** | o | | o | – **Accounting act: Implementation Fourth EC Directive (1983)** | ++ | |
| 1985–1989 | +++ | | ++ | | ++ | – Joint project of the IASC and CICA (1988) | +++ | – **Companies Act: Implementation Seventh EC Directive; ASB & FRC (1989)** | +++ | – **Implementation Fourth and Seventh EC Directive (1985)** | +++ | – **Implementation Seventh EC Directive (1985)** | +++ | |

*Table 5.4* (Continued)

| | | | | | | | | | | | | |
|---|---|---|---|---|---|---|---|---|---|---|---|---|
| 1990–1994 | o | – Comparability and Improvement Project (1993)<br>– Advisory Council (1994) | o | | + | – AcSB(1991)<br>– MJDS (1991)<br>– NAFTA (1994) | o | | o | – WpHG (1994) | ++ | | o | – Amendment Commercial Code (1993) |
| 1995–1999 | ++ | – Endorsement of a core set of IAS by the IOSCO (1995) | +++ | | ++ | | +++ | | +++ | – **KonTraG: GASC, use of int. acc. standards (1998)** | ++ | – Restructuring CNC (1996)<br>– **CRC (1998)**<br>– **decree: use of int. acc. standards (1998)** | +++ | – Japanese Financial Services Agency (JFSA) (1998) |
| 2000–2004 | o | – Lamfalussy Report (2000)<br>– **IASB/IFRIC (2001)**<br>– **EFRAG (2001)**<br>– **EC 1606/2002**<br>– **Norwalk A. (2002)** | o | – Sarbanes-Oxley Act (SOA) (2002) | o | – AcSOC (2000) | o | – FSMA (2000) | o | – Transparency and Disclosure Act (2002)<br>– Investor Protection Improvement Act (2004) | o | – Law on Financial Security (2003)<br>– Financial Markets Authority (*Autorité des Marchés Financiers* AMF) (2003) | o | – **FSAS/ASBJ (2001)**<br>– CPA law amended (2004) |
| 2005–2007 | ++ | | ++ | – SEC Release NOS. 33–8879 (2007) | +++ | – **Decision to use IFRS from 2011 on (2006)** | +++ | | ++ | – Transparency Directive Implementation Act (2007)<br>– first draft BilMoG (2007) | +++ | | + | – Convergence project ASBJ/IASB (2005) |

*Notes*: Major events in bold; **o**, GR $\leq$ 1; +, 1< GR $\leq$ 1.1; ++, 1.1 < GR $\leq$ 1.25; +++, GR > 1.25.
*Source*: Authors' own contribution.

the 16 events classified as major events, the concurrence of globalisation and accounting harmonisation is evident. Eight events are observed after periods of high and very high growth, respectively. At the national level, legislators in Germany and France issued laws or degrees for the acceptance of IFRS at the end of the high growth period from 1995 to 1999. Moreover, all three insider economies set up a private standard-setting body at the end or after the high globalisation phase at the end of the 1990s (France and Germany in 1998, Japan in 2001). Also, the latest phase of high globalisation growth, from 2005 to 2007, has initiated harmonisation developments: for instance, Canada decided in 2006 to use IFRS from 2011 on, and the US allowed foreign private issuers to use IFRS from 2007 on, and in 2008 discussed prescribing the use of IFRS by all SEC-registered companies from 2014, an initiative that has now come to a halt.

## 5.5 Conclusion

Canada, France, Germany, Japan, the UK and the US have experienced different waves of globalisation since the beginning of the 1970s. Companies increasingly became active on international (capital) markets and now have subsidiaries around the globe. These developments are also crucial for accounting systems: we have seen that there is a concurrence between globalisation and the harmonisation of accounting in the six sample countries. Financial globalisation thus seems to be an important driver for the convergence of accounting systems.

Globalisation puts pressure on MNEs to adopt the accounting rules used by leading competitors in the process of raising equity capital. This pressure arises because markets are integrated, and companies cannot only attract local investors but have to rely on investment from around the world. Firms also want to operate in very liquid markets, to lower their cost of capital further. Investors demand comparable, information-accounting rule sets to be able to use financial numbers to calculate their expected returns. Local GAAP privileges national investors and is thus not able to minimise information asymmetries. Foreign investors may have difficulties understanding the financial accounts of a company and thus insist on a higher risk premium or decide not to invest at all in these markets. Hence, companies that want to attract international investors have to prepare financial reports on the basis of internationally accepted accounting standards. If companies have to use more than one set of rules, transaction costs will rise. Therefore, they demand that national regulators accept IAS. The pressure on national regulators is increased by the liberalisation of capital flows and financial globalisation, which sparked competition between capital markets to attract companies and investors. Nation states are required to adjust their regulatory system to ensure the competitiveness of the domestic market, as otherwise domestic companies may migrate to foreign markets and foreign investors avoid the domestic ones.

Financial globalisation puts not only the sets of rules but also the institutional setting of accounting systems under pressure. Accounting standards set by private, professional standard-setting bodies have been thought of as having a greater legitimacy than rules set by state law. Therefore, nation states have sacrificed competencies in the standard-setting process and assigned tasks to private or transnational bodies. This holds true not only for France and Germany, as parts of the EU, but is also observable in Japan. As we show in Table 5.3, pressure on the institutional setting is especially large at the end of, and after, periods of high globalisation growth rates, respectively.

# 6
# Mimetic Isomorphism: Crisis as a Driver of Change and Convergence

## 6.1 Introduction

This chapter shows that regulatory mimicking after outbreaks of crises is an important driver of change and global convergence in regulatory structures. By their very nature, crises are unforeseen events which negatively affect the well-being of at least parts of society. They are often perceived as exogenous shocks, even though their emergence is frequently inherent to the political, societal or technical systems at place. They are often direct outcomes of previously unobserved or disregarded system dysfunctionalities. Crises can be related to natural and technical disasters, riots and political turmoil, instability of the financial and banking system, a stock market crash or serious fraud at the corporate level, to name just a few examples. A common feature of crises, however, is that there are serious and significant negative externalities which make them not only a locally confined problem of some individuals but also one for wider society: a meltdown of a nuclear power plant, for instance, not only negatively affects the financial results of the operating company but also has a negative impact on the environment and the well-being of everyone living in the wider neighbourhood. Likewise, the bankruptcy of a system-relevant bank negatively affects not only its shareholders, creditors and employees (some of whom may even be insured against this risk) but also the well-being of many other economic actors who are not part of the direct nexus of contracts of these institutions: other banks may collapse, and the corporate lending business may come to a halt. The occurrence of a crisis is, by definition, beyond rational expectations. It is *not* a realisation of an uncertain yet anticipated state of nature; rather, it can be characterised as an unanticipated hazard that suddenly occurs and was not regarded as a possible future state of affairs in rational decision-making processes. It involves an accumulation of adverse conditions and is characterised by uncertainty and severe threat (Rosenthal and Kouzmin 1997).

In the following, we develop some hypotheses about how crises can have an impact on regulatory structures. We first hypothesise that corporate crises are likely to trigger regulatory change. We then argue that any legal amendment may be an innovation but is more likely to be an adaptation to seemingly more successful regulation found abroad: in other words, mimicking. We then present some empirical evidence for these hypotheses from our sample countries before discussing our findings and the role of mimetic isomorphism in accounting regulation.

## 6.2 Crises as catalysts for isomorphic change in regulation

Let us first consider two different economic explanations for the emergence of regulation in general (for the following see Stigler 1971). According to the first, regulators – or the 'state' – enact regulations to increase public welfare. The state and its regulatory agencies act altruistically, aiming at achieving Pareto-optimal solutions when intervening in society and the economy. This view, commonly referred to as the 'normative' theory of regulation, is still common in some branches of welfare economics. An intervention is regarded as required and justified if it can increase the economy's allocative efficiency or contributes to financial stability. A justified intervention can also change the distribution of economic resources in order to increase equity and fairness in the economy.

The second view rejects the assumption that the state or its agencies act in an altruistic fashion. This is referred to as the 'positive' theory of regulation and argues that conceiving the state as a single, identifiable institution is a fallacy. What is called 'the state' is rather a set of institutions which allow highly legitimated interventions into the private sphere of individuals. These institutions are used by individual political actors or bureaucrats (i.e., the government, broadly speaking) as a vehicle to intervene in private decision-making. Responsible actors may change over time and be affiliated with different parties, but what is important to stress is that all actors are assumed to have their own incentives and to be trying to maximise their own individual utility. This poses the question of what the incentives of regulatory actors such as politicians and bureaucrats are. One important incentive is to stay in office. One means to this end is maintaining or increasing the number of voters, but another might be gaining donations or the support of opinion-formers. Thereby, the general aim is to increase the resources controlled by the government or by the respective branch of government where the regulatory actors work, such as an agency (Watts and Zimmerman 1986). To maximise their own utility, political actors thus behave rationally when offering regulations of the kind and at the point in time when required by powerful groups in society. Watts and Zimmerman (1986) thus describe the political process as a 'competition for wealth transfers'.

Assuming that political actors behave as utility-maximising individuals is a simple but powerful adaptation of standard economics to the political sphere. However, standard economic theory is not very helpful in explaining processes of change. The assumption of efficiency assures that all kinds of markets – including those for regulations – are always in equilibrium and that any changes in preferences and beliefs will lead to the emergence of a new equilibrium without much delay or relevant transaction costs. However, processes in particular are important to understand, especially as they are not purely mechanical but can be shaped and designed by individuals. This is especially true for processes of change that involve deliberations and interactions of a limited number of individuals, which is the case with organisations or politics. Drawing on the organisational literature, change induced by individuals is likely to be of an incremental nature (Cyert and March 1963). The reason is that actors within organisations tend to look for local rather than global optima and that they aim at avoiding uncertainty. Revolutionary change is thus unlikely to occur; instead, incremental steps are undertaken, which particularly involve the application of solutions already known and which have been proved to work previously, in other branches or under similar environmental conditions. This step-by-step behaviour may be challenged in crisis situations.

There are basically three explanations of why crises may lead to governmental reactions. The first is that they are likely to change individuals' preferences and beliefs. A new equilibrium has to be found. An adjustment of some form or other has to take place. Indeed, crises are likely to challenge individuals' 'tacit beliefs about [...] the character of the environment (social and physical) and the adequacy of existing organisational and political arrangements to cope with that environment' (Stern 1997). Per se, this change of underlying beliefs can be a driver of governmental action observable after crises. The second explanation is that a crisis – as a 'focusing event' (Birkland 2004) – undermines the legitimacy of government authorities since they proved unable to prevent the occurrence of the crisis (Rosenthal and Kouzmin 1997). Thus, a demand for better regulation emerges within society. Moreover, from a legitimacy perspective, the regulator is threatened by a loss of confidence in the ability 'to maintain or establish effective normative structures in the extent required' (Habermas 1973) once such cases have attracted public interest. By announcing and implementing reforms, the regulator focuses the public's attention on administrative issues, preventing the institution itself from receiving scrutiny (Sikka and Willmott 1995). Supply of regulation thus contributes to the goal of governmental actors, which is to increase the likelihood of staying in office. However, the outcome of this process – that is, the actual type and content of regulation offered – is hard to predict, as society consists of various interest groups who are differently affected by regulations and will thus engage in different lobbying activities to influence the outcomes of the regulatory process. The third explanation for governmental reactions after a crisis is that crises establish a 'window of opportunity' for intervention or for the adoption of measures already on the agenda of some political actors. While any attempt to increase the resources controlled by government in normal times will prompt a sceptical reaction from constituencies, they are likely to be appreciated in times of a crisis. Watts and Zimmerman (1986) provide an appealing example of such incentives and behaviour, albeit one not directly contributing to what could be called a 'crisis theory' of regulation. They refer to the Great Crash of 1929 – a stock market and financial crisis – when explaining why and how regulation emerges. They argue that the crash 'created an opportunity for politicians to earn votes by appearing to be preventing future stock market crashes'. Note that this idea does not necessarily imply that regulators *really* aimed at preventing future crises. What regulators were in fact doing was creating a very powerful agency, the SEC, and by this means 'transfer[ring] resources to their own control' (Watts and Zimmerman 1986). Regulatory reactions are never compelling but provide windows of opportunity for regulatory interventions which, in the end, aim at increasing the resources controlled by regulators. Accordingly, Rosenthal and Kouzmin (1997) argue that crises are 'political events par excellence', not only in requiring decisions to be made but also by providing 'occasions for a restructuring of power relations'.

## 6.3 New regulation: Innovation versus mimicking

New regulations can either be regulatory innovations or regulatory adaptations. A regulatory innovation is a regulation that breaks new ground. Such innovations are not necessarily caused by crises. In general, they co-evolve along with other innovations in society and economy. Accounting standards are an example: as Basu and Waymire (2006) postulate, 'recordkeeping and accounting co-evolve with the scale of exchange, complexity in the division of labor, and changes in law and other economic institutions that sustain cooperation.' The bypassing of regulation in place by inventing financial innovations is another case in point (Moshirian 2011). Because of such behaviour, regulators are forced to keep pace, which leads to new regulation co-evolving with financial innovations. Competition between regulatory institutions may facilitate the emergence of such innovations (Sunder 2002), but generally – and probably also as a consequence of a lack of regulatory competition – the regulatory system's ability to produce innovations is very restricted. Innovations are not in line with incremental change and thus are not very likely to occur in any organisation, as the behavioural theory of organisations according to Cyert and March (1963) suggests.

However, crises may be catalysts for innovation. Again, the Great Crash of 1929 can serve as an example. Indeed, the introduction of a powerful supervisory agency, the SEC, represented an innovation in the organisation of financial and capital markets. Further examples include the increasing usage of international benchmarking (Lodge 2005) and compliance-oriented regulation (Parker 2000). Both represent innovative regulatory tools, and their emergence can largely be traced to the occurrence of crises. Benchmarking with good corporate governance practices was a reaction to fraud (Jesover and Kirkpatrick 2005); focusing on compliance-oriented regulation aims at dealing with the shortcomings of more traditional forms of intervention which failed in several corporate scandals. Indeed, regulatory innovations are more likely to happen after crises, when there is simply no possibility for incremental solutions, as muddling through is no longer a tenable option. The problem, however, is that in situations of crisis there is often no time to engage in 'searching for optimality or synoptic rationalism' (Rosenthal and Kouzmin 1997). This makes incremental decision-making by regulators very likely and leads to a paradoxical situation. Without crises, there is no need to innovate; in times of crises, time, resources and other factors which are required to innovate are lacking. Indeed, the absence of true innovation also becomes apparent when reconsidering the previous examples. Creating the SEC was indeed an innovation in US capital market regulation, but the mode of hierarchical governance reflected in control by agencies was not at all new. While benchmarking indeed represents a novel instrument applied by regulators, its main purpose is simply to identify best practices already applied somewhere else and to adapt them. Finally, compliance-oriented regulation is at first glance an innovation, but can be recognised at a second glance to build on well-established mechanisms of self-regulation.

While all of these regulatory mechanisms have at some point in time been true innovations, regulatory innovations are mostly adaptations of regulation found elsewhere. They are new only to the system under scrutiny. Accordingly, Lodge (2005) defines regulatory innovation 'as a process that seeks to encourage the development of domestic regulation according to "best practice" standards, however defined'. In the regulatory context, best practices may be provided by international or professional organisations (such as the OECD, the IOSCO, the World Bank), but they may also simply represent identified best practices. That is, they may consist of seemingly more successful regulation found somewhere else: international standards, other branches of regulation, other countries or other periods of time.

Mimicking is in line with individuals' preference for choosing alternatives already known and searching for local instead of global optima. But it requires regulatory actors to learn about potential alternative solutions. To become adaptable, regulatory alternatives need to be detected. There is a broad literature on learning in politics and policy, also revolving around the question of whether institutions and organisations (i.e., non-human beings) are at all able to learn (Bushman et al. 2006, and Stern 1997 review the related literature). Following Stern (1997), policy learning may come in different forms and even includes what Stern calls 'virtual' experience, which includes experience gathered by simulations, scenarios, cases or communication in networks described in Chapter 7. Obviously, it also embodies learning from crises that happen somewhere else, particularly if they are regarded as threatening, owing either to a contagion or to the risk that a similar crisis might occur in the organisation's own system. Learning and mimicking are in line with findings in the literature on behaviour of and in organisations (Mizruchi and Fein 1999; Barreto and Baden-Fuller 2006). Such behaviour is also consistent with the positive theory of regulation: regulators' generic alternatives are to develop innovative forms of regulation or to adapt existing ones.

However, mimicking requires that alternative solutions or perceived best practice can be identified. The more local a crisis is, the more likely is it to identify alternative regulatory solutions, for example, in other countries not suffering from a crisis at that point in time. Moreover, the more specific the local regulatory landscape, the more likely it is to find a benchmark solution that can be adapted. Mimicking is hardly possible when regulators have to tackle problems of high complexity and novelty. Globalisation, for instance, poses such problems. At the national level, financial markets are strongly regulated, but the increasing financial integration and globalisation of capital markets provide opportunities for constituencies to bypass such regulation. National regulation cannot simply be mimicked on global markets, as there is a lack of a 'world state' that would be responsible for enacting and enforcing such regulations (Werner 2010). As a consequence, new regulatory structures have to be found, which necessarily need to be innovative as such structures have not existed before. If there is no variation in regulatory approach, there is also nothing that can be mimicked. Thus, ongoing harmonisation and the existence of international organisations decrease competition between regulatory approaches and diminish the potential for mimicking.

## 6.4 Regulators' reactions to crises: Some evidence

In what follows we provide some evidence for mimetic isomorphism. We focus on incidents of serious fraud, mainly in our sample countries, that gave rise to regulatory change and, in many cases, furthered harmonisation of accounting regimes. We also shed light on the latest financial crisis, which began in 2007 and had a global outreach and thus made simple learning from regulatory practices in other countries more difficult.

*United States*: In the US there were several severe crises in the early 2000s, including the infamous cases of Enron, Adelphia, Global Crossing, WorldCom and Qwest. These cases, most notably the fall of Enron (Zimmermann 2002; Healy and Palepu 2003), raised concerns about whether investors had been sufficiently protected by the regulations in place. The regulatory reaction to these concerns came quite quickly as, in response to public indignation following the failure of such a large enterprise, politicians began to seek renewed legitimacy in the eyes of their voters. As little as two weeks after the public disclosure that Enron was filing for bankruptcy, congressional hearings on the case began. Six months later, Congress enacted H.R. 3763, the Sarbanes-Oxley Act. With this piece of legislation a fundamental transformation of the US securities legislation had begun. The act was said to be 'the most extensive regulation of the securities markets since the SA of 1933 and the SEA of 1934', which also were responses to crises (Ball 2009). The Sarbanes-Oxley Act was a case of forced innovation, because regulations already in place were supposed to provide the highest level of investor protection in the world. This hypothesis is broadly supported in the literature, probably beginning with La Porta et al. (1997), but this will be examined more closely and critically in Part IV. To some extent, it was therefore surprising that large corporate scandals could occur within this system. Enron's fall in a system of seemingly tight oversight raised questions of whether the regulation of financial reporting, external auditing and the internal governance structures of corporations in the US were still appropriate. Indeed, some reactions point to attempts at regulatory learning. For instance, there was a review of whether principle-based regulation, as it exists in European countries, outperforms the US approach of rule-based regulation (Schipper 2003). Some provisions, including the requirement to maintain risk management and internal control systems, were modelled on prototypes found abroad. But there is no strong evidence that regulatory reaction in general mimicked regulation found abroad. Rather, it incrementally adjusted the regulation in place by introducing some new elements. These built on strong securities laws and enforcement mechanisms that have traditionally been observable in the US. The US regulatory reaction, however, have themselves been imitated in many countries.

*Canada*: So far, no big corporate scandal has dramatically changed the regulatory landscape in Canada (Nicholls 2006). This does not mean, though, that no scandals have occurred here. Canadian accounting scandals of the 1990s include, among others, Bre-X Minerals Ltd, Cinar Corp., Livent Inc. and YBM Magnex International Inc. (Grey 2002). Also the case of Nortel Networks was widely recognised (Fogarty et al. 2008). But the literature does not point to any regulatory consequences of these scandals. This may be explained by a distinct feature of Canadian securities regulation, discussed in Chapter 4, which is that it is fragmented, since Canada regulates securities at the provincial and territorial level. As a consequence, there are different provincial approaches towards regulation and more or less loose attempts of harmonisation. This also explains why there was no unified Canadian reaction to the events at Enron and WorldCom. Instead, several regulatory measures have been proposed and enacted by the different Canadian securities regulators. These measures had to meet the challenge of restoring investor confidence on the one hand but also, on the other, not overburden Canadian firms, which tend to be smaller than their US counterparts. Nicholls (2006) thus describes the reforms undertaken as 'not designed as a response to a problem but rather, a response to a "solution"' – namely, the

Sarbanes-Oxley Act. This notion also implies that the home-grown accounting scandals themselves would not have resulted in reforms (Nicholls 2006). Canadian regulators thus responded to experiences abroad. There is also evidence for learning, even though this resulted in a regulatory solution that can be called customised mimicking.

The Canadian reform process is driven more fundamentally than just by responses to Enron. For a long time there was dissatisfaction with the fragmented Canadian approach to regulation, which does not chime with international practice. Comparing Canadian with other regulatory solutions and thereby learning from them has been the task of several commissions. In 2005 the Investment Dealers Association of Canada set up the 'Task Force to Modernize Securities Legislation in Canada', which was commissioned to make recommendations on how to modernise securities regulation. The final report, issued in October 2006, mentions the need to re-examine 'governance requirements, in part in the light of rethinking Sarbanes/Oxley in the US'. However, the commission's mandate explicitly excluded the issue of regulatory fragmentation.

In recent years there has also been a tendency to uncouple from US regulation. While there were plans in the early 2000s to converge Canadian GAAP with US GAAP, in 2006 the decision was made to converge with IFRS instead. US regulation was increasingly regarded as too burdensome. With the budget of 2007, the Canadian government issued a plan to further enhance domestic capital market regulation. One element was to set up the 'Expert Panel on Securities Regulation', which was mandated to review the regulations in place. It concluded that enforcement mechanisms in Canada were looser than in other countries, and it raised concerns that investors were not adequately protected. The Panel's work is not related to a specific corporate event, but regarding the sub-prime crisis it has already expressed concerns that the absence of 'a national Canadian securities regulator also raises wider concerns about systemic risk as there is no national entity accountable for the stability of our national capital markets' (Expert Panel on Securities Regulation 2009). Eventually, the report led to the proposal for a Federal SA in May 2010 by the Minister of Finance (Lee 2011). It was immediately sent to the Supreme Court to assess whether it is in line with the constitution (Lee 2011). The Supreme Court has ruled in December 2011 that it was outside the authority of the Parliament of Canada to nationalise securities regulation. But the attempt to enact such a law is the clear outcome of a learning process and of the aim to adapt to what is perceived as international best practice.

*Japan and other Asian countries*: The introduction of group accounts in Japan in 1977 can be traced not only to the globalisation of Japanese firms but also to the bankruptcy of Sanjo Special Steel Company, Nippon Special Steel Company and Sun Wave Industry in the late 1960s. At least in part, the regulatory reforms thus seem to be a reaction to the occurrence of a spectacular crisis. As McKinnon (1984), argues, it was not only this bankruptcy itself but 'the widespread publicity surrounding this and similar cases occurring at approximately the same time' that increased regulatory pressure. Consistent with our previous reasoning, the Japanese regulator learned and adopted perceived international best practice. Consistently, the consolidation requirements introduced in 1977 build on information accounting and thus Anglo-American practice. Some 20 years later another crisis, this time caused by the collapse of the Japanese banking sector, marked the beginning of a reform process that began in 1996 with the Japanese Prime Minister's announcement of several financial market reforms (Hoshi and Kashyap 2001). These reforms, sometimes referred to as the 'big bang' (Shiba 2004), aimed at restoring investor confidence (Anderson and Campbell Ii 2000). They put a strong focus on ensuring fair capital markets. As a means to this end, the institutional framework was reviewed and amended to bring it into alignment with international best practice in law, accounting and supervision (Honda 2003). The reforms imposed significant changes in accounting and enforcement regulation (Shiba 2004). For instance, the establishment of the ASBJ in 2001 reflected perceived international best practice. Moreover, developing accounting standards of high quality, similar to international standards such as IFRS or US GAAP (Benston et al. 2006b), is a learning outcome. As Suda (2011) says, '[a]ccounting scandals that have occurred since the 1980s have heavily influenced accounting institutions. In particular, they have caused new accounting standard setting, the reorganisation of audit firms and the establishment of internal control systems.' These reforms are largely in line with other countries' reforms in accountancy in the 2000s.

*Germany*: The German financial system was shaken by a series of accounting scandals in and around the 1990s. Infamous cases include those of Co-op (1988), Balsam (1994), Bremer Vulkan Verbund (1995), Philipp Holzmann (1999), Flowtex (2000) and ComRoad (2001). Lenz (2011) reviews these cases and also discusses immediate regulatory responses. Among other things, these cases led to serious doubts about the appropriateness of the investor protection mechanisms in place. There were concerns, in particular, about the supervisory board's role, the effectiveness of annual audits, financial reporting's ability to provide timely signals about the worsening of company's financial condition and a lack of transparency in regards to risk factors. KonTraG, in 1998, was the first in a series of legal amendments, described in more detail in Chapter 4, that aimed at improving corporate governance, accounting and auditing regulation. As Lenz (2011) points out, this 'Act was a direct regulatory response to accounting scandals'. Establishing the GASC is parallel to what was perceived as international best practice. KonTraG also forced companies to establish internal control and risk management systems and preceded similar (but not identical) rules to those which have been introduced by the SOA (Dobler 2004). A more complete review of the regulatory framework was undertaken by the 'Baums Commission'. This was set up in 2000 by the German Chancellor, who argued that experiences with the case of Philipp Holzmann point to the need to inquire into potential defects of the German corporate governance system. The final report of the Baums Commission was published in 2001 and contains several recommendations based on an in-depth analysis of alternative corporate governance solutions in foreign countries. This is an outstanding example of regulatory learning. The recommendations of the Baums Commission finally were the backbone of the German federal government's ten-point programme of 2003, which aimed at further improving investor protection and corporate integrity.

The programme put forward various measures that would improve investors' rights to file an action as well as increasing the duties and liability risks of the board of directors and supervisors. These measures were addressed by an assortment of minor laws. The main focus, however, was on two main issues. The first of these was the strengthening of accounting laws and their alignment to international standards, which were achieved by the laws listed in Chapter 4. The second was the legislator's intention to create a legal basis for the enforcement of accounting standards: in other words, the supervision of the accuracy of accounts by an independent authority. This measure was implemented in December 2004 with the German Accounting Control Act (*Bilanzkontrollgesetz,* BilKoG). This law gave rise to the Financial Reporting Enforcement Panel (FREP), a private-law body, which was empowered by law to audit single and group accounts of capital-market-oriented companies additionally to the regular auditor.[1] If FERP notices a violation within the accounts, a joint solution between it and the company involved should be found. If the company blocks such a solution, BaFin is able to intervene. BaFin looks into the incident as well and may enforce corrections and potential sanctions by public authority. Thus, the law has set up a two-step enforcement system (Pellens et al. 2011). In general, the programme and the connected legal reforms can be understood as, in part, a reaction to the Sarbanes-Oxley-Act; other elements have their origin in initiatives at the European level.

*France*: The international literature only rarely looks at French accounting scandals, even though France has experienced several cases of fraud. One of the cases that gained international recognition is the case of Vivendi in 2002 (Henselmann and Hofmann 2010). Further events include the Banque Pallas Stern scandal (mentioned in Konishi 2010), but also scandals of (at the time) public sector companies such as Crédit Lyonnais, Crédit foncier de France, Air France and France Télécom. But compared with Enron, the cases were of minor importance. As Stolowy (2005) explains, the French profession initially did not even consider the Enron case as a relevant lesson. The domestic financial market was perceived to be more tightly regulated.

In particular, control by auditors was perceived to be stronger because of the stipulation that 'two joint auditors must be appointed if the company publishes consolidated financial statements' (Stolowy 2005). Doubts about the appropriateness of financial market regulations and their respective enforcement described in more detail in Chapter 4 arose, however, and this eventually resulted in the passing of a new act – the Financial Security Law of 2003 (Konishi 2010). Its regulations are very much in line with reforms undertaken after Enron in the US and other countries. While the process of reviewing the architecture of French financial market regulation may have started even before the events at Enron became public (Stolowy 2005), hearings in the law-making process clearly indicate that the Enron case influenced the project and was considered by regulators. In the Senate debate two French ministers made explicit reference to occurrences at Enron when moving the legal amendment.[2] In their view, there was a need to review the institutions in place to ensure that nothing like Enron would happen in France. The explicit mention of the Enron case, again, points to regulatory learning.

*United Kingdom*: The UK has experienced several large-scale accounting scandals, including the cases of Polly Peck, the Bank of Credit and Commerce International and the Mirror Group. These cases are discussed in Gwilliam and Jackson (2011), who conclude that these scandals, among other things, 'no doubt contributed to strengthening the hand of the newly formed ASB'. In the UK there was a plethora of reforms concerning corporate governance, statutory audit and disclosure. These reforms can be explained in part, by the home-grown accounting scandals but can also be seen as, in part, a reaction to the collapse of Enron. For regulators, the Enron debacle clarified that even a very high level of investor protection, as had been supposed to exist in the US pre-Enron, would not automatically prevent the occurrence of fraud. It followed that the British system was no longer regarded as being immune to such events (Fearnley and Beattie 2004). This new perspective became clear in a speech by the then Secretary of Trade and Industry, Patricia Hewitt, who argued that 'the collapse of Enron is of such scale that it requires us carefully to review our arrangements for financial reporting and auditing'.[3] As a consequence, the government initiated several reviews into necessary changes to the regulation of UK audit and corporate governance (Dewing and Russell 2004). These reviews and the regulatory changes clearly indicate that the British system learned from the US experience and partly mimicked regulation abroad, particularly in regard to independent standard-setters. Again details are set out in Chapter 4.

*European level*: Supranational organisations also react to crises. An example is the EU, which issued its own regulation in the 2000s. This can partly be explained as a reaction to other European corporate crises, such as the case of Parmalat in 2003, but also to Enron and the Sarbanes-Oxley Act. In this context it is helpful to look at the guiding political criteria formulated in a communication by the EC in 2003, entitled 'Modernising Company Law and Enhancing Corporate Governance in the European Union – A Plan to Move Forward' (COM (2003) 284 final). The Commission emphasises, on the one hand, that, taking into account the member states' various traditions, their own European approach to corporate governance has to be developed. On the other hand, the Commission also stresses that it has to be borne in mind that corporate governance rules are increasingly set at an international level and that regulations in other countries, especially the US, might have a significant impact on economic actors domiciled in the EU (COM (2003) 284 final: 5). These statements again clarify that the new US regulation can be regarded as a driver for worldwide convergence in the fields of both financial reporting and corporate governance. It put European regulators under pressure, and also has had direct consequences for both European companies listed at US stock exchanges and European auditors.

*International crises*: Chapter 5 showed how, in recent years, financial markets have become increasingly global and integrated. However, owing to the absence of a global state, new forms of regulation had to be devised. Indeed, several international organisations and collaborative arrangements have emerged, but the recent financial crisis has raised the question whether the governance of global markets is in good shape. Crises of a global scale impose the problem that learning from them is almost impossible, which makes reactions to them much more complex than with regional ones. So far, there is no clear regulatory answer on how to proceed. On the one hand, there is evidence that the strong nation state again re-entered the stage. On the other, collaborative arrangements played important roles in dealing with the crisis: the G20, established in 1999 to deal with the Asian financial crisis, held several summits and obviously was an arena for regulatory cooperation and innovation. Existing institutions such as the IMF and the EU also played important roles. However, the reactions of these and other institutions in dealing with the sub-prime and financial crisis, to some extent, reinforces the argument that regulatory learning is the typical outcome after local crises and that the impossibility of learning becomes more likely with the increased scale of the regulatory problem and may lead to forced innovation.

The possible answer to this shortcoming of ever closer convergence and integration is a switch back to national solutions. Here there will be a long-standing tradition of national regulations to build on and observable alternatives to learn from. There are also risks attached, as there are almost no examples of successful attempts at de-harmonisation. The most likely outcome is therefore to change the harmonised regulation in place. Incremental steps may be undertaken, but owing to the fact that there is no regulatory solution to learn from, this process can only be one of innovative change.

## 6.5 Conclusion

Every kind of crisis highlights the fact that there are deficits in the regulatory system in place. Politicians and regulators, who are held responsible for maintaining and assuring workability of the systems, have incentives to react to crises to demonstrate regulatory capabilities and to meet demand for regulation. Particularly in a severe crisis, it is likely that political actors will respond to them by supplying new regulation. In our sample countries there is large evidence that regulators reacted directly to corporate crises, irrespective of their origin. While there is stronger evidence that regulators respond to domestic crises, there is also ample evidence that they reacted to crises abroad, particularly when occurring in culturally close countries and when the likelihood seems to be fairly high that similar events might also occur at home.

Mimicking of regulation found in other countries and introducing regulatory innovations proposed by international organisations can be regarded as drivers of international convergence of regulatory regimes and isomorphic change. This chapter has highlighted several cases in which regulators mimicked regulation from other countries. Imitation of Sarbanes-Oxley is the most prominent example in this area. Such examples generally support our argument that crises make mimetic isomorphism likely and, in the end, impose (further) convergence of regulatory patterns across nation states. There are conditions in which mimicking is hardly possible. This is true for the sub-prime and financial crisis that started in 2007. Its widely felt repercussions can be regarded as an outcome of increased globalisation: increasing financial globalisation links formerly autonomous systems and crises in individual nation states become crises of every (or the global) financial system. One problem with international events such as the recent banking and financial crisis is that regulatory learning is almost impossible. There are simply no national regulatory solutions that could easily be applied to crises on a global scale when the origin of the crisis is a lack of regulation on a global scale. In this respect, the difficulties in finding a regulatory answer to such crises underline the initial argument that the most likely reaction of regulatory actors is mimicking – and that regulators are unsure how to proceed if mimicking is not possible.

# 7
# Normative Isomorphism: The Role of International Networks for Convergence in Accounting Regulation

## 7.1 Introduction

Previous chapters have provided explanations for convergence of accounting regulation around the globe. Chapter 5 explained convergence in relation to the increasing globalisation and integration of financial markets. The perspective on convergence was extended by Chapter 6, where convergence was related to the mimicry behaviour of accounting regulators in times of crises and scandals. This chapter now looks at the structural foundations of accounting convergence, the creation and maintenance of networks in which normative ideas are disseminated.

Convergence constitutes more than a simple and spontaneous agreement between countries to use similar rules. Convergence also ensues because underlying normative ideas have spread before and are now shared. IFRS rest on two of those normative ideas. The first idea is that financial accounting should be information-oriented in such a way that it serves the efficiency and integration of capital market investors. The second idea is that standard-setting for financial accounting should be professionally self-regulated. This assumes that experts know best how accounting rules for companies and capital markets should look. Both ideas originate with the Anglo-Saxon paradigm of accounting regulation as described in previous chapters. The IASB has not only transported the overarching idea of globally standardised accounting rules but also an idea of a specific content and institutional setup. Consequently, when states agree on IFRS, they also sign up to the two normative ideas promulgated by the IASB. The extension of the use of IFRS, therefore, also equates to the successful dissemination of the two overarching ideas of information accounting and professional self-regulation.

Diffusion of ideas does not take place in a vacuum, indeed what is called 'diffusion' is very often dissemination. A crucial element is the effective communication between and integration of pertinent actors supporting the idea. Explanations attach great importance to the existence of network structures for the diffusion of normative (policy) ideas. Thus, networks serve as a mechanism with normative pressure that mediates change towards (policy) convergence in the long run. Furthermore, networks do not emerge by coincidence. They rather result from a factual need which is generated by exogenous forces. Financial globalisation, in particular, discussed in Chapter 5, is such a force.

To examine the role of networks for accounting regulation, this chapter is organised as follows. First, the role of networks for the diffusion of ideas is examined. The following section briefly summarises the globalisation of accounting service firms, as they are important actors who have established a network for the diffusion of ideas, and their expansion is closely connected to the foundation of the IASB and the idea of information-oriented accounting rules set by experts. Then the development of the network around the IASB is analysed in regard to our six country cases: we analyse and compare the make-up of the network in the 1970s and 2000s. Structural changes of the network are examined in the light of their contribution to the dissemination of the IASB's ideas of accounting regulation.

## 7.2 The role of networks in the diffusion of ideas

Convergence in accounting is often explained by structural changes relating to economic issues such as globalisation and crises. However, there is a need to understand the process whereby these structural forces translate into policy convergence. This pertains, in particular, to the intermediate mechanism that affects domestic arrangements in such a way that convergence across countries occurs. In this regard the concept of (policy) diffusion or transfer is used to understand how national arrangements are influenced, and by which intermediate mechanisms (Busch and Jörgens 2005).[1]

Diffusion is generally defined as the socially mediated spread across and within social systems encompassing communication and influence processes (Rogers 1995). The processes largely deal with the diffusion or transfer of knowledge. To be more precise, the objects of transfer can be policies, institutions or negative lessons but also, more importantly, ideologies as well as attitudes and ideas (Dolowitz 1997). The communication of changes takes place through certain channels and implies their spreading or dissemination from a common source or point of origin. Diffusion does not refer to a specific 'spread mediation', because all conceivable channels are possible (Knill 2005). Consequently, diffusion can be triggered by a large number of factors.

A key feature of the diffusion process is that it takes place without formal or contractual obligations. Moreover, diffusion manifests itself through a cumulative imitation and emulation process but also, more importantly, through social learning with respect to a specific issue (Busch and Jörgens

2005). Learning helps to support the diffusion of ideas, as it encapsulates cognitive changes and the redefinition of interests on the basis of knowledge affecting the beliefs and ideas attached to the pursuit of solutions (Hall 1993). In this sense diffusion and learning are more continuous and gradual than the learning referred to in Chapter 6. Diffusion and transfer of 'new' ideas can be regarded as supported by a prior process of learning as well as being a result of it, which may result in a coherent diffusion of ideas (Stone 2004). Learning often culminates in consensual knowledge by experts about the functioning of social arrangements, but also of other actors as the learning process also influences their behaviour and cognitive attitudes. The process of learning about policy innovations takes place not randomly but through common affiliations, negotiations and institutional memberships (Simmons and Elkins 2004). Thus, social and collective processes are involved which rely on the exchange of information between actors (Knoepfel and Kissling-Näf 1998). In general, this type of diffusion or transfer can be regarded as a process that DiMaggio and Powell (1983) label 'normative isomorphism'.

Conceptually, the exchange of information is the pivotal determinant for learning and, with it, the engine for the diffusion or transfer of new ideas. In this respect, communication and learning conditioned in networks are regarded as the central mechanism behind the diffusion of ideas (e.g., Rogers 1995 as well as Simmons and Elkins 2004). This makes networks formal or informal structures that link experts sharing a common interest on a specific issue or problem and a common set of (normative) beliefs and values (Bennett 1991; Haas 1992).

Networks are important means for the spread of ideas because networks typically evolve from a shared problem and the attempt to find a common solution (Knoepfel and Kissling-Näf 1998). They bring together representatives from several domains and assist communication between them. Rhodes (1997) describes networks as the commitment of independent actors to the delivery of services, which builds on the exchange of resources (e.g., information and expertise) to achieve a common purpose, but also to maximise their influence over outcomes or to preserve their independence from other actors. Moreover, networks serve as filters and amplifiers of ideas (Portes and Yeo 2001). The filter function refers mainly to the decision about which ideas are worth paying attention to and how to organise information. The amplifier function makes little-known or poorly understood ideas more accessible to others.

Networks also play an important role at the international level (Loft and Humphrey 2011). They are fruitful means for facilitating transnational communication and transnational problem-solving, which lead to the international spread and dissemination of ideas and paradigms (Bennett 1991). The key advantage of transnational network structures is that the actors are able to operate beyond their domestic borders. Transnational structures enable them to disseminate their ideas across states and within global or regional forums (Stone 2004). Networks thus deliver an enormous potential for facilitating joint operations and for gathering information detached from geographical, legal or institutional barriers. Transnational network structures, therefore, promote the formulation of a common perception of shared domestic problems and the development of collective solutions by adoption at national levels (Holzinger and Knill 2005).

Simmons and Elkins (2004) argue that international institutions play a significant role in transnational network structures. An international institution presents a forum that allows for regular discussions about shared problems and facilitates the mechanism of joint transnational problem-solving (Holzinger and Knill 2005). International institutions, in particular, open up an opportunity to find solutions in areas that do not necessarily need regulation by law. The strategic position that international institutions assume in networks also allows them to act as entrepreneurs of ideas. That is, international institutions, in particular in policy arenas, are able to forge the terms of debate, produce arguments, cross-link with decision-makers and communicate their ideas to potential (political) followers (Stone 2004). In this vein, the active integration of political decision-makers promotes the likelihood of political influence through networks. But even without political involvement, the norms and values that spread through the network can radiate a significant normative influence on public opinions and debates.

Over all, transnational networks accelerate the spread of models and solutions, compared with horizontal communication between countries, and create the basis for a subsequent international convergence within the relevant field of activity. Diffusion and network studies already have a long-standing tradition in the study of national policy convergence in federal systems (e.g., Gray 1973 as well as Walker 1969). Recently this concept has also been increasingly applied to the international level and research into policy convergence between states (e.g., Kern 2000 as well as Way 2005).

## 7.3 International auditing networks as international accounting entrepreneurs

Economic reasoning can link the internationalisation of auditing firms and the internationalisation of accounting: common IAS facilitate and support cross-border activities of auditing companies, and this generates business income and economies of scale (Mandler 1994). Thus the debate about the possibilities and consequences of IAS emerged as soon as the internationalisation process of the auditing sector began. This process, which led to the development of several global accounting firm networks, can be split into two phases: an internationalisation phase, followed by a subsequent concentration phase, which eventually formed the Big 4.

The internationalisation phase began with FDI of British companies in North and South America at the end of the 19th century (Mandler 1999). In 1880 Deloitte, Dever, Griffiths & Co. opened its first office in New York, and shortly afterwards two other leading UK accounting firms followed: Price Waterhouse and Touche Ross. The earliest (international) merger between two accounting firms took place in 1911 and goes back to the firms William Barclay Peat & Co. (UK) and Marwick, Mitchell & Co. (US). In 1926 the nationally important firm Cooper Brothers (UK) also established an office in the US (Wise 1966). The global expansion of the British industry, therefore, heralded the first wave of internationalisation of accounting firms, which was directed from the UK to the US and lasted approximately from 1890 to 1945 (Daniels et al. 1989).

A second wave of internationalisation took place in the 1950s and 1960s and was directed from the US to Continental Europe. This time the process was triggered by overseas direct investments of the US industry (Lück and Holzer 1981). Audit companies originally from the UK now penetrated the Continental European market under the name of their US company labels. In addition, two original US firms – Arthur Andersen and Arthur Young – joined. The expansions activities preceded several larger mergers between UK and US auditing firms (Daniels et al. 1989). For instance, in 1952 Deloitte, Haskins & Sells was formed by a merger between Deloitte, Plender, Griffiths & Co.[2] (UK) and Haskins & Sells (US), and Coopers & Lybrand emanated from the merger between Coopers Brothers (UK) and Lybrand, Ross & Montgomery (US) in 1957.

In the following years large accounting service firms successively expanded their international service networks, mostly by cooperating and integrating firms that operated only nationally (for a detail discussion see Wootton et al. 2003). Coopers & Lybrand, for instance, founded about 170 offices worldwide between 1957 and 1973 and quadrupled their foreign offices. In about the same period the international network of Arthur Andersen grew from 2 to more than 180 foreign offices (Mandler 1999). During this period 'the Big 8' became the general name for the international networks of the eight leading accounting firms, encompassing Arthur Andersen, Arthur Young, Coopers & Lybrand, Deloitte Haskins & Sells, Ernst & Whinney, Peat Marwick International, Price Waterhouse and Touche Ross (Simons 2005). Since then, an incremental consolidation process between these companies took place, leading to the 'Big 6' group in the 1990s and the 'Big 4' in the 2000s, consisting today of (ordered by size): Price Waterhouse Coopers, Deloitte, Ernst & Young and KPMG. Figure 7.1 briefly outlines the consolidation process.

Following the merger between Arthur Young (US) and Ernst & Whinney (UK), and the closure of Arthur Andersen (US) because of the Enron scandal in 2002, the remaining Big 4 all have a British background (Benston and Hartgraves 2002). Today Price Waterhouse Coopers is the largest firm in

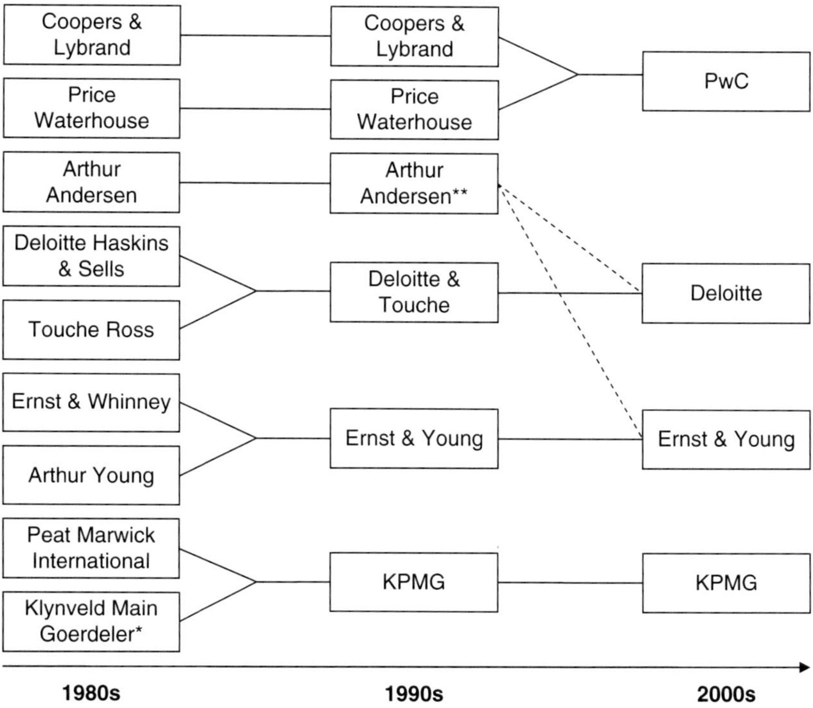


*Figure 7.1* Consolidation process of the Big 8 to the Big 4
*Source*: Müller-Stewens et al. (1999).
*Notes*: *Klynveld Main Goerdeler did not belong to the former group of Big 8. **The Arthur Andersen network was dissolved owing to its involvement in the accounting scandal of Enron in 2002. The main parts of the network were taken over either by Deloitte – for example, in Spain and the UK – or by Ernst & Young – for example, in France and Germany.

terms of annual income and the number of countries served, followed by Deloitte, Ernst & Young and KPMG, as can be seen in Table 7.1. Beside the Big 4, several other international accounting groups developed, in which single smaller national auditing firms, also referred to as second- and third-tier companies, cooperate (Mandler 1999). The Big 4 stand out as they constitute by far the largest groups in terms of income, the countries in which they are active and professional staff (Smith 2009). For instance, the total annual income of the companies ranked from 6 to 10 ($22,768 million) barely exceeds the annual income of the fourth-ranked member, KMPG. Similar proportions exist for the number of professional staff.

The early expansion and internationalisation activities of accounting firms are especially remarkable as the accounting landscape was highly fragmented. National accounting standards showed a high degree of diversity, as did the professional requirements of auditors. Market-related reasons,

*Table 7.1* Top 10 accounting firms worldwide in 2009

| **Rank 2009 (2008)** | **Company name** | **Income in $ million** | **Number of countries active** | **Professional staff** |
|---|---|---|---|---|
| 1 (1) | Price Waterhouse Coopers | 28,185 | 153 | 116,935 |
| 2 (2) | Deloitte | 27,400 | 140 | 124,000 |
| 3 (3) | Ernst & Young | 24,500 | 140 | 107,447 |
| 4 (4) | KPMG | 22,690 | 144 | 104,057 |
| 5 (5) | BDO Int. | 5,145 | 110 | 33,436 |
| 6 (7) | Grant Thornton Int. | 4,000 | 100 | 21,822 |
| 7 (8) | Geneva Group Int. | 3,707 | 72 | 14,005 |
| 8 (6) | RSM Int. | 3,620 | 64 | 21,401 |
| 9 (9) | Praxity | 3,233 | 72 | 17,934 |
| 10 (10) | Crowe Horwarth Int. | 3,063 | 101 | 16,456 |
| **Total sum** | | **125,543** | | **577,493** |

*Source*: Smith (2009).

that is, the relationship of auditor and audited firm, must therefore play an important role in relation to cost-related advantages, which simply brings about a cheaper delivery of the service by economies of scale and scope. Indeed, the (almost) reciprocal relationship between the internationalising company and its auditor amplified the demand for seamless global accounting services. This demand arose with uncertainties about the professional quality as well as reliability of foreign auditing firms in the host countries (Mandler 1994). As a result, a simultaneous international expansion of auditing companies, on the one hand, guaranteed their clients horizontal quality consistency and, on the other, was able to save their clients transactions costs (Nusbaumer 1987; Mandler 1994). The 'follow-your-client strategy' by accounting firms was not fully voluntary. They were in fact forced into this position if they did not want to run the risk of losing their (local) clients. Even today reliability of quality and consistent corporate auditing remain the standard factors in choosing the annual auditor (Williams 1988; Coenenberg and Marten 1993). Thus, the internationalisation waves of UK and US commercial firms required auditors to extend their reach to avoid market share losses.

Internationalisation also facilitated the acquisition of new clients and fostered further growth. The largest international group was able to solidify customer retention and guarantee the largest potential for the acquisition of new clients (Mandler 1995). Accordingly, accounting firms switched their strategy from 'follow-your-client' to 'follow-your-competitor' as tapping into markets that their original clients had not (yet) entered provided advantages (Mandler 1999). The potential for horizontal quality consistency and the scale effect went in hand in hand and improved the competitive position of globally acting accounting service firms compared with firms that operated only nationally. The competitive advantages that international companies obtained were, however, to quite some extent a coercive necessity and induced by the globalisation of their local clients (Nachum 2003; Grewe 2008).

International expansion enabled accounting firms also to realise some cost advantages even though the degree of diversity in accounting was high. The advantages arose from economies of scope and scale as resources or infrastructures could be used more efficiently by the integration of cross-border activities (Coenenberg and Marten 1993; Mandler 1994). The global transfer of expert knowledge between employees, for instance, improved not only the availability of an all-embracing customer support but also the ability to acquire new clients. Likewise, cost advantages could be gained from the utilisation of shared staff sections, such as special teams for complex corporate accounting issues (Hachmeister 2001). The deployment of international administrative units also allowed international personnel development. This in turn generated a cost advantage in the way that auditing companies could more easily adapt to country specific demand cycles and the seasonality of the accounting services. With more flexibility to share resources peak capacity could be reduced and the overall capacity utilisation was improved. Bottlenecks during peak seasons could be avoided due to more efficient deployment, which subsequently allowed for a more efficient distribution of a fixed cost (Coenenberg and Marten 1993; Eitzen 1996).

Internationalisation made accounting firms aware at an early stage of the differences between accounting systems and highlighted barriers and difficulties associated with these differences. Auditing companies recognised the costs and difficulties of accounting diversity not only for their clients but also for their supply of services (Mandler 1994). The fragmentation of the accounting landscape constituted an impediment to realising the full potential of internationalisation. Every expansion, for instance, required a search for competent partners as it would have been burdensome for each company to build up its own competence in the respective national accounting system (Daniels et al. 1989). Moreover, to offer a homogenous product worldwide was largely impossible. Accounting firms had to pay special attention to the assurance of the demanded international quality consistency while accounting diversity significantly complicated its maintenance and made country-by-country differentiation necessary. The satisfaction of customer demands, therefore, meant relatively high transaction costs for accounting companies (Mandler 1994).

The accounting profession therefore began to discuss the advantages and practicalities of international comparable accounting standards as soon as the first transatlantic investments of industrial companies began. The accounting profession, in this respect, can be seen as the source of the idea of international standardised accounting standards (Samuels and Piper 1985; Daniels et al. 1989). Although having a positive effect in terms of the public interest, the origins of the idea of convergence can be seen as having been motivated by economic self-interest based on the advantages international accounting companies would gain from standardised accounting standards for large companies (Botzem 2010).

However, the attempts at harmonisation made by the international accounting profession were marginal until the 1970s. The big accounting companies, for instance, could not harness their outstanding position in regional and international accounting markets to exert influence on national regulators to harmonise accounting systems. Moreover, there was no (international) forum to provide such issues an arena for discussion – only forums with a purely regional focus, which lacked clout, and occasional international auditor conventions (for details see Botzem and Quack 2005b).

## 7.4 Evidence of an international accounting standard-setting network

The foundation of the IASC in 1973, at the initiative of the British accounting profession and some other national accounting and auditing associations (Mennicken and Heßling 2007), marked the accounting profession's attempt to increase its material output with respect to internationally comparable accounting standards (Flower 2004). In this respect, the IASC was also a vehicle to promote the idea of professionally set standards in accounting. Its founder members were employees or partners of leading accounting service firms, whose internationalisation had reached a new peak in this period. Sir Henry Benson, first chairman of the IASC, for instance, was senior partner at Coopers & Lybrand, who had opened their 173rd international office in the same year (Walton 2008). Similar observations could be made for all those who signed the memorandum of association.

It is conjectured that promoting standardised accounting standards was not the only aim of the IASC: it was also a protective measure on the part of the accounting profession. International political institutions such as the UN and OECD had also recognised the need for IAS (Camfferman and Zeff 2007). The foundation of the IASC, therefore, would secure the influence of the accounting profession on an issue where regulation would have a large impact on the supply of their services. The initiative would protect their field of activity from intrusion by political actors, in particular in those countries where political influence was traditionally low (Willmott et al. 1993).

Establishing harmonised accounting standards and self-regulation for the accounting profession at the international level required the integration of supporting and legitimising partners. Harmonising accounting rules would cut deep into national sovereignty, in particular in Continental European countries. Expert knowledge in itself is not sufficient for the creation of legitimacy. Unlike international political institutions, the IASC could not rely on a pre-existing network of legitimising affiliated and pivotal members who supported their ideas. The IASC, therefore, faced not only the challenge of creating high-quality accounting standards for international use (Samuels and Piper 1985), but also that of establishing relationships with national actors in order to disseminate its idea of standard-setting and to gain acceptance and legitimacy.

Network analysis can provide an explanation of the stages by which this was brought about (e.g., Knoke and Yang (2008) as well as Richardson (2009) and Scott (2005)). We will reconstruct and document the development of the international standard-setting network in accounting, using the method of social network analysis. We will show the growth of the network and the shift in the actors' constellation during the development process. From this we draw conclusions about how shifts in the actors' constellation contributed to the increased importance of the IASC, the promulgation of its ideas and, finally, to the success of the IASC in shaping international standard-setting. The results add a further facet to our explanation of the observed process of accounting convergence, and they additionally highlight the extent to which the IASC network contributed to accounting convergence.

Most of the data for the network analysis were extracted from chapters 3 and 5, which is why only governmental and non-governmental actors are represented in the network. The network analysis is limited to these actors as they are typically directly involved in the process of standard-setting at the national level. Private actors (lobbying groups) such as accounting service companies were not explicitly captured, on the assumption that these actors are indirectly represented in the network by their respective professional associations. These limitations set the boundaries of the network and also define a fixed sample of actors for the networks under consideration.

The connections between the organisations were established by 'link-tracing' – that is, we examined whether or not an actor has a relation with any of the other actors in the sample (Spreen 1992). Any kind of relationship between the actors was incorporated into the link-tracing processes. The nature of relationships considered, therefore, ranges from annotation, assistance and guidance in the standard-setting process to cooperation and partnerships between actors, their direct membership as well as the appointment and election of members of an institution. They are formalised in the most straightforward way, namely a binary and undirected form (symmetric relations). This implies that information flows in both directions (Haas and Malang 2010). This method limits the analytical spectrum to the disclosure of the formed relationships and the possible channels through which the ideas of the IASB could be diffused and how these links altered over time. Positions of power and control are beyond our analysis.

The comparative analysis of the network development refers to three points in time: 1973, 2001 and 2010. The analysis for the 1973 network is further split up into one part without the IASC and one part with. Three two-way comparisons will be made: the pre-IASC network (constructed by fading out the IASC) and the 1973 network are compared in order to understand the significance of the formation of the IASC in 1973 for international accounting standard-setting. Next, the 1973 network is compared with the 2001 network. The 2001 network was chosen as a benchmark as the IASC finished a significant restructuring process and achieved a breakthrough regarding the acceptance of its standards in that year, as was documented in Chapter 2. The 2001 network, in turn, is compared with the present 2010 network, to establish whether the network has reached a steady state.

For analytical purposes we discuss not only the network as a whole, but also its constituent parts (sub-networks). These should provide additional insights into the extent to which changes in the actors' constellations of the network helped to disseminate the promulgated policy ideas of the IASB and vice versa. We consider national networks and the EU network as well as the egocentric network of the IASB. The egocentric network of the IASB incorporates all actors that are in its direct neighbourhood (geodesic distance equals 1.0). The examination of the egocentric network will shed light on the relevance attached to the IASB by the relevant national or international actors and how the actor's constellation contributed to the legitimacy of the IASB. As the network illustrations will show, the egocentric network constitutes the core of the international standard-setting network.

The qualitative analysis of the structural changes and the comparison of the networks will be supported and supplemented by the core measures for social network analysis, which are listed and defined in Table 7.2. These quantitative measures give information about the information diffusion and processing characteristics of the network as well as the positioning of actors within the network, which points to their role in the dissemination of ideas.

### 7.4.1 The rise of an international standard-setting network

Figure 7.2 displays the national standard-setting networks with regard to our six national case studies before the formation of the IASC in 1973. The drawing illustrates that the number of actors as well as the type of actors who participate in the respective standard-setting process varies from country to country. The number ranges from only two actors in the UK to six in the US. The US government and the SEC were not fully committed to the standard-setting process but limited their commitment to put other institutions in charge: that is, the US government made the SEC responsible for organising standard-setting, and the SEC finally handed over the responsibility to the FASB – a private standard-setting body.

The network first illustrates that in each country accounting associations are involved in the standard-setting process. The distinctive feature

*Table 7.2* Definition of basic network measures

| Measure | Definition |
|---|---|
| Average Distance | Path distance or geodesic distance is a cohesion measure. It is defined as the length of the shortest path between two actors: the distance between two directly connected actors equals 1.0. The average distance as a macro-characteristic is the average sum of all the shortest paths between all pairs of actors and indicates how closely each actor is connected to any other actor in the network. The greater the average distance, the fewer direct connections will exist between actors and the longer it will take for ideas or information to diffuse across a network, all other factors being equal (Scott 2005). |
| Between-ness | Between-ness is a centrality measure. Centrality measures, in general, describe structural attributes of actors and provide information about their strategic position in the network: that is, they reflect the potential influence that actors can have on the network flow. Between-ness, in particular, describes the intermediation centrality of an actor by measuring to what extent an actor is located on the shortest path between two actors. The more frequently an actor is represented as a broker in the network, the higher his between-ness figure (Freeman 1977). |
| Compactness | Compactness is a distance-based cohesion measure for the whole network. The parameter amounts to 1.0 if every actor is connected with every other and 0.0 if all actors in the network are isolated. The more compact a network is, the more quickly information will be disseminated across a network, all other factors being equal (cf. average distance). |
| Max. Distance/ Diameter | The maximum distance or diameter is the largest distance between two actors in the network. Accordingly, the diameter indicates how large a network is and how many steps are needed for information to cross a network (Jansen 2006). That is, the higher the diameter, the longer it takes for ideas or information to cross the network from one side to the other. |
| Mean of Relations | The number of actors' relations indicates an actor's surroundings and displays how many direct neighbours he or she has. This measure, therefore, is an indicator of the potential for an actor to undertake activities, or rather exchange ideas, with other actors. It therefore values in- and outgoing paths, which is akin to the degree of centrality (Freeman 1979). Thus, the average value indicates the average size of the neighbourhood an actor has. |
| Network Density | The network density is an index value for the proportion of links of the network relative to the total number of links possible. It is calculated by the number of actual relations divided by the number of all theoretically possible relations. It follows that the lower the network density, the more loosely knit a network is, and the lower the relatedness of actors respectively (Scott 2005). This measure indicates the degree of cooperation and the level of similarity. |

*Table 7.2* (Continued)

| Measure | Definition |
|---|---|
| Structural Hole | Structural holes describe absent or weak relations in networks. Actors who strategically fill these holes often gain an advantage owing to their location in the social structure. These advantages result from control and monitoring advantages and information arbitrage. Moreover, bridging actors are able to circulate ideas and information across actors (Burt 1995, 2004). |

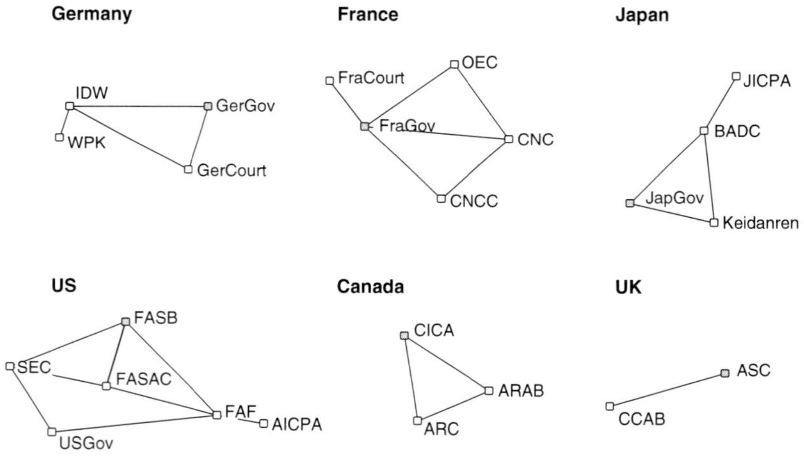


*Figure 7.2* National standard-setting networks before the formation of IASC in 1973
*Source*: Own contribution.

of Canada, which distinguishes its standard-setting network from that of all other countries, is that standard-setting is not separated from the accounting association. The network drawing also reflects the typical country dichotomy of standard-setting. The actors responsible for standard-setting (grey nodes) are private in Anglo-Saxon countries and governmental in Continental European ones (Volmer et al. 2007; Nobes and Parker 2008).

Figure 7.2 also reveals that regulative solutions for accounting were produced by local standalone networks, although the six countries advanced to mutually important economic and financial centres. There was neither a direct relationship between the national standard-setting bodies nor a subordinate actor in the form of an international player that coordinated standard-setting activities between countries. Consequently, standard-setting in each country took place in a closed system. This setting contrasted

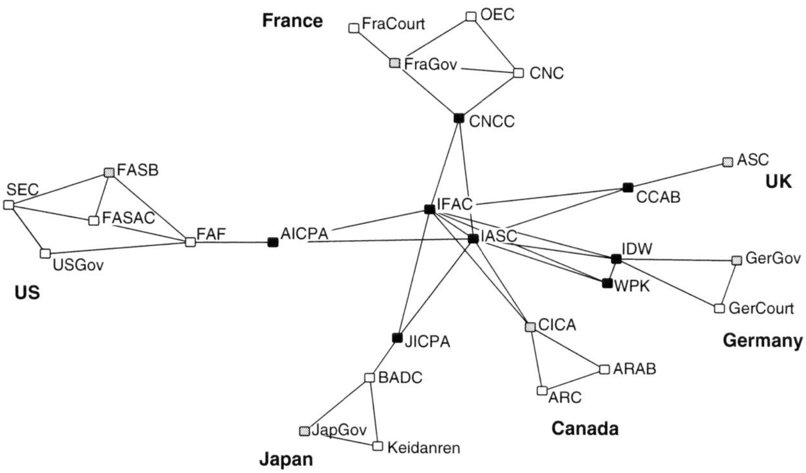


*Figure 7.3* The international accounting standard-setting after the formation of IASC in 1973
*Source*: Own contribution.

with the increasing aggregation of markets and organisations.[3] Figure 7.2, therefore, shows quite clearly the existence of an institutional void (or structural hole) at the beginning of the 1970s in terms of international financial accounting and its standard-setting (Djelic and Quack 2007).

The institutional void was filled by the foundation of the IASC, which is illustrated in Figure 7.3. The self-image of the IASC with regard to standard-setting differed considerably from that of the UN or the OECD, which had put international accounting on their agenda (Camfferman and Zeff 2007). On the one hand, there were differences in the targeted role that these institutions wanted to carry out. While the IASC committed itself directly to standard-setting, the UN and OECD focused on a more indirect role by influencing public opinion about the direction of standard-setting. On the other hand, the IASC's perspective on standard-setting was more all-embracing. While the UN concentrated only on accounting standards for developing countries and the OECD only on standards for already industrialised countries, the IASC focused on the idea – at least in the beginning – of developing a common set of standards for every type of company and country. However, over the course of their activities the IASC realised that this project was too ambitious. The IASC, therefore, changed its directions and concentrated on the development of standards for capital markets and capital-market-oriented companies (Flower 2004).

The formation of the IASC can be understood as the formation of a new, path-generating institution. Moreover, an autonomous organisation rooted in the profession such as the IASC provided an opportunity for the profession to share their experiences in the discussion of IAS (Botzem and Quack 2005a). It was a forum for articulating and discussing national and sectoral accounting norms as well as different accounting philosophies. Accounting experts were given the platform and the opportunity to exchange information and to gain a better understanding of accounting practices in other countries. The IASC progressed to become a receptacle for approaches and ideas on how to achieve the overarching aim of developing a new set of standards for global application (Tamm Hallström 2004).

Figure 7.3 shows how the creation of the IASC led to the formation of a star-shaped network with a 'hub-and-spoke type' character. The star-shaped structure applies first and foremost to the egocentric network of the IASC. Actors belonging to the egocentric network are marked with black nodes, while actors who belong to the core and simultaneously fulfil a standard-setting task in their country remain grey. Table 7.3 summarises some basic network metrics about the IASC's egocentric network and the structure of the network as a whole in 1973. The egocentric network, which exhibits the core of the international standard-setting network at this point in time, is determined by nine actors, of whom the IASC and IFAC are the only international ones. The remaining actors include the respective national accounting associations (founder members). Germany is the only country represented by two associations. The egocentric network contains a third of all actors in the network as a whole, which includes a total number of 26 actors. Each actor in the egocentric network has on average 3.6 relations, and the average distance between these actors is 1.6. In the network as a whole the average sum of relations drops slightly to 3.2, and the distance averages 3.5. This means that, although the degree of centrality is relatively equal, the

*Table 7.3* Basic statistics for the 1973 network of the IASC

| | **Egocentric network 1973** | **Complete network 1973** |
|---|---|---|
| Actors | 9 | 26 |
| – international level[a] | 2 | 2 |
| – national level | 7 | 24 |
| Actors as a percentage of the network as a whole | 35 | 100 |
| No. of relations[b] | 32 | 82 |
| Mean of relations | 3.6 | 3.2 |
| Average distance | 1.6 | 3.5 |
| Network density | 44% | 13% |

*Source*: Own calculations.

[a]Even though the IFAC was not established until 1977, it was already included in the network as it developed a strong relationship with the IASC since its formation.

[b]Links are counted twice in order to grasp the relation as in- and outgoing flow of ideas and information.

ability of actors in the network as a whole to exchange ideas or information directly is more limited owing to the greater distance. Actors in the core network are virtually able to communicate with all the others through their direct neighbour (IASC or IFAC), which does not hold true for the network as a whole. Thus the relative frequency and efficiency of the information exchange can be categorised as higher in the egocentric network than in the network as a whole.

The network density amounts to 44 per cent for the egocentric network and 13 per cent for the network as a whole. This shows that the 1973 network as a whole is relatively loosely knit compared with the egocentric network. This has structural reasons. The formation of the IASC did connect actors, but the IASC did not establish direct connections between all of them. The IASC instead functions as a hub between the countries, which is shown by the star-shaped network structure. The structural feature also explains the huge difference between the densities of the egocentric network and the network as a whole, as with an increasing number of actors the number of possible links increases exponentially. Consequently, the emergence of new actors in the network either at the national or at the international level would further decrease the network density if the new actors maintain links to only a small group of existing actors: for example, solely to the IASC.

The IASC maintains also the highest number of relations in the network as a whole, with a total of eight relations, which means that it is related to 35 per cent of the others. This underlines the central position that the IASC assumes in the newly formed network. As the hub, the IASC centrally functions as a communication interface between the different spokes – in this case, national accounting associations – and as the distributor for centrally arranged activities. More importantly, the IASC institutionally connected, for the first time ever, accounting actors from the largest industrial countries and from different accounting traditions to work jointly on international accounting regulation.

The founder members of the IASC had agreed on their function as mediator and spokesperson at their respective national levels to arouse public interest in the work of the IASC (Camfferman and Zeff 2007), and they had many channels through which to do so (Zimmermann et al. 2008). First, national accounting associations were engaged in the education of the profession, which provided the chance to discuss new technical expertise from the international arena and introduce it into local education. Second, through the active participation of most of the members in the accounting associations, they were able to spark an interest in the IASC's work in companies and to campaign for their support. Third, accounting associations were integrated and involved in the national standard-setting processes, such as the development of new rules and the interpretation of standards. This provided them also with the chance to promote new ideas in the national standard-setting process, and they were able to influence established patterns of thought about accounting standards and how they were set. So national accounting associations were able to initiate and support the process of 'policy' learning at the national level. The learning process is in several stages, starting as a mutual learning process at the level of the IASC, spreading to the national links, the accounting associations and from these actors flowing to other actors embedded in the national network.

Such a learning process was important for the IASC in two respects. It contributed to the diffusion of the IASC's ideas, typified by the published standards and the organisation of standard-setting. Further, the process made it possible for their efforts to gain recognition and legitimacy, in particular from the standard-setting authorities at the national level. This was of vital importance as companies are not usually free to choose their reporting standards but are compelled to apply their respective national standards. Therefore the creation of a societal and national political awareness of the IASC was very important for the dissemination of their ideas and the success of the network (Luthardt and Zimmermann 2009).

### 7.4.2 The 1973 network and 2001 network compared

Figure 7.4 shows the international accounting standard-setting network in 2001, the year that marked the breakthrough of international standards as laid out in Chapter 2. A simple visual comparison between the 1973 network and the 2001 network reveals straight away that the network has changed considerably. These changes relate above all to a growth in complexity

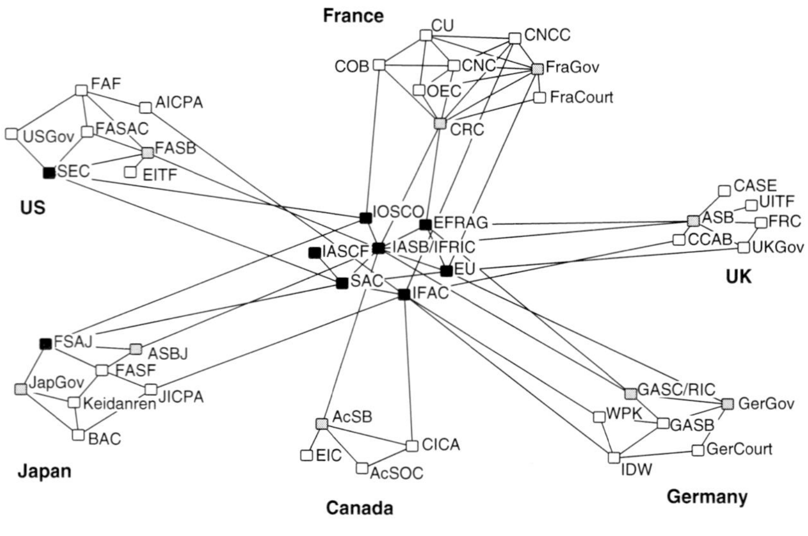


*Figure 7.4* International accounting standard-setting network in 2001
*Source*: Own contribution.

*Table 7.4* Comparison between the 1973 network and 2001 network

| | Egocentric network 1973 | Egocentric network 2001 | Network as a whole 1973 | Network as a whole 2001 |
|---|---|---|---|---|
| No. of actors | 9 | 15 | 26 | 45 |
| – international level | 2 | 7 | 2 | 7 |
| – national level | 7 | 8 | 24 | 38 |
| Actors as a percentage of the network as a whole | 35 | 33 | 100 | 100 |
| No. of links | 32 | 48 | 82 | 176 |
| Mean of relations | 3.6 | 3.2 | 3.2 | 4.0 |
| Average distance | 1.6 | 2.0 | 3.5 | 3.0 |
| Network density | 44% | 23% | 13% | 9% |

*Source*: Own calculations.

at the international level and in the respective national standard-setting networks as well as to the type of actors participating in the respective networks.

Table 7.4 juxtaposes the key facts of the 1973 network and 2001 network in order to characterise the changes by 2001. The increase in the total number of participating actors from 26 to 45 actors in the network as a whole mirrors the increase in complexity of standard-setting worldwide. Despite this jump, the fraction of actors in the egocentric network remained almost constant. That is, the proportion of actors still accounts for about a third of the total network: the egocentric network and the network as a whole have grown by the same amount. The increase in internationality of the actors in the network is particularly remarkable: the proportion of international to national actors in the network as a whole increased from 1:12 in 1973 to roughly 1:5 in 2001. Likewise, the proportion in the egocentric network increased from roughly 1:4 in 1973 to almost parity in 2001.

The growth in complexity is also mirrored in the average values of actor relationships. In the egocentric network the mean of relations dropped from 3.6 to 3.2, and the average distance increased from 1.6 to 2.0 compared with 1973. Likewise, the maximum distance between two actors enlarged from two steps in 1973 to three in 2001: for example, between the Financial Services Agency of Japan (FSAJ) and the EFRAG. There are two main reasons for this. First, the number of relations did not grow to the same extent as the number of actors in the core network. As a consequence, the mean number of relations decreases. And second, the average distance increased owing to the changes in the actors' constellation. That is, the IASB and its subgroups (IASCF and Standard Advisory Council (SAC)) advanced to become the sole juncture among the actors in the core network. Previously, there were two junctures for actors to reach one another: the IASC and IFAC. The

*Table 7.5* Centralities of the IASC/IASB and IFAC compared over time

| Between-ness (normalised)[a] | Egocentric network 1973 | Egocentric network 2001 | Network as a whole 1973 | Network as a whole 2001 |
|---|---|---|---|---|
| IASB/IFRIC | 35.7 | 64.7 | 39.2 | 37.0 |
| IFAC | 35.7 | 0.0 | 39.2 | 25.8 |

*Source*: Own calculations.
[a]In each network the IASC or rather IASB/IFRAC has the highest Between-ness score, which is quite normal as the network has a star-shaped structure.

IASB managed to strengthen its position in the egocentric network, which is also shown in the centrality measure of the IASB in Table 7.5.

The network as a whole shows a different development. Compared with 1973, there are more and closer relations: the average number of relations rises from 3.2 to 4.0, and the average distance decreases from 3.5 to 3.0. The average number of relations increased as the number of links from periphery actors to the core network actors increased, as did the connections between actors in the national networks. This can be seen by comparing the network drawings in Figures 7.3 and 7.4. It also shows that the connectivity between actors of different countries increased as additional actors appeared at the international level: EFRAG, for instance, connects the standard-setting actors from France, Germany and the UK to allow for joint action concerning the transformation of the IAS into European law. These four actors form a European standard-setting network, which is embedded in the wider international network. EFRAG, therefore, filled a structural hole in the network as it assumes a role in the network that was formerly filled only by the IASB. This type of development decreases the distance between (national) actors. Nevertheless, the centrality of the IASB remains stable.

One might suppose that the 2001 network would be denser than its predecessor. However, the network is actually less dense, as the values for network density in Table 7.4 indicate. The reason is that the formerly star-shaped structure of the network with the IASB as linchpin of the network did not change at all, while other influential actors joined the network.

### 7.4.3 Changes in the fractional networks: Indications for the diffusion of the idea of the IASB

We now discuss the changes and developments of the network as a whole in more detail by referring to the fractional networks. The additional analyses ask whether the changes in the fractional networks are an indication of the diffusion or increased importance of the ideas promulgated by the IASB.

Table 7.6 shows the growth of the respective fractional national standard-setting networks between 1973 and 2001. On average the number of actors increased at the national level from four actors to just over six. The largest

*Table 7.6* Growth of the standard-setting networks at the national level

| Country | No. of actors in 1973 | No. of actors in 2001 | Absolute change | Relative change |
|---|---|---|---|---|
| US | 6 | 7 | 1 | 17% |
| Canada | 3 | 4 | 1 | 33% |
| UK[a] | 2 | 6 | 4 | 200% |
| Germany[a] | 4 | 6 | 2 | 50% |
| France[a] | 5 | 8 | 3 | 60% |
| Japan | 4 | 7 | 3 | 75% |
| **No. of actors** | **24** | **38** | **14** | **58%** |
| **Mean** | **4.0** | **6.3** | **2.3** | |
| Mean Anglo-Saxon tradition | 3.7 | 5.7 | 2.0 | 55% |
| Mean Cont.-European tradition | 4.3 | 7.0 | 2.7 | 62% |

*Source*: Own calculations.
[a]European institutions such as EFRAG are excluded, as these are transnational actors.

increase is observable in the UK, where the number of actors trebled from two actors to six. Over all, though, the growth of the networks in the group of countries with an Anglo-Saxon accounting tradition turns out to be smaller than that in the group of countries with a Continental European accounting tradition. In the Anglo-Saxon group growth is 55 per cent, while growth in the Continental European group amounts to 62 per cent. Also, the average number of actors in the standard-setting networks of countries with an Anglo-Saxon tradition is lower than in countries with a Continental European one.

The growth of the national networks is due to the subdivision of the standard-setting responsibility, which comes with the appearance of new actors. Enlargements in the Anglo-Saxon group of countries can largely be traced back to new actors supporting the non-governmental standard-setter on special issues, such as the Urgent Issues Task Force (UITF) and the Committee on Accounting for Smaller Entities (CASE) in the UK. In contrast, the enlargements in the group with a Continental European tradition relate to the fragmentation of the standard-setting responsibility, which in every case coincides with the transfer of responsibility to a privately organised standard-setter. The German network, for instance, now comes with two main standard-setting actors. A similar shift to more professional self-regulation took also place in France and Japan with the integration of the CRC and ASBJ into standard-setting. Additionally, the French and Japanese standard-setting networks were supplemented by financial market regulators.

Accordingly, non-state actors now assume the main standard-setting role in all countries. The network diagram, therefore, underlines the institutional aspects of the convergence process described in Chapter 4. Moreover, the developments are an indication of how normative ideas have advanced: professional self-regulation has increased, and the incorporation of capital market regulators mirrors the reorientation of accounting towards informing capital markets in countries such as France, Germany and Japan. All this is consistent with the view of the IASB.

Changes in the relations between the actors are observable not only in the national networks. Table 7.4 shows that the number of participating actors in the core network increased from 9 actors to 15. This increase is almost exclusively triggered by further international players entering the direct neighbourhood of the IASB, which are shown in Table 7.7. The network, formerly shaped by national actors, is now virtually on a par with actors at the national and international level. The IASB managed to spark the interest of transnational and international institutions, which are themselves concerned with the issue of regulatory convergence. The IOSCO, for instance, as an association of national securities regulators, works towards the integrity of global securities markets (Flower 2004). The interest of the EU is in setting up a single European market, including a common regulatory framework (Zimmermann 2010b). The participation of these actors in the network and in the discussion about common IAS suggests that these actors shared the ideas and beliefs of the IASB. Altogether, the IASB was able to win important actors for the promotion of the IAS. This became evident shortly afterwards, when the EU decided to adopt IFRS and European capital-market-oriented companies to prepare their consolidated accounts according to these standards from 2005 on.

However, the changes within the egocentric network relate not only to an increase in the number of direct connections between the IASB and further

*Table 7.7* Changes of the actors in the egocentric network

| Origin | Actors in 1973 | Actors in 2001 |
|---|---|---|
| International[a] | IASC, IFAC | IASCF, IASB/IFRIC, SAC, IFAC, IOSCO, EFRAG, EU |
| US | AICPA | FASB, SEC |
| Canada | CICA | AcSB |
| UK | CCAB | ASB |
| Germany | IDW, WPK | GASC/RIC |
| France | CNCC | CRC |
| Japan | JICPA | ASBJ, FASJ |

*Source*: Own calculations.

[a]Enlargements of the international group are also driven by the fact that the IASC is split up into three subgroups (IASCF, IASB/IFRIC, SAC). The division was retained in the drawing for the reason of consistency regarding the relationships of the actors. The same applies to the national networks.

actors but also to its composition. Table 7.7 shows that the constellation in relation to how the national and international levels were linked changed fundamentally. After nearly 30 years the IASB severed the link with the founder members. The national accounting associations lost their function as bridge between the IASB and the national standard-setting networks as they were detached from the direct domain of the IASB. The only representative remaining from the accounting professions with a direct connection to committees of the IASB is their international association, the IFAC. The decreased significance of national accounting associations translates also into a loss of centrality within the network as a whole shown in Table 7.8.

These developments can be explained by the IASB's active quest for acceptance and legitimacy (Djelic and Quack 2007). Amendments to the IASB's constitution in 1977 and 1982 had already decreased the exclusive influence of the founder members. Parallel to this, the liaisons with actors that are closer to the state were expanded and intensified. These developments culminated in a complete revision of the organisational structure in 2001, resulting in a wholesale shift away from the national accounting associations. The connections were substituted by a (further) accretion of actors close to the state: that is, the respective national, state-legitimated accounting bodies, such as the ASBJ or ASB. It followed that the remaining egocentric network – apart from the EU as an institution – is now composed of two clusters of actors: accounting regulators and financial market regulators. These actors can be further distinguished into actors from the national level – such as FASB and SEC – and those from the international level – such as EFRAG and IOSCO. Thus the IASB was able not only to establish direct relations to relevant actors in the international scene but also to promote their idea at the national level by attracting the national standard-setters. The IASB was thus able to form connections to the respective standard-setter which is relevant at the minimum for the rules of group accounting in each country.

The developments at both the national and international level reflect a rise in the importance of the ideas promulgated by the IASB: accounting standard-setting by a professional body and the orientation towards investor protection and capital markets. The developments also show that the founder IASB members were willing to give up their original place in the

*Table 7.8* Centralities of the accounting associations compared over time

| **Between-ness (normalised)** | **IDW** | **WPK** | **CICA** | **JICPA** | **AICPA** | **CNCC** | **CCAB** |
|---|---|---|---|---|---|---|---|
| 1973 | 15.3 | 0.0 | 15.3 | 15.3 | 33.3 | 28.0 | 8.0 |
| 2001 | 3.0 | 0.9 | 3.2 | 6.1 | 2.5 | 6.7 | 3.3 |

*Source*: Own calculations.

core network and to weaken their autonomy in standard-setting in order to gain institutional acceptance and legitimacy.

### 7.4.4 Benchmarking the 2001 network with the 2010 network

Figure 7.5 shows the international standard-setting network in the year 2010. Compared with the 2001 network, only slight changes show in the metrics for the egocentric network and the network as a whole over this period. These are displayed in Table 7.9. The number of actors remained practically constant, as did the number of links. Consequently, the density of the 2010 network also remained nearly the same as that for 2001. By contrast, the egocentric network became more dense, which stems from the reduction of actors by one (FSAJ), reducing the number of possible links and a simultaneous increase of the number of actual links. This also influenced the average values of the other network statistics.

A very similar picture emerges for the national networks. In four countries the standard-setting networks remained unaltered. In France and Japan changes have occurred, which are, however, by and large marginal. In France the number of actors dropped by one, as the functions of the CRC, CNC and the Emergency Committee (the *Comité d'urgence*, or CU) were consolidated in two new institutions: the ANC and CC. In Japan the formation of the IFRS Council expanded the national network. While these changes led to a reduction in compactness in France, compactness in Japan has increased, as is shown in Table 7.10.

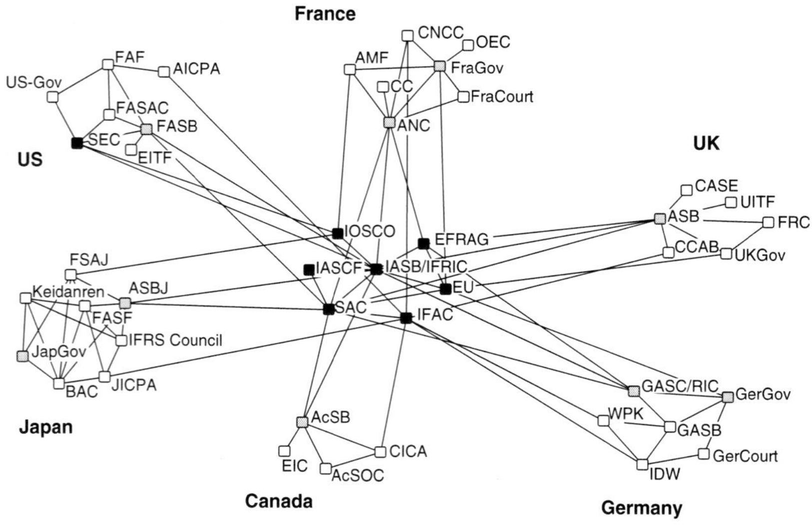


*Figure 7.5* International accounting standard-setting network in 2010
*Source*: Own contribution.

*Table 7.9* Comparison between the 2001 network and the 2010 network

| | Egocentric network 2001 | Egocentric network 2010 | Network as a whole 2001 | Network as a whole 2010 |
|---|---|---|---|---|
| No. of actors | 15 | 14 | 45 | 45 |
| – international level | 7 | 7 | 7 | 7 |
| – national level | 8 | 7 | 38 | 38 |
| Actors as a percentage of the network as a whole | 33 | 31 | 100 | 100 |
| No. of links | 48 | 54 | 176 | 178 |
| Mean of relations | 3.2 | 3.9 | 3.9 | 4.0 |
| Average distance | 2.0 | 1.7 | 3.0 | 3.0 |
| Network density | 23% | 30% | 9% | 9% |

*Source*: Own calculations.

*Table 7.10* Compactness changes in the French and Japanese networks

| | France 2001 | France 2010 | Japan 2001 | Japan 2010 |
|---|---|---|---|---|
| Average distance | 1.4 | 1.6 | 1.6 | 1.4 |
| Compactness | 0.8 | 0.7 | 0.7 | 0.8 |

*Source*: Own calculations.

Viewed from the perspective of the network as a whole, the two changes virtually cancel each other out. Overall, the network(s) are in stasis in 2001, as the actors' constellations as well as their relations have remained by and large stable.

## 7.5 Conclusion

The developments of the network as a whole as well as the changes in the fractional networks show radical changes between the 1970s and the 2000s. In general, the complexity of the networks increased as the size of the networks increased, as well as the connections among actors. Furthermore, the type and number of actors as well as the relation between them have changed fundamentally since the formation of the IASB. Its formation led to a reorganisation of the participating actors in standard-setting at both the national and international level. At the national level accounting standard-setting gained more weight as the number of actors increased in each country. The network analysis shows that this led to an amalgamation between state and non-state actors primarily in countries with a Continental European tradition. Hence, the original dichotomy between the two archetypes in accounting regulation dissolves.

The most fundamental changes, in particular with regard to the success of the ideas promulgated by the IASB, took place at the international level. Relevant actors from the international and national scene joined the network of the IASB. Simultaneously, the direct link between the IASB and the national networks changed. That is, the links between the national accounting associations, which functioned as bridging posts, were replaced by direct links to the respective national standard-setter in charge. These changes, on the one hand, pinpoint the IASB's increase in popularity and, on the other hand, indicate that the ideas promulgated by the IASB found favour at the level of national and international regulators. The increase in importance is also reflected by the adoption of IFRS by the EU and the several convergence projects under way between the IASB and the other non-European countries in the network.

The emergence of the IASB network at the beginning of the 1970s can be seen as a result of normative isomorphism. Voluntary associations such as the IASB can only evolve provided that similar interests and intentions between the participating actors exist – in this case, between national accounting associations. Subsequently, the formation of the IASB as a central instance of international accounting standard-setting can be interpreted as the result of an effective normative isomorphism. Network structures allow for the interests and ideas of the existing members to be assimilated further by means of permanent exchange. Additionally, these actors exert collective normative pressure on unaligned actors.

In this regard, the centrality of the IASB appeared to be of vital importance for the subsequent effectiveness of the network in many respects. First, national or international organisations had a central point of contact. Second, the members of the core network were able to communicate their ideas in a concerted manner through the IASB. The IASB as platform favoured the central coordination of interests as well as the development of a common framework for international accounting. This process of mutual consent shows further alignment of interests between parties involved as well as a process of normative isomorphism within the network structure. Third, the centrality of the IASB was vital in order to establish the acceptance and legitimacy of the standard-setter, which is by far the most important aspect. The IASB increased its legitimacy by imposing normative pressure on close-state actors unaligned to the egocentric network. That is, the IASB actively canvassed its activities among relevant actors and offered membership status as a means of co-opting these actors.

This pressure initiated a process of reassessing local accounting solutions against the new normative background and, in the end, triggered these actors now actively taking part in the international discourse of accounting by directly connecting with the IASB network. In this regard, the established centrality of the IASB was even more beneficial as it allowed for the restructuring of the egocentric network in order to solidify the achieved acceptance and legitimacy. Power and influence could be shifted away from the representatives of the various national professional associations without suffering a loss of centrality. Consequently, the centrality of the IASB can be seen as key factor for exerting normative pressure on relevant actors and for the positive effectiveness of the network in converging accounting.

Nevertheless, the evolvement and transmission of normative isomorphism at the national level would not have been possible without the basic need for new paths of accounting regulation. The wave of globalisation as well as (accounting) crises and scandals with regional and even international consequences for the financial community highlighted this need. These circumstances questioned national standalone accounting solutions and raised public concern about whether single accounting solutions by national regulators were still an appropriate way to handle these problems. A need for joint actions across borders seemed necessary and was also demanded socially. At the national level, a reorientation of standard-setting and redirection of national accounting solutions were required.

The emergence of the IASB network provided a point of reference for standard-setters. The reshaping of fractional networks – for example, the restructuring of the national or European accounting networks – showed how the ideas promulgated by the IASB were successfully disseminated through the network. The direct commitment of national standard-setters and other actors to the IASB network is a further indicator that they commonly share the principal ideas of the IASB for accounting standard-setting. This, in turn, argues for an alignment of the ideas concerning accounting regulation: that is, normative isomorphism triggered by networks, assuming that through the affiliation in networks ideas are usually shared.

The IASB network stimulated national self-transformation, which simultaneously involved changes of the network and relations among actors over time. Generally speaking, these changes are responsible for the development of accounting standard-setting from being the domain of formerly national standalone solutions to one of joint action organised in a large international standard-setting network whose actors rely on a shared normative mindset.

# Part IV
# Explaining National Preference

Our empirical data show that many elements in accounting regulation have not converged. This is because the driving forces that we considered in Part III are moderated by country-specific institutional frameworks which still differ from country to country. They have an impact on the decisions of economic actors in regards to system change, as the institutional structures shape the regulatory demands of actors within the system. In the following, we examine how the legal and financial systems and the type of welfare state moderate change or do not allow it to happen.

Chapter 8 analyses the role of the legal system. Local accounting practices in civil-law countries still focus on the maintenance of legal capital. The standards are set by the state and support the long-term stability of companies by restricting corporate payouts. The accounting rules fit into the prevailing governance mechanism; they are complementary in this respect. The same holds for the accounting regulation in common-law countries. The protection of equity investors through information is supported by unbiased or neutral financial reporting numbers. Following from that, some parts of the accounting systems are sticky, particularly stalling the process of change in civil-law countries. Civil-law countries place particular emphasis on the conflict-solving role of corporate law and need accounting to mitigate conflicts. However, the civil law countries have extended the reach of securities law, which is now qualitatively on a par with the common-law ones. As Chapter 8 reveals, we thus observe the emergence of two parallel systems of accounting regulation inside the civil-law countries: the traditional local GAAPs for individual accounts and the IFRS for group accounts of listed entities. In the common-law countries not much change in the general orientation of accounting regulation is observable: for example, the UK allows IFRS instead of UK GAAP for single accounts.

Chapter 9 examines the role of financial systems, which fall into market- and bank-based systems. Firms and stakeholders from bank-based systems do not demand information accounting to the same extent as their counterparts in market-based economies. This contributes to the explanation of why the convergence of accounting regimes is limited to the reporting of listed groups. Chapter 9 provides evidence for three moderating effects: the different demands of investors and lenders in general (e.g., the asymmetric loss function of creditors and the information demand of shareholders); the closer relationship of debt holders to lending entities in bank-based economies; and the different demands of short- and long-term investors, respectively. We also provide evidence that systems as such do not converge, but distinctive features remain. All this makes convergence of the entire accounting regimes unlikely.

Chapter 10 shows that there is a connection between the type of welfare state and the degree to which interests of corporate constituencies are balanced by accounting. Institutional welfare states, exemplified by the case of Germany, rank the role of prudent accounting in balancing interests higher than its informational role. In comparison, residual welfare states, exemplified by the UK, emphasise its informational role. Prudent accounting protects, and informational accounting enables; this is the dichotomy that exists in the respective welfare states. Institutional welfare states have a higher degree of state intervention, as is also witnessed in accounting. Societally approved intervention requires the regulation of company accounts, driving the hybridisation of accounting systems further. Group accounts are legally irrelevant and can elude the state as regulator, but company accounts must not. The social conception of welfare and the extent of the desire to allow the market to operate freely explain further why accounting has only converged for listed groups.

# 8
# Legal Backing of Equity Investment

This chapter deals with the question of whether national legal systems can be identified as a constraint to harmonisation and whether they lead to path dependencies which explain persisting cross-country variation in accounting regulation. We focus on the legal backing of equity investments and how accounting is connected to and influenced by the organisation of national legal systems in this context. Following the structure of Chapter 3, we identify three legal fields that are connected to accounting regulation: company law, securities law and tax law. Each of these attends to core conflicts in business relationships, but legislators use different legal instruments and combine in a different way measures from company law, securities law, corporate governance codes, listing rules, self-regulation by markets and accounting regulation.

## 8.1 Introduction

In Part II we outlined the way several drivers of change lead to a convergence in the organisation of accounting standard-setting and, following from that, most notably to a convergence of applicable rules. Part III will now clarify how the convergence process may be constrained by national particularities that will cause path dependence in two respects: first, the application of harmonised rules may differ because of persisting national particularities; second, some accounts (particularly single accounts) are subject to a lesser degree – if at all – to harmonisation. While financial statements of group accounts of publicly traded firms are converging worldwide, single accounts still differ widely.

Concerning the focus, organisation and configuration of national legal systems, states can be divided into two major categories: common-law and civil-law countries (David and Brierley 1996; La Porta et al. 1997). Anglo-Saxon countries such as Canada, the UK and the US are classified as common-law countries, whereas Continental European countries and Japan are classified as civil-law countries.[1] Common law is based on English law, which is formed above all by judges and legal practice. In contrast, civil law originated from Roman law and uses statutes and comprehensive codes as the primary sources (La Porta et al. 1998). Also the protective mechanisms concerning equity investors differ between the two systems. This becomes apparent in the different use of two key instruments which are implemented in laws and regulations for the legal backing of investors: information and participation. Information is provided by mandatory corporate disclosure and is directed to all stakeholders, whereas participation rights are a protection mechanism for (long-term) equity investors. In diminishing order of importance, mandatory disclosure is regulated in securities law, listing rules, corporate governance codes and company law. Company law ranks last, as it focuses more on rules for participation and decision rights of shareholders, such as pre-emptive rights, voting rights or the division of management and control.

Based on rights stipulated by law, shareholders can use the options of 'voice or exit' to respond to management decisions (Hirschman 1970; Kostant 1999). The voice or exit concept can be used to describe two different shareholder strategies if they do not agree with decisions made by the management or if they are dissatisfied with the company's performance. Subject to the institutional setting and depending on how the instruments of information and participation are pronounced in the legal system, either one or both options could be available to investors. Options are reduced when no liquid market exists for the shareholder to sell her shares in a timely fashion, applying the exit option, or when the legal system does not provide shareholders with enough participation rights to permit a sufficient voice option.[2]

Exit and voice options are present in common-law and civil-law countries. However, each system has a specific focus on either participation rights or information of equity investors. Common-law countries focus on shareholder information, emphasising the exit possibility in case of unsatisfactory management. In contrast, civil-law countries show a strong focus on participation rights given by company law so that equity holders can use their voice.

Previous research on the legal backing of equity investors has typically analysed regulation from securities and company law jointly (Lele and Siems 2007). This conflates the different approaches in legal cultures and introduces bias into the analysis. Consequently, we will split the legal backing of investors into protection by company law and protection by securities law. Therefore, we will present two measures showing the embodiment of company law (Section 2) and the embodiment of securities law (Section 3) in our national case studies. Based on these results, the consequences for accounting regulation will be discussed in Section 4. Section 5 concludes.

## 8.2 Developments in company law

Company law regulates how corporations are formed, operated and terminated in legal terms (Heiser 2000), and it constitutes different corporate personalities by providing rules on incorporation and statutes for the protection of the involved parties. While differing in detail, all company laws contain similar basic characteristics. These are legal personality, limited liability, transferable shares, delegated management under a board structure, and investor ownership. Differences exist owing to different legal paradigms in company law, including essentially different ideas about important characteristics of corporations, relevant problems to be solved and the legal instruments to address those problems (Heine and Kerber 2002). Accordingly, company laws vary with regard to the type of stakeholder that should primarily be protected (Cheffins 2001). The respective protection mechanisms in place can be explained as an answer to the dominant contracting problems within the economic system (resulting, for example, from the separation of ownership and control), hence as a mechanism to reduce transaction costs and to contribute to economic welfare. They can also be an expression of the general volition of society, an argument put forward in greater detail in Chapter 10.

Company law helps to mitigate conflicts between investors and the firm by assigning decision and profit participation rights to shareholders. As shown in Chapter 3, legislators either use the option to design company law in a flexible way with default rules that contractual parties can individually modify or they set mandatory rules with binding clauses. Both designs can exist in one legal system; however, each of the above-mentioned systems focuses either on modifiable default rules or on mandatory rules. The extent of binding decision and profit participations rights for shareholders, giving them the option of voice, is a good yardstick by which to measure a legal system.

In the following we compare the participation rights of equity investors in France, Germany, the UK and the US. A 'leximetric' company-law index allows us to analyse country-specific differences and similarities in the legal system. The approach has been designed to compare laws and regulations on a quantitative basis. The term 'leximetric' was created by Cooter and Ginsburg (2003). However, the method itself was used much earlier, by Cooke and Wallace (1990) or in the seminal work of La Porta et al. (1997). It provides a good means by which to compare legal systems over time and between countries (Lele and Siems 2007), even though its often more summary methods have given rise to criticism (Siems 2005b).

The following index is based on the work of Lele and Siems (2007). They quantified shareholder protection by examining company law, securities law, listing rules and corporate governance codes for France, Germany, the UK, the US (here: Delaware General Corporation Law) and India from 1970 to

2005. We take 12 variables from Lele and Siems (2007), which measure core elements of company law – such as voting rights, minority shareholder protection or monitoring rights (see Table 8.1) – and extended the index to the year 2010. The focus of the extracted variables is on ownership control rights through participation. We group the variables into three broad categories, which reflect the decision and profit participations rights

*Table 8.1* Variable description for company-law index

| | **Variables** | **Description** |
|---|---|---|
| **Claims on Assets** | $V_1$: Pre-emptive rights (Dilution) | Equals 1 if the law grants shareholders the first opportunity to buy new issue of shares, and if this right can be waived only by the general meeting; 0 otherwise. |
| | $V_2$: Dividend Distribution | Equals 1 if the general meeting can effectively influence the amount of dividends (i.e., if it decides about the annual accounts and annual dividend, and if the board has no significant possibility of 'manipulating' the accounts); equals 0.5 if there is some participation in the general meeting; equals 0 if it is only the board that decides about the dividend. |
| | $V_3$: Expropriation (squeeze-out) | Equals 0 if a shareholder holding 90 per cent or more can 'squeeze out' the minority; equals 1 otherwise. |
| | $V_4$: Power of the general meeting for de facto changes | If the sale of more than 50 per cent of the company's assets requires approval of the general meeting it equals 1; if no specific percentage is given but the courts speak of 'substantially' it equals 0.75; if the sale of more than 80 per cent of the assets requires approval it equals 0.5; 0 otherwise. |
| | $V_5$: Remuneration Directors | Equals 1 if the general meeting has to approve all compensation schemes; equals 0.5 if this is limited (e.g., if it applies to stock option plans only, or if some directors are excluded); 0 otherwise. |
| | **Claims on Assets** | **Mean of variables $V_1$–$V_5$** |
| **Board Composition** | $V_6$: Division between management and control | Equals 1 if there is a two-tier system or at least half of the board members are non-executive; equals 0.5 if at least 25 per cent of the board-members are non-executive, 0 otherwise (intermediate step 0.75 for France introduced by Lele and Siems 2007). |

| | | |
|---|---|---|
| | $V_7$: Independent board members | Equals 1 if at least half of the board members must be independent; equals 0.5 if 25 per cent of them must be independent; 0.25 if members of some special committees of the board need to be independent (e.g., compensation or audit committee), so that it is indirectly prescribed that some members of the board are independent; 0 otherwise. |
| | **Board Composition** | **Mean of variables $V_6$–$V_7$** |
| **Voting Rights and General Meeting** | $V_8$: Prohibition of Multiple Voting Rights | Equals 1 if there is a prohibition of multiple voting rights; equals 2/3 if only companies which already have multiple voting rights can keep them; equals 1/3 if state approval is necessary, 0.5 if shareholders who hold shares longer than two years can be given multiple voting rights, 0 otherwise (may be regulated in securities law!). |
| | $V_9$: Voting right ceilings | Prohibition of capped voting rights: Equals 1 if there is a prohibition; equals 2/3 if only companies which already have voting caps can keep them; equals 1/3 if state approval is necessary; 0 otherwise. |
| | $V_{10}$: Extraordinary shareholder meeting | Equals 1 if the minimum percentage of share capital to demand an extraordinary meeting is less than or equal to 5 per cent; equals 0.5 if it is more than 5 per cent but less or equal than 10 per cent; 0 otherwise. |
| | $V_{11}$: Quorum | Equals 1 if there is a 50 per cent quorum for the extraordinary shareholder meeting (when called for the first time); equals 0.5 if the quorum is 33 per cent; equals 0.25 if the quorum is 25 per cent; 0 otherwise. |
| | $V_{12}$: Supermajority requirements | Equals 1 if there are supermajority requirements (e.g., 2/3 or 3/4) for amendments of the articles of association, mergers, and voluntary liquidations; equals 0 if they do not exist. |
| | **Voting Rights and General Meeting** | **Mean of variables $V_8$–$V_{12}$** |
| | **Company-Law Index** | **Mean of Claims on Assets, Board Composition and Voting Rights** |

*Source*: Based on the index of Lele and Siems (2007), adapted.

provided by company law: claims on assets; board composition; and general meeting and voting rights. The variables can take the range of values between zero and 1. Some are coded in binary (0, 1), others are coded in a non-binary way (e.g., 0, 0.25, 0.5, 0.75, 1). This allows legal rules to be translated into more than just a 'no' (rule/regulation does not exist) or 'yes' (rule/regulation exists), as it applies a more detailed measurement of the content of rules. Variables in the index are not weighted. This is because weighting of variables might introduce bias into the index.

The index is calculated from 1985 to 2010 for each year and country. The variables can change their value every year. However, if there is no adjustment in company law, the values remain unchanged.[3] As shown in Table 8.1, the arithmetic mean of the (sub-) variables pre-emptive rights, dividend distribution, expropriation, power of the general meeting for de facto changes and remuneration gives the annual value for claims on assets. The arithmetic mean of the variables division between management and control and independent board members gives the annual value for board composition. The arithmetic mean of the variables prohibition of multiple voting rights, voting right ceilings, extraordinary shareholder meeting, quorum and supermajority requirements gives the annual value for voting rights. The mean value of the three group variables gives the company-law index value for country *n* in year *t*.

The value for the company-law index is between 0 and 1. The latter is the highest possible value and would point to a very strong legal backing of equity investors through participation rights in company law, giving investors the option of voice. An index value close to 0 would indicate a very poor equity investor protection by company law, leaving only the option of exit to equity investors. However, we have to bear in mind that investor protection also depends on securities law, corporate governance codes or accounting regulation. What we focus on here is the legal backing of equity investors by company law. In Section 4 these legal instruments will be discussed together.

With the quantification of law we are now able to compare company law in the four countries. Figure 8.1 presents an overview of how participation rights in France, Germany, the UK and the US have developed. The civil-law countries have a more interventionist company-law system than the common-law countries, and the significant difference between the civil-law and common-law countries does not get narrower. Index values are relatively stable, especially in the common-law countries. Table 8.2, presenting the grouped variable values, emphasises the overall picture: France and Germany have higher values in nearly all observation points than the UK and the US. German company law assures shareholders the greatest rights in terms of participation, influence on management decisions and protection of minority shareholders. France only has higher values in the group variable 'general meeting and voting rights'. French company law itself is still very different from UK and US law.

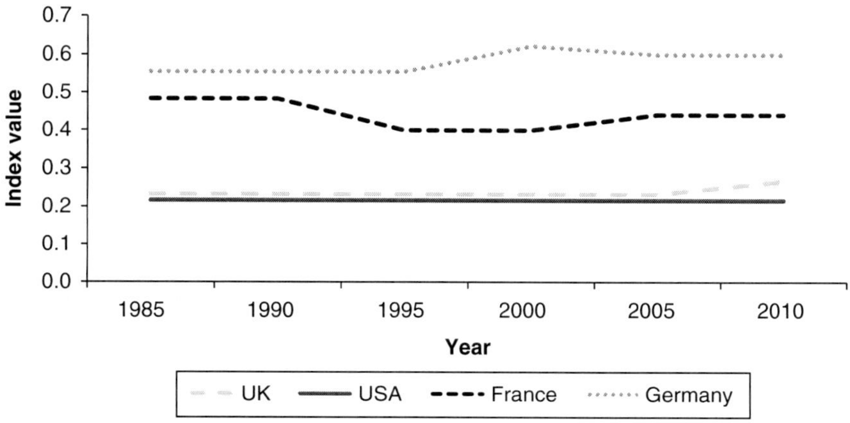


*Figure 8.1* Legal backing of equity investors by company law
*Source*: Based on the index of Lele and Siems (2007), adapted.

*Table 8.2* Group variable values company-law index

| Group Variable | Year | UK | USA | France | Germany |
|---|---|---|---|---|---|
| Claims on Assets | 1985 | 0.40 | 0.25 | 0.60 | 0.70 |
| | 1990 | 0.40 | 0.25 | 0.60 | 0.70 |
| | 1995 | 0.40 | 0.25 | 0.40 | 0.70 |
| | 2000 | 0.40 | 0.25 | 0.40 | 0.70 |
| | 2005 | 0.40 | 0.25 | 0.40 | 0.50 |
| | 2010 | 0.40 | 0.25 | 0.40 | 0.50 |
| Board Composition | 1985 | 0.00 | 0.00 | 0.25 | 0.50 |
| | 1990 | 0.00 | 0.00 | 0.25 | 0.50 |
| | 1995 | 0.00 | 0.00 | 0.25 | 0.50 |
| | 2000 | 0.00 | 0.00 | 0.25 | 0.50 |
| | 2005 | 0.00 | 0.00 | 0.38 | 0.50 |
| | 2010 | 0.00 | 0.00 | 0.38 | 0.50 |
| Voting Rights and General Meeting | 1985 | 0.30 | 0.40 | 0.60 | 0.47 |
| | 1990 | 0.30 | 0.40 | 0.60 | 0.47 |
| | 1995 | 0.30 | 0.40 | 0.55 | 0.47 |
| | 2000 | 0.30 | 0.40 | 0.55 | 0.67 |
| | 2005 | 0.30 | 0.40 | 0.55 | 0.80 |
| | 2010 | 0.40 | 0.40 | 0.55 | 0.80 |

*Source*: Own calculations.

Looking at the participation rights of the countries in greater detail, we observe that the index value declined in France and increased in Germany throughout the 1990s, which made the regulation over all more different. This is due to two separate developments. In France, the requirements for squeezing out minority shareholders were lowered in 1993 (Law 93–1444). The slight increase in Germany's index value at the end of the 1990s results from a stricter regulation of voting rights (KonTraG amended §12(2) AktG). However, the two countries slightly narrowed the regulatory gap in the period from 2000 to 2005. In Germany a squeeze-out rule was inserted into the commercial code in 2001 (*Unternehmensübernahme-Regelungsgesetz* amended §327a AktG). Therefore, the value of the variable expropriation was set from 1 to 0. In France two moderate changes increased the index value. The division of management and control was slightly enhanced in 2001, and the minimum of shares needed to demand an extraordinary shareholder meeting was lowered to under 5 per cent in the same year (Law 01–420).

Looking at the participation rights in the civil-law countries, we note that US (Delaware General Corporation Law)[4] as well as UK company laws are relatively deregulated. The two index values remain constant at around 0.25. In both countries the value of the group variable 'board composition' is 0 over the total period. Company law in the two countries does not demand independence of board members and has no greater requirements for the division of management and control. Furthermore, the group variable 'claims on assets' is relatively weak for equity holders in the US. The mean of variables $V_1$–$V_5$ is only 0.25 for the total period. In the UK the value for claims on assets is 0.4 from 1985 to 2010. The value for the group variable 'general meeting and voting rights' is 0.3 until 2005 and was the lowest of all sample countries.

In conclusion, the data show that equity investors in France and Germany have a more direct influence on the corporation through binding decision- and profit participations rights than investors in the UK or the US. The governance function of law is pronounced in the two civil-law countries. The legislator assures the rights of equity investors by mandatory rules giving investors the voice option. The company-law rule systems of France and Germany focus on interventionist rules and explicit control; management and shareholders both have power in the administration of the entity (Zetzsche 2004). In contrast, company law in the UK and in the US only provides default rules and does not give shareholders direct influence on the corporation through binding decision and profit participations rights. The directors have more independence in corporate management and, regarding governance, the legislator rather relies on market forces and bilateral agreements (Coffee 2000b). The company-law rule system can be characterised as liberal and implicit and the voice option is relatively weak.

## 8.3 Developments in securities law

In this section the analysis of the legal backing of equity investors will be expanded by looking at the respective national securities law. The protection of equity investors is not only codified in company law; securities law is another important legal source. It regulates the issuance of capital on primary markets and the trading of ownership rights as well as (public) debt titles on secondary markets. Securities law aims to reduce information asymmetries by supplying investors with all relevant information about the company and by prohibiting people with private information from trading; for example, on primary markets – in the case of an IPO – securities law regulates the issue of the listing prospectus or on secondary markets the disclosure of ad-hoc news is regulated by securities law. Besides disclosure requirements, the enforcement of the rules is an important part of securities law to ensure the application of the rules. In contrast to company law, securities law is only relevant for publicly traded entities. Its main function is to ensure the functionality and liquidity of capital markets, which is a vital precondition for the exit option to be attainable for investors. Moreover, the focus of its provisions is not on the long-term survival of companies and their various stakeholders. Rather, securities law will assure the supply of capital by fostering efficient capital markets (Goshen 2003). It governs 'investors' interest in capital market transactions', and it has hence a focus on shareholder protection and stability of capital markets (Heiser 2000). The backing of investors by securities law is mainly achieved through giving information to shareholders, and minimum levels are set by mandatory disclosure rules and their enforcement. Hence, a strong securities law provides investors with information, ensures market liquidity and enables investors to use the exit option rather than the voice option to respond to management decisions.

Again, an index will be used to quantify and compare the securities laws of France, Germany, the UK and the US over time. We draw on the work of La Porta et al. (2006). They studied whether capital market development is connected to investor protection for a sample of 49 countries. Investor protection is measured by disclosure requirements and their enforcement, which is important to ensure the compliance with the regulations. Their data are based on questionnaires answered by attorneys.[5] However, the La Porta et al. (2006) data are limited to the regulation as of December 2000, and no time-series data are available. For the following analyses we take the year 2000 as a starting point and expand the index from 1990 to 2009. Moreover, we dropped, added or modified some variables to make the analysis more suitable for our four countries. This and the definition of the variables are presented in Table 8.3.

Activity in changing securities law was low during the 1970s and 1980s. Moreover, in the civil-law countries the securities law only started to become relevant in the 1970s. It is therefore sufficient, in contrast to the company-law index, to capture the period from the beginning of the 1990s. Owing to the larger amount of variable value changes, we display annual values from 1995 on, instead of five-year periods, as was done in the analyses of company law.

The allocation of variable values and the calculation of the index are similar to the company-law index: variables can take the range of values between 0 and 1 and can change their value every year. Some variables

*Table 8.3* Variable description for securities-law index

| | Variables | Description |
|---|---|---|
| **Disclosure Index** | $V_1$: Prospectus | Equals 1 if the law prohibits selling securities that are going to be listed on the largest stock exchange of the country without delivering a prospectus to potential investors; equals 0 otherwise. *(adopted)* |
| | $V_2$: Inside Ownership | Equals 1 if the law or the listing rules require that the ownership of the Issuer's shares by each of its director and key officers be disclosed; equals 0.5 if only the aggregate number of the issuer's shares owned by its directors and key officers must be disclosed; equals 0 when the ownership of issuer's shares by its directors and key officers need not be disclosed. *(adopted)* |
| | $V_3$: Transactions | Equals 1 if the law or the listing rules require that all transactions in which related parties have, or will have, an interest be disclosed; equals 0.5 if only some transactions between the Issuer and related parties must be disclosed; equals 0 if transactions between the issuer and related parties need not be disclosed. *(adopted)* |
| | $V_4$: Responsibility Statement | Equals 1 if the directors have to sign for the material accuracy of financial statements; equals 0 otherwise. *(added)* |
| | $V_5$: Internal Control | Equals 1 if an internal control system is mandatory for listed companies and this system has to be continuously observed by auditors and management; equals 0.5 if a system has to be set up but without continuous observation; equals 0 if no internal control system is mandatory. *(added)* |
| | $V_6$: Quarterly Reports | Equals 1 if companies have to publish quarterly reports; equals 0.5 if reports have to be published every six months; equals 0 otherwise. *(added)* |
| | $V_7$: MD&A | Rating for the complexity of the Management Discussion and Analysis (as it is named in the US – for example, in the UK it is named 'Operating and Financial Review' or in Germany the *Lagebericht*). Equals 1, 0.75, 0.5, 0.25 or, if no such report exit, 0. *(added)* |
| | **Disclosure Index** | **Mean of variables $V_1$–$V_7$** |
| Enforcement Index | $V_8$: Appointment Supervisor | Equals 1 if a majority of the members of the supervisor are unilaterally appointed by the executive branch of government; equals 0 otherwise. *(adopted)* |
| | $V_9$: Tenure | Equals 1 if members of the supervisor cannot be dismissed at the will of the appointing authority; equals 0 otherwise. *(adopted)* |

| | |
|---|---|
| $V_{10}$: Focus | Equals 1 if separate government agencies or official authorities are in charge of supervising commercial banks and stock exchanges; equals 0 otherwise. *(adopted)* |
| $V_{11}$: Rule-making power | Equals 1 if the supervisor can generally issue regulations regarding primary offerings and/or listing rules on stock exchanges without prior approval of other government authorities. Equals 0.5 if the supervisor can generally issue regulations regarding primary offerings and/or listing rules on stock exchanges only with the prior approval of other governmental authorities; equals 0 otherwise. *(adopted)* |
| $V_{12}$: Document | Equals 1 if the supervisor can generally issue an administrative order commanding all persons to turn over documents; equals 0.5 if the supervisor can generally issue an administrative order commanding publicly traded corporations and/or their directors to turn over documents; equals 0 otherwise. *(adopted)* |
| $V_{13}$: Witness | Equals 1 if the supervisor can generally subpoena all persons to give testimony; equals 0.5 if the supervisor can generally subpoena the directors of publicly traded corporations to give testimony; equals 0 otherwise. *(adopted)* |
| $V_{14}$: Penalty Companies | Equals 1 if the supervisor has far-reaching competencies to impose financial and other legal penalties on companies; equals 0.5 if the supervisor can only impose financial penalties; equals 0 otherwise. *(modified)* |
| $V_{15}$: Penalty Management | Equals 0 if the accountant/management cannot be held criminally liable when the financial statements are misleading. Equals 0 if the accountant/management can be held criminally liable when aware that the financial statements are misleading. Equals 1 if the accountant/management can also be held criminally liable when negligently unaware that the financial statements are misleading. *(modified)* |
| $V_{16}$: Independent auditor | Equals 1 if far-reaching rules concerning the independence of auditors exist; equals 0.5 if there are only weak independence criteria; equals 0 if there are nearly no independence criteria. *(added)* |
| **Enforcement Index** | **Mean of variables $V_8$–$V_{16}$** |
| **Securities-Law Index** | **Mean of Disclosure Index and Enforcement Index** |

*Source*: Based on the index of La Porta et al. (2006), adapted.

are coded in binary, others are coded in a more than binary fashion, with values of 0, 0.25, 0.5, 0.75 and 1. Variable values or modification of values were conducted by examining changes in laws and regulations, information by regulatory authorities and by analysing secondary literature. Moreover, listing rules from the major stock exchange in a country and corporate governance rules are included in the index if they are mandatory for public companies. Most of the changes in laws, regulations and the responsible actors for the enforcement have already been described in Part II and are not presented here in greater detail.[6]

As Table 8.3 shows, the index consists of 16 (sub-)variables; the arithmetic mean of the first seven variables gives the country-specific value for disclosure regulation, and the arithmetic mean of the other nine variables measures enforcement. The arithmetic mean of the disclosure index and the enforcement index gives the overall securities-law index. A value close to 1 indicates a very high legal backing of equity investors by securities law and a value close to 0 indicates a poor legal backing.

Figure 8.2 presents the securities-law index values for the four analysed countries from 1990 to 2010.[7] In contrast to company law, the securities-law regulation has experienced significant changes since 1995. In every country regulation has increased significantly. The German government, in particular, enacted several laws which created new mandatory provisions for listed companies or improved enforcement. In 1990 the index value of Germany was approximately 0.05. Hence, the legal backing of equity investors by securities law could be classified as nearly non-existent. This slightly changed with the enactment of the *Wertpapierhandelsgesetz* (WpHG) in 1995, which introduced higher disclosure rules as well as an enforcement agency. Numerous new laws and regulations have followed

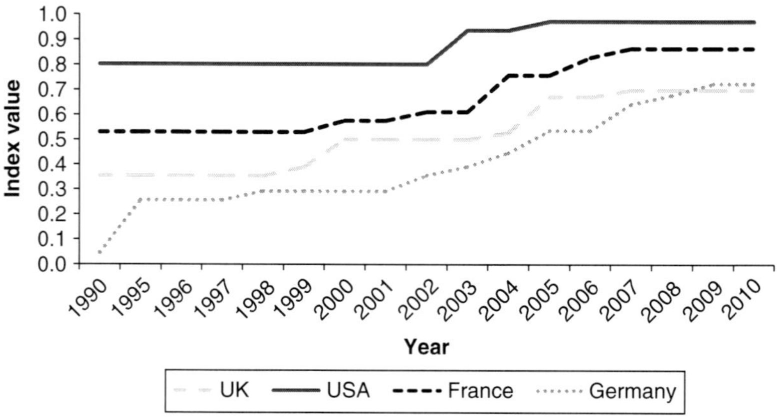


*Figure 8.2* Securities-law index
*Source*: Based on the index of La Porta et al. (2006), adapted.

since 1998, and today the legal backing of equity investors is as high as in the UK. US regulation was already high in 1990. Disclosure rules as well as enforcement were pronounced. The basis for the high regulation was set in the 1930s with the enactment of the SA and the SEA. Despite this high regulation, a further increase of mandatory rules followed after the collapse of Enron and other large US entities with the enactment of the Sarbanes-Oxley Act (SOA) in 2002. Today the securities-law index value of the USA is 0.97 and, in respect to our definition of the variables, close to the maximum.

The results for the French and UK index values are also quite remarkable. The regulation in France is relatively strong: the index value of France is higher than the UK value over the whole period. As France is classified as a civil-law country we would not necessarily expect the high regulation in the area of securities law. Furthermore, the high distance to the German index value in 1990 is surprising at first glance. However, the index values of France, Germany and the UK have grown more or less in step with each other. An important factor for the convergence of securities law in France, Germany and the UK is the process of Europeanisation, triggered, for example, by the Financial Services Action Plan from 1999 (Hellgardt and Ringe 2009). Moreover, in contrast to company-law regulation, the securities laws seem to converge to a certain degree.[8] All four countries enacted a variety of laws and regulations during the last two decades which increased mandatory disclosure provisions and their enforcement. There is a clear trend towards constraining publicly traded entities by law to publish more information, and thus the regulation of the four countries is becoming more similar. This becomes evident by looking at the aggregated differences of the securities-law index values from the US to France, the US to Germany and the US to the UK. The aggregated 'distance' between the US and the other three countries was 1.48 in 1990, 1.04 in 2000 and 0.63 in 2010. This shows that securities-law regulation converges towards the US model or in general to a high regulation level.

A closer look at the sub-indices is presented in Table 8.4. The mandatory disclosure rules and the enforcement of the rules are presented separately. This gives a better explanation for the high index value for France in 1990, as it shows that the high value of France is mainly due to the strong enforcement of the laws. In contrast to Germany and the UK, France established a national securities commission, the Securities and Exchange Commission (*Commission des Opérations de Bourse,* COB), as early as 1967. Germany only did so in 1995. However, France and Germany have a comparable level of disclosure regulation. Both countries did not demand extensive mandatory disclosure information from publicly traded entities. Mandatory disclosure was relatively low in the two civil-law countries until the beginning of the 21st century. In contrast, the values are higher for the two common-law countries; again the US stands out with a value of 0.71 in the 1990s and the maximum value of 1 since 2005.

*Table 8.4* Group variable values securities-law index

| Group Variable | Year | UK | USA | France | Germany |
|---|---|---|---|---|---|
| Disclosure Index | 1990 | 0.43 | 0.71 | 0.39 | 0.04 |
| | 1995 | 0.43 | 0.71 | 0.39 | 0.18 |
| | 2000 | 0.50 | 0.71 | 0.43 | 0.25 |
| | 2005 | 0.79 | 1.00 | 0.57 | 0.57 |
| | 2010 | 0.79 | 1.00 | 0.79 | 0.89 |
| Enforcement Index | 1990 | 0.28 | 0.89 | 0.67 | 0.06 |
| | 1995 | 0.28 | 0.89 | 0.67 | 0.33 |
| | 2000 | 0.50 | 0.89 | 0.72 | 0.33 |
| | 2005 | 0.56 | 0.94 | 0.94 | 0.50 |
| | 2010 | 0.61 | 0.94 | 0.94 | 0.56 |

*Source*: Own calculations.

In conclusion, there were broad differences in the shape and relevance of securities laws. The mandatory provision of information for shareholders by listed companies was low in civil-law countries until the end of the 1990s. In contrast, the disclosure requirements for public companies were higher in the UK and the US. However, the historical development of enforcement is rather different inside the two country groups. Regarding enforcement, the distinction between civil-law and common-law systems does not explain the former countries' differences, which are due to a higher level of enforcement. The differences in the mandatory provision of information between the common-law and civil-law countries are in line with the results from the company-law analyses: the legal backing of equity investors in civil-law countries focuses on participation and direct influence on the corporation. In contrast, the legislators in common-law countries rely on market forces. To ensure the functioning of the markets, the legislator constrains public entities to support (outside) investors with sufficient information, and this regulation, as the provided leximetric analysis shows, converges in securities law.

## 8.4 Consequences for accounting

The analysis of the legal systems of France, Germany, the UK and the US showed that civil-law and common-law countries have organised the legal backing of equity investors in a different way. Participation and monitoring rights, set by company law, are more pronounced in civil-law countries. Shareholders have rights to monitor or even control management and thus have the opportunity to express their grievances if they are dissatisfied with the performance of the company (Zetzsche 2004). Securities law and capital market institutions were less developed in civil-law countries for a long time. As the efficiency of capital markets was relatively low, the exit opportunity was a costly option. The opposite holds for common-law countries. They rely on market forces, and equity investors are supplied with information instead of having extensive participation rights. Capital markets were developed early on, and disclosure provisions are pronounced. Equity investors are more left to their own devices in the relationship with managers; but the legislator ensures their supply with information. Hence, the exit opportunity is the prevailing mechanism by which equity investors can respond to management decisions.

This regulatory approach is reflected in the accounting standards used in common-law countries: the local GAAP of the UK and the US historically placed emphasis on information that is decision-relevant. Valuation rules use fair-value accounting wherever expedient. An unbiased or neutral presentation is of greater importance than prudent financial reports. Financial reporting is thus designed to provide decision-relevant information to pursue entry and exit strategies. They are facilitated by the greater ability to predict future cash flows by analysing financial reports presented on the basis of information accounting. Hence, group accounts are the dominant reporting form, and financial reporting mainly serves as a means of protecting (outside) investors. Like the focus of the legal system, the accounting system is more oriented towards securing the efficiency of markets and on short-term economic goals (Heiser 2000). Annual reports are mostly an information source and do not have direct payout consequences. Many disclosed elements, such as cash flow statements, interim reports or even the consolidated annual reports, are not relevant for calculating tax or dividends (Nobes 1998).

In contrast, the accounting systems of civil-law countries were designed in connection to the regulatory approach of participation and voice: the local GAAPs of civil-law countries historically focus on verifiable and therefore less disputable data. The accounting rules are conservative and support the long-term stability of companies by restricting corporate payouts. The calculation of these corporate payouts was the primary use of financial reports in civil-law countries. Consequently, single accounts dominated for a long time over group accounts, and asset valuation rules are dominated by historical cost accounting instead of fair-value accounting; the reliability of accounting numbers is more important than their relevance.

Over all, accounting systems differ in nation states because they co-evolved with other elements of corporate governance. The corporate governance system is then a system of complementary elements (Schmidt and Spindler 2002). The interaction of the system components, with the accounting system as an important element, yields an effective set-up for the corporate governance system as a whole.

Nevertheless, as shown in Section 3 of this chapter, the differences between the securities laws in common- and civil-law countries have become smaller. The regulatory system, the ownership and the financial structure of listed entities have changed during the last decades, as was shown in Chapter 5. Today, not only the voice but also the exit opportunity is of importance for the legal backing of equity investors in civil-law countries. The need for information accounting has become more pressing. With the increase of mandatory disclosure provisions through securities law, the use of information accounting rule-sets started to find its way into the corporate governance regulation. Consequently, the civil-law states, France and Germany, accepted the use of either IFRS or US GAAP at the end of the 1990s. It is therefore observable that the legal system had virtually no decelerating effect on the harmonisation of accounting standards for consolidated financial statements of listed firms. One important explanation is that one legal field, securities law, is itself subject to change.

However, in the area of unlisted firms and individual accounts the legal systems in place have an important moderating effect on the convergence of accounting regulation. Securities law does not apply to unlisted firms. These entities are only subject to the governance of company law, which has not experienced significant changes over the last decades. Hence, the regulatory system of unlisted firms has not changed. In this context Cheffins (2001) argues that, if a legal system of a country does not offer favourable conditions for a new type of corporate governance structure, a full convergence towards this model could not be expected and differences will remain. Indeed, this is observable for accounting regulation: company law as the primary source of regulation remains stable in the civil-law countries. Company law did not change – the focus remains on monitoring, participation and standardised contracts – and single accounts keep their important role. The accounting standards applicable for single accounts still have the function of maintaining legal capital and helping resolve possible disputes. An important explanation is that for stakeholders of non-listed companies in civil-law countries information accounts are of minor importance. The timely presentation of information does not provide additional utility or might even be unsuitable in terms of the organisation of corporate governance, for instance, if it starts favouring payouts over the maintenance of capital by neutral instead of prudent reporting.

Considering the concept of complementarity, the question arises whether a change in the accounting system – as long as it is connected to a stable legal system – might even lead to an inefficient system of governance (Schmidt and Spindler 2002). The system fit of the different components of corporate governance elements might become disordered. Nobes (1998) already speaks in this context of an 'inappropriate transfer [...] of technology'. This may be an important reason why national governments do not allow the preparation of individual accounts on the basis of IFRS: in Germany individual financial statements still have to be prepared on the basis of the commercial code. The state still sets the accounting standards and enforces the rules. Notwithstanding the enactment of the BilMoG in 2009, which introduces elements of decision-usefulness into the commercial code, the principle of (unconditional) conservatism is still the basic objective of German GAAP. The same holds for France: a public decree from December 2004 prohibits the application of IFRS for individual accounts, and hence companies have to prepare single accounts on the basis of the PCG (Hoarau 2009).

Besides the moderating effect of company law, governments of civil-law countries insist on the preparation of individual accounts on the basis of local GAAP because of the close link between financial and tax reports (Schaub 2005; Goncharov et al. 2009). The annual profit from the financial report is the starting point for the calculation of payable tax. For the calculation of tax, reported numbers should be verifiable in case of conflict and they should be prudent so that no overtaxing occurs; the decision-relevance for shareholders is of minor importance. The amount of tax payable should not fluctuate due to outside developments – as is the case in fair value reporting – and companies should only pay taxes from realised income (Schön 2005). A change of the accounting rules for individual accounts would entail a change of the tax law or the preparation of individual tax accounts.

In conclusion, for the vast majority of firms in civil-law countries the traditional governance has changed very little during the last two decades: company law ensures participation as well as monitoring rights, and accounting regulation is geared to the maintenance of legal capital. The imposition of an information-accounting set of rules for all companies on a system with a detailed interventionist company-law system would introduce inefficiencies, as the latter have purposes other than information (Delvaille et al. 2005). Today sees the hybridisation of accounting in civil-law countries with the local GAAP as the dominant system. Group accounts developed as an important additional (information) tool for equity investors of listed companies. They became a complement to the changing securities laws. This dichotomy is likely to persist under the current regulatory regime.

## 8.5 Conclusion

We showed that the legal systems differ in the way equity investors are protected. The prevailing governance mechanisms in civil-law countries are participation and monitoring rights, which are codified in company law. The rules are interventionist and form standardised contracts between management and owners. The focus of the governance is long-term orientation, and hence equity investors have a voice in case of unsatisfactory management work. In contrast, common-law countries show a strong focus on information ensured by securities law and an efficient capital market so that equity holders can use the exit opportunity.

The organisation of the legal system is reflected in accounting regulation. The local GAAPs of the civil-law countries, France and Germany, still focus on the maintenance of legal capital. The standards are set by the state and support the long-term stability of companies by restricting corporate payouts. The accounting rules fit into the prevailing governance mechanism; they are complementary. The same holds for the accounting regulation in common-law countries. The protection of equity investors through information is supported by unbiased or neutral financial reporting numbers. If the legal systems remain stable, a change in accounting harmonisation may lead to system inefficiencies. As shown in Section 3, there is indeed a change in a part of the legal system of civil-law countries. Securities law, especially the mandatory disclosure provisions, have been significantly expanded for listed entities in civil-law countries. However, the primary source of regulation remains stable, and the legal rules in civil-law countries only change for listed groups. Therefore, full convergence of accounting rules for single and group accounts is likely to be inefficient regarding the organisation of corporate governance. As a consequence, there is a hybrid system of accounting regulation inside the civil-law countries: the traditional local GAAPs for individual accounts and the IFRS for group accounts of listed entities. In the common-law countries accounting regulation remains stable. Few if any constraints on the adoption of IFRS can be traced back to the legal system of common-law countries.

# 9
# Financial Systems and Corporate Credit Arrangements

Ongoing differences between financial systems across countries may explain why financial reporting systems have not yet fully converged. This chapter begins with a discussion of the traditional types of financial system in the six sample countries, Canada, France, Germany, Japan, the UK and the US. Evidence for persisting differences between the six countries' financial systems will be presented by comparing country-specific data; in particular, we compare the importance of capital markets as against debt capital and the role of deposit money banks. Based on this analysis, we discuss the accounting system as a subsystem of the financial system and the consequences for accounting regulation. Three main arguments for the continuing divergence between accounting regimes will be discussed: first, the different demands of equity investors and lenders in general; second, different interests of short-term and long-term investors; and third, the different affiliation between debt holders and lending entities, respectively.

## 9.1 Introduction

Chapter 8 analysed country specifics in legal systems, and this chapter follows on by looking at the financial system to explain persisting divergences in accounting. Indeed, comparative accounting research prefers the type of a nation state's financial system to the legal system as a driver shaping local accounting practice and regulation (Ball 2001).

Analogously to the legal system classification of countries (common law vs. civil law), nation states can be subdivided by their financial systems into two major categories: the more market-based, outsider-control systems and the more bank-based, insider-control systems (Franks and Mayer 1994). In outsider economies equity capital is more important than debt capital (Wüstemann 2003), and debt raised on markets is more important than credit raised through banks. Outsider systems show a dispersed ownership/holdership in contrast to family-dominated and bank-financed entities in insider economies. As a result, the information asymmetries between shareholders and the firm are higher in outsider economies. Shares in insider economies are instead held by well-informed block-holders such as families, other companies or the state (Dutzi 2005). The same is true for debt.

Hence, nation states as well as the involved private actors have different interests concerning financial reporting and its regulation. Consequently, the focus and preconception of accounting, as discussed in Chapter 3, are not identical for firms and users in the different financial systems. In outsider systems the demand for investor protection is higher, and the basic objective of accounting has been to provide useful information for making financial decisions to secure the efficiency of capital markets. In contrast, owing to the different ownership structure and the dominant role of the banks, the basic objective of accounting in insider economies has been to support relationship-based financing. Prudence has been the most important fundamental principle to guide accounting. Each system shows a specific configuration of different actors with dissimilar participation in the regulation of accounting.

As described in Chapter 5, financial markets are globalised today, and ever more companies start to raise capital on (international) equity markets. We showed that this development favours the harmonisation of accounting regimes. However, in Chapter 5 we focused on larger public companies and the rules and regulations for group accounting. We now need to consider the whole system to explain the findings of Part II, which showed that harmonisation developments are considerably less pronounced for private companies and single accounts. Examples of continuing variation in national accounting systems include the setting and content of accounting rules for non-listed companies and the rules applicable for single (i.e., unconsolidated) accounts for all firms, listed and non-listed alike.

## 9.2 Characteristics of outsider and insider economies

There are two analytical perspectives on financial regimes: namely, the macro-level analysis of the financial system as a whole and the micro-level analysis of companies' financial structure. The starting point for the latter was set by Modigliani and Miller's (1958) study of the cost of capital, corporation finance and the theory of investment. Examples of recent literature are Desai et al. (2004), who analyse the capital structures of foreign affiliates of multinational corporations, or Mittoo and Zhang (2008), who compare the leverage of large Canadian and US companies. The classification of different financial systems at the macro-level is often closely linked to scholarly work on corporate ownership and dates back to Berle and Means (1932), who observed that most US companies had substantially increased the dispersion of ownership.

In a cross-country analysis, Rybczynski (1984) distinguished systems where capital is primarily distributed by financial intermediaries and systems where companies obtain capital on markets. He highlighted the (inter-) dependency of companies and banks in the former and introduced the term 'bank-orientated systems'. For the latter he emphasised the importance of capital markets and established the term 'market-orientated system'. Furthermore, Rybczynski (1984) concludes that these systems developed owing to the different regulatory frameworks of nation states during industrialisation. In bank-oriented countries the development was 'state-assisted', most notably by, for example, the creation of banks providing risky finance by means of long-term debt. Banks in market-oriented countries only provided working capital, and hence larger capital markets developed. Franks and Mayer (1994) classified countries into outsider-control systems and insider-control systems and thus connected the corporate finance perspective with corporate governance. Berglöf (1997) strengthened this connection by stressing that corporate ownership and control are relevant for the distinction of the two systems and not different sources of finance: companies in market-based countries can have similarly high amounts of debt, but their control is differently organised. Therefore, he suggested the terms 'control-orientated' vs. 'arm's-length' finance. We will use the terminology interchangeably.

Canada, the UK and the US are historically classified as outsider systems, while France, Germany and (with some distinctive features) Japan are insider systems. Classification is therefore the same as in Chapter 8. Some scholars argue that the differences between the two groups have begun to fade since globalisation has shaped integrated financial markets: equity financing has become more important in insider economies, and entities show a more dispersed ownership (Hall and Soskice 2001). This is also in line with the results we presented in Chapter 5. Some researchers even see a convergence of the financial systems: for example, Murinde et al. (2004) found a convergence of seven EU financial systems to a variant of the Anglo-Saxon model using a panel of flow of funds data for the period 1972–1996. However, more literature indicates that these changes are incremental at best or a short-lived phenomenon owing to the stock market peak in 2000. Over all, the systems remain divergent (Krahnen and Schmidt 2004; Antzoulatos et al. 2008). At this stage we posit that the environment for larger international companies alters while at least unlisted and smaller companies do not change their financial structure.

Owing to the ambiguous results and obsolete data in the existing literature, respectively, we first look at the development of the financial systems by analysing empirical data and then discuss the impact of the financial system on the accounting regimes. In the existing literature there is no clear definition of how to capture the financial system. Thus we provide a broad selection of indicators. For the analysis we have subdivided the capital market into equity and debt capital markets. In both, capital is raised through public and private placements of various financial instruments such as shares or bonds. We particularly look at the role of public and private financing of the debt and equity and the distinctive role of banks. Differences and changes in financial systems are measured by contrasting countries' equity and bond markets, by analysing the size and activity of the banking sector and by comparing the quantitative part of banks in the process of capital allocation.

### 9.2.1 Equity capital

As presented in Chapter 5, capital markets throughout the OECD have internationalised since the 1970s: for example, the share of market capitalisation relative to GDP presented in Figure 5.4 illustrated the general growth of equity markets. However, we also showed that the outsider economies still have larger equity markets than the insider economies. In the following we will take a closer look at whether the differences between outsider economies and insider economies are still in place today.

Besides market capitalisation, a further indicator for the use and liquidity of capital markets is the rate of share turnover. This ratio is calculated as the amount of shares traded, divided by the number of outstanding shares. Figure 9.1 shows the average ratio for the three outsider economies, two insider economies (Germany and France) and Japan. The main share indices are used to represent the countries: the TSE 60 (Canada), FTSE 100 (UK), S&P 100 (USA), CAC 40 (France), HDAX (Germany) and Nikkei 225 (Japan). Over all, the turnover rate increases in most of the years shown, and the ratio of both systems is considerably higher in 2010 than in 1992. This points to

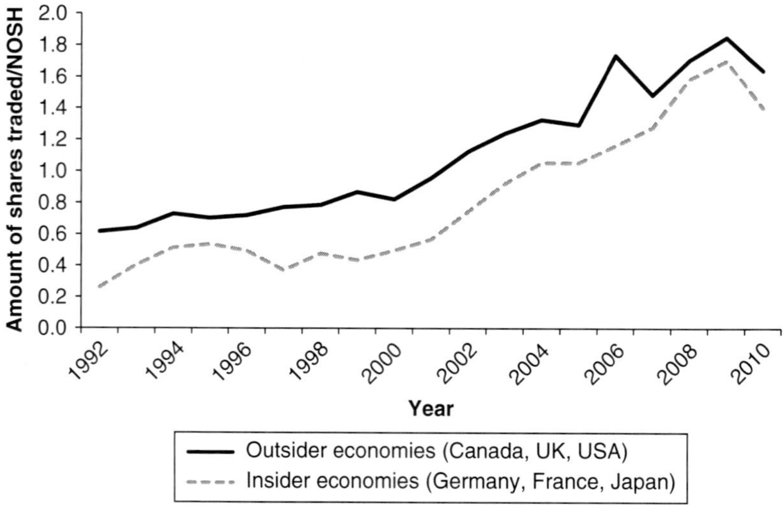


*Figure 9.1* Rate of share turnover for companies listed on TSE 60 (Canada), FTSE 100 (UK), S&P 100 (USA), CAC 40 (France), HDAX (Germany) and Nikkei 225 (Japan)
*Source*: Thomson Reuters Datastream.

a growing liquidity of capital markets. In line with the results for market capitalisation, the turnover rate of shares is lower in bank-based economies. In 1992 the ratio value of the outsider economies was nearly three times higher than the aggregated turnover of the insider economies. The indicator increased a little more strongly in the insider economies, and share turnover is converging between the two systems to some extent. Moreover, the rate of share turnover gives some insight into the different investment strategies of capital suppliers in outsider and insider economies. If the volume of traded shares relative to the amount of outstanding shares grows, this indicates a more frequent change in ownership and thus points to shorter holding periods of companies' shares and a stronger short-term orientation of investors. Hence Figure 9.1 also shows that investors in outsider economies have traditionally been more short-term-oriented (speculative investment), while investors in insider economies have been more long-term-oriented (strategic investment). This disparity has, at least for the largest listed companies in the two systems, diminished since 1992.

A look at IPOs in France, Germany, the UK and the US (Table 9.1) shows that the use of public equity has become more important for company financing in both systems since 1981. In Germany and France IPOs were rare events during the 1980s. Only since the middle of the 1990s have a significant number of firms started to raise capital by issuing shares to the public. The UK also had not seen a lot of firms going public in the 1980s. Here the increase was very strong between the middle and the end of the 1990s. Numbers have declined over all after the turn of the millennium, but the decline since 2000 has not been as strong as in the two insider economies, France and Germany. An important reason for this development is the availability of the lightly regulated AIM at the LSE, which attracts a substantial number of foreign firms; the UK figures are thus somewhat distorted. Only the US already had a high amount of IPOs in the 1980s. However, even here the amount of IPOs more than doubled from the period 1981–1985 to the period 1996–2000. The difference between the amounts of IPOs in the two economic systems is still notable today.

*Table 9.1* Number of IPOs since 1981

| | IPOs | | | | | |
|---|---|---|---|---|---|---|
| | **1981–1985** | **1986–1990** | **1991–1995** | **1996–2000** | **2001–2005** | **2006–2009** |
| USA | 2,022 | 2,564 | 3,830 | 4,337 | 1,423 | 1,206 |
| UK | 24 | 73 | 330 | 1,008 | 927 | 386 |
| Germany | 3 | 10 | 74 | 849 | 135 | 148 |
| France | 1 | 35 | 124 | 648 | 284 | 245 |

*Source*: Thomson One Deals.

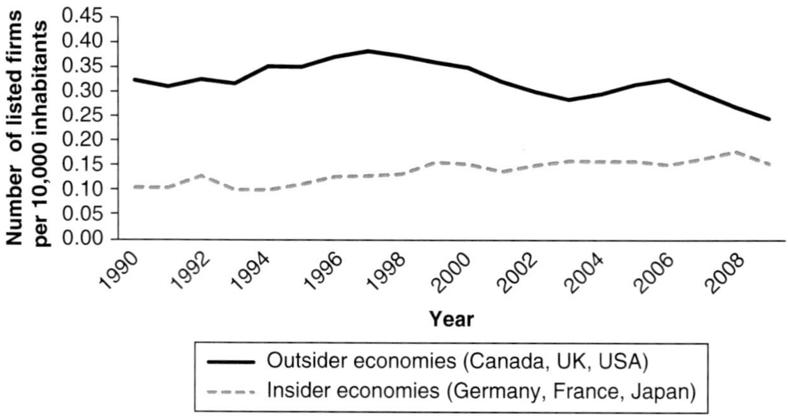


*Figure 9.2* Number of listed firms per 10,000 inhabitants since 2002 excluding Canada
*Source*: World Bank (World Development Indicators Online, 2009).

The total amount of domestic listed companies per capita also displays ongoing differences. The figures support the argument that listed equity capital is more important in outsider economies. As Figure 9.2 shows, the amount of listed companies per 10,000 inhabitants is about twice as high in capital-market-oriented countries as in insider economies. This gap has remained relatively constant over time.

### 9.2.2 Debt capital

Bond markets are available for company finance in both outsider countries and insider countries. With the issuance of bonds, companies raise debt capital on capital markets. Bonds are fixed-interest securities with no voting rights but a guaranteed interest payment and a guaranteed redemption of the contributed capital. Like shares, bonds can be traded on public markets, but often they are traded 'over the counter' (OTC) on bilateral, private arrangements between the investor and the issuer or with financial institutions as intermediaries. Corporate bonds have a lower liquidity than shares. While they are an instrument of arm's-length finance, they differ considerably from equity securities.

Table 9.2 shows the annual amount of corporate bond issues relative to our countries' GDP for the years 1990, 1995, 2000, 2005, 2008 and the mean value over the period 1990 to 2008. The use of the corporate bond market is in general larger in outsider economies. The mean value of this ratio in the three outsider economies was about 2 per cent in 1990, over 5 per cent in 2000 and 4 per cent in 2008. In contrast, the ratio from the three insider economies was less than 1 per cent in 1990 and around 2 per cent in the years 2000 and 2008. The use of corporate bonds is especially marginal

*Table 9.2* Corporate bond issues relative to GDP, excluding financial institutions

| Year | France | Germany | Japan | Canada | UK | USA |
|---|---|---|---|---|---|---|
| 1990 | 0.23% | 0.07% | 1.56% | 2.74% | 0.64% | 3.24% |
| 1995 | 0.38% | 0.09% | 1.19% | 3.28% | 1.53% | 4.12% |
| 2000 | 2.50% | 1.43% | 4.21% | 3.37% | 6.97% | 6.25% |
| 2005 | 1.78% | 0.95% | 3.46% | 2.52% | 2.37% | 4.16% |
| 2008 | 2.30% | 0.41% | 4.24% | 5.74% | 3.00% | 3.25% |
| Avg. 1990–2008 | 1.44% | 0.55% | 3.09% | 4.36% | 2.70% | 5.60% |

*Source*: Thomson One Deals, IMF World Economic Outlook Database.

in Germany. Japan again is an outlier. The issue of corporate bonds has approached the values of outsider economies since the end of the 1990s. Over all, there is no clear trend of convergence.

The second important source of debt capital is bank lending. This is captured by the degree of financial intermediation in the six economies. We use the bank intermediation ratio of non-financial companies. This indicator does not include consumer credits and thus focuses only on the corporate world. It expresses the importance of *corporate* debt finance through banks in an economy. This ratio is based on the flow-of-funds between the different economic sectors and indicates which portion of financial liabilities from non-financial companies is channelled through banks as financial intermediaries (Schmidt et al. 1999). It is calculated by dividing the total bank liabilities of non-financial companies by total liabilities of non-financial companies. The liabilities include securitised and non-securitised instruments. Figure 9.3 shows that the ratio is considerably higher in insider economies. Even though the gap has diminished since the middle of the 1990s – again Japan shows the largest decline – this ratio indicates that the importance of banks is today still higher in insider systems. Here banks play a more significant role in the financing of companies. Indeed, there seems to be a tendency towards convergence between the roles of banks in the two systems. However, the bank intermediation ratio of non-financial companies so far does not indicate a transformation of bank-based systems into market-based systems or other way around.

### 9.2.3 Overall assessment

A final indicator directly contrasting the role of capital markets vs. banks in the two different economic systems is the share of market capitalisation to GDP divided by bank credit to GDP. A higher ratio value indicates a higher importance of capital markets relative to banks in an economy and thus points to a more market-based financial system. The index value is above 1 in most years in the outsider economies, and it shows that stock markets

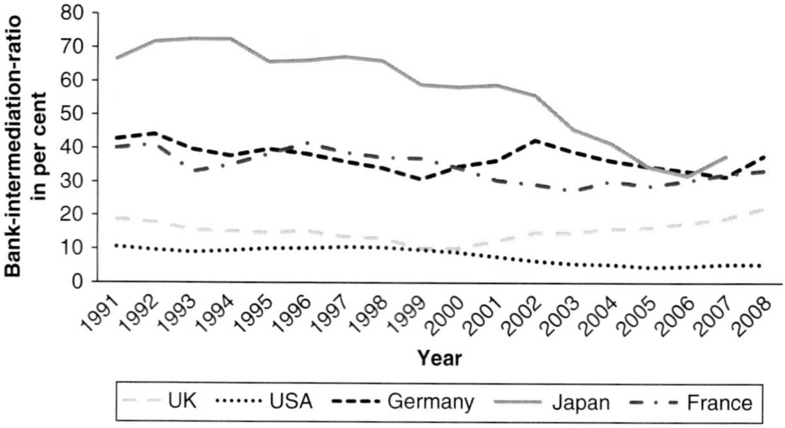


*Figure 9.3* Bank Intermediation Ratio of non-financial companies
*Source*: UK Office for National Statistics, US Federal Reserve Bank, Deutsche Bundesbank, Statistics Bureau of Japan, Banque de France.

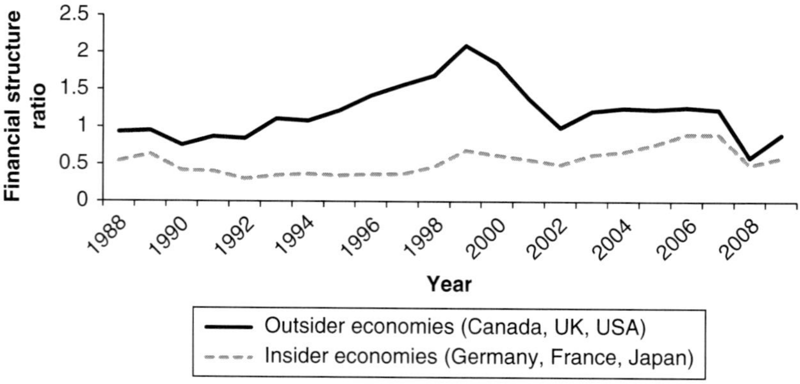


*Figure 9.4* Share of market capitalisation to GDP divided by bank credit to GDP
*Source*: World Bank, Beck and Demirgüc-Kunt (2009).

have a higher importance relative to banks. The opposite holds true for insider economies. Only in 2008 does the value for the outsider economies drop substantially below 1. However, this is due to the financial crisis and the strong devaluation of shares. The financial structure ratio of outsider economies goes up to 0.9 in 2009. Hence Figure 9.4 also does not point to a convergence of financial systems.

The aim of the analysis of the financial systems was to investigate whether there is a convergence between market-based and bank-based economies. In both, the demand for capital has risen considerably during the last few decades, and globally active firms increasingly use international capital markets to raise capital. Furthermore, the size and activity of the commercial banking sector has increased in both systems since the 1980s, with a specific reaction in Japan.

The presented data do not point to a transition of bank-based economies into market-based economies or the other way around. Over all, the financial systems have at best changed incrementally. Some indicators point to more similarities between bank- and market-based economies, but we cannot talk of convergence. In outsider economies equity capital is still relatively more important than debt capital, and debt raised on markets is more important than credit raised through banks. In insider systems the majority of the companies still rely on non-public debt finance. As the bank intermediation ratios show, banks remain the most important source of finance.

## 9.3 Consequences for accounting

The relative stability of financial systems with different characteristics is a further important factor in explaining why accounting regimes have not converged more strongly. Market-based and bank-based economies still differ in terms of access to capital markets, in the time-scale of investors and in the importance of the banking system and the affiliation between debt holders and lending entities. In each feature the two systems vary significantly in the way capital is allocated between capital supply and demand.

Chapter 3 has shown how accounting regulation in a country is an answer to the dominant informational and contractual needs within the system. These arise out of the particular information asymmetries between capital suppliers and companies and different regulatory interests of the state. Abstracting away from the distributional aspects, accounting regulation should reflect the prevalent demands of economic agents who are users of financial reports. These demands vary significantly between different groups of users: for example, between shareholders and debt holders or between short-term and long-term providers of funds.

### 9.3.1 Prevailing corporate financing strategy

Equity investors request high-quality information accounting sets of rules. This is achieved by providing group accounts that use rules of unbiased information. This is particularly important for outside investors. Publicly listed firms have a reasonable interest in meeting this demand. Higher public disclosure lowers the information asymmetries between investors and the firm and enhances the liquidity of capital markets. This lowers investors' monitoring and transaction costs (Raskop 2004). Hence the risk premium demanded by investors is lower, the demand for shares is higher and the cost of capital for the listed firm declines (Vernimmen 2005). Thus information accounting is crucial in outsider systems in order to diminish information asymmetries between investors and listed companies (Leuz 2010).

The high number of privately held firms and the importance of bank-based credit finance reduce the demand for informational accounting standards. Instead, standardised creditor protection rules gain in importance. Creditors, as the major stakeholders in bank-based systems, are best served by conservative accounting standards focusing on maintaining legal capital, at least when standardised contracts, as in company law, are written. Creditors have the incentive that payouts to shareholders are delayed until future periods (Fülbier et al. 2008). One explanation is the asymmetric loss function of creditors (Watts 2003): creditors do not benefit from positive accounting information, in the sense of receiving any additional payouts, but will be strongly affected if the debtor is illiquid at maturity. Another one is the lack of exit options that debt contracts provide.

The absence of capital markets reduces the incentive to publish detailed information. Disclosure has little rewards and may even lead to competitive disadvantage, for example by the publication of proprietary information to competitors (Hackethal and Schmidt 2000). A limited distribution of information can therefore even be beneficial. Moreover, providing detailed information raises the compliance costs of companies (Marosi and Massoud 2007).

To conclude, and expand the theoretical argument from Chapter 3, in countries in which the majority of firms rely on arm's-length finance, the demand for information-accounting sets of rules is high. These rules give a better solution to the dominant contracting problem – the relationship of outside equity investors and firm's management. In contrast, in countries where the majority of firms focus on debt capital, the demand for information accounting is small. Here the dominant contracting problem – the relationship of debt holders and lending entities – can be solved more effectively by prudent accounting rules.

### 9.3.2 Different interests of short-term and long-term investors

Figure 9.1, which depicts the rate of share turnover, hinted at the different investment interests of equity capital suppliers in market-based and bank-based economies. The higher turnover of shares in market-based economies points to shorter holding periods. Hence the equity market of these economies is rather dominated by short-term investors, while the equity markets of bank-based economies also have a higher quota of long-term equity investors. The two groups of capital suppliers have dissimilar investment strategies. Short-term investors have a focus on short-term returns by means of their price movements; they are rather speculative investors and act on share markets by trading future returns. The reversibility is much more important for short-term investors. By contrast, long-term investors are interested in sustainable returns by means of cash flows such as dividends.

Long-term investors typically have a closer, more direct connection to the management and the insider information. Owing to their strategic focus, long-term investors have an interest in dividends only being paid on the basis of realised profits, to avoid financial distress by virtue of capital outflows (Berglöf and Thadden 1994). Hence they tend to prefer prudent financial reports. Therefore, it is arguable that the majority of investors from insider economies do not necessarily have an interest in switching from local rules to IFRS or US GAAP. This conflict is mitigated when information accounts play no role in determining dividends.

Their outsider status leaves short-term investors higher information asymmetries than long-term investors. Hence the information presented in financial reports is of higher interest for them (Küting and Kaiser 2010). Unbiased representation is more helpful for predicting future cash flows and future returns.

### 9.3.3 Affiliation between debt holders and lending entities

Figures 9.3 and 9.4 showed that the importance of (unlisted) debt capital and the general role of banks as financial intermediaries are still more pronounced in bank-based economies. If debt is not publicly traded, the creditor and the lending entity have a bilateral relation, which also differs between the two systems. In general, lending entities in bank-based economies have closer relationships to the debt holder. A single bank is often a company's major financial source. Banks lend short-term as well as long-term funds, and the borrowing firm is to a certain degree dependent on the bank. Sometimes a bank representative is even a member of the firm's supervisory board. In Germany the close relationship between main banks and firms is called the *Hausbanken-System*: that is, companies themselves have a main bank that conducts most of their financial business (Schmidt 2007).[1] This system is also dominant in the Japanese *Keiretsu* (Cooke 1996). Superior information is available to the main bank. Other stakeholders may get this information only at a high price, if at all. These close affiliations between firms and banks are usually not found in market-based economies. Hence the agency conflicts between the major debt holders and firms differ between the two systems.

The affiliation between debt capital suppliers and firms has a significant influence on the way agency conflicts are reduced. In general, banks demand information about the liquidity and future solvency of a debtor (Guay 2008). Both will be strongly affected if unrealised revenues are distributed. Hence banks require prudent accounting. Furthermore, banks demand the right to access recoverable assets in the event of a debtor's illiquidity. These demands are adequately satisfied in bank-based economies by the close relationship between banks and firms, supplemented by legal regulations that focus on creditor protection. In case of imminent illiquidity, *Hausbanken* are informed earlier, have more chance to demand counteractions and greater access to the debt holder's capital reserves than do banks in market-based economies. Furthermore, company law is more strongly oriented towards creditor protection, and the local GAAPs in France, Germany and Japan focus on reliable and prudent numbers supporting the long-term stability of companies. This entails a tendency to undervalue assets and to overvalue liabilities, inducing hidden reserves and higher recoverable assets. Over all, the insider relation, higher hidden reserves and a good protection of legal capital sufficiently reduce agency conflicts between borrowers and lending entities.

While the rules, regulations and restrictions in bank-based economies are predominantly mandated by company law, governance in outsider economies is strongly supplemented by or even primarily based on bilateral debt covenants (Leuz et al. 1998; Armour 2006). These are additional private agreements between the debtor and the bank which add supplementary conditions to debt contracts. Covenants require the borrower to meet certain, mostly financial, criteria. If covenants are not met by the borrower, penalty payments or a call in of the loan may result. Debt covenants thus serve as a compensation for weak creditor protection by company law (Qi and Wald 2008). Covenants allow the creditors to recognise earlier signs that the debtor may be in financial distress and to take corrective actions. Earlier counteractions might also be beneficial for the debtor, and covenants can thus lead to lower cost of capital (Zimmermann et al. 2011).

This argument primarily holds for the regulatory set-up of market-based economies. As the primary contracting problem in market-based economies is the protection of outside equity investors, the accounting rules provide unbiased representation and creditor protection is rather weak. Owing to the focus on information and relevance, creditors in market-based economies often demand additional debt covenants, increasing control over the assets. While debt covenants are also used in bank-based economies, their complexity and frequency are still much less pronounced in bank-based economies. Arguably, traditional local GAAPs seems to be better at meeting the reporting demands of firms and most stakeholders in bank-based economies. Hence the local GAAPs of the bank-based economies are an ideal solution to one of the dominant contracting needs within these systems (Kilian 2011).

The regulation of credit financing is still shaped differently in the two systems. The above argument suggests that this is appropriate given the different financial systems. In bank-based economies the reduction of agency problems between the creditor and the firm are predominantly mandated and the contracting parties rely on standardised regulation, whereas private debt covenants are regularly used in market-based economies. A switch to information accounting for non-public firms in bank-based economies seems a poor fit and would result in an extended need of bilateral debt covenants, possibly resulting in higher transaction costs.

## 9.4 Conclusion

Financial systems and accounting regimes are closely linked; the nature of a nation state's financial system shapes local accounting practice and regulation (Ball 2001; Werner and Zimmermann 2009). Therefore a convergence of the financial systems will probably entail a convergence of accounting regimes.

The available data do not suggest a convergence of the different financial systems into one single global system. Financial systems have only changed incrementally. We showed in this chapter that most firms from bank-based systems do not demand information-accounting sets of rules to the same extent as their counterparts in market-based economies. The main function of accounting in these economies is the information of outside shareholders to support the efficiency of public capital markets. By contrast, the main function of accounting in bank-based economies is its use in standard contracts formulated by company law. Different demands of investors and lenders in general, different interests of short-term and long-term investors and the different affiliation between debt holders and lending entities will make it likely that there will continue to be differences between accounting systems.

This is in line with the results concerning the legal system, presented in Chapter 8. As we showed there, the prevailing governance mechanisms in a country determine investors' ability to exercise the options of voicing their concerns or exiting, leading to a stronger demand for information accounting in common-law- and market-based countries and for prudent accounting in bank-based and civil-law countries respectively. This consonance amplifies the fit of the prevailing accounting regimes to the relatively persistent environment of companies. Over all, similar demands on accounting data arise out of the legal and financial system.

# 10 National Values and Political Systems

Accounting regulation, viewed within the context of the financial system, shows that different interests of corporate stakeholders exist, which trigger different demands for accounting information. These demands are typically satisfied by regulation, but an analysis of the financial system alone cannot derive implications for a demand nor a supply of *state* intervention in accounting. The same holds true for the legal system. In general terms, the legal-system approach reveals to which part of the law accounting is a complement and to which extent accounting is part of the law. This indicates differences in the intensity of state intervention, but the different intentions and intensities of state intervention in accounting regulation cannot be fully understood on this basis. We therefore need to analyse societal motive and values, which can be captured by the type of welfare-state. The societal aspect is often ignored or subsumed under the generic interests of stylised actors in the traditional approaches – shareholders or other providers of capital are reduced to their role – but the following will show that societal motives and values play a substantial role in determining accounting systems. This broadens our perspective on comparative accounting, as it provides an opportunity to shed some light on the general role of accounting in society.

## 10.1 Introduction

Nation states differ with respect to the ideas of distribution and social justice that form the foundation of their political institutions. These basic societal ideals and values characterise a country's policy tradition and serve as a benchmark indicating the extent to which enforced distributions are perceived as acceptable and societally legitimate. These societal attitudes can be captured by a country's welfare state. Welfare states do not only reflect principles of providing social security; they also embody the societal–political ideals and values that determine the extent of allocative and distributive activities. They stand for different understandings and interpretations of social fairness and freedom, which build the foundation of that society. Their influence will thus not be restricted to the area of social security but will also influence any kind of state activity.

Societal values and motives will therefore also play a key role in the policy arena of accounting. We will show that the societal volition expressed in welfare-state types is reflected in a country's prevalent aims and goals of accounting. The focus is especially on the distributive effects emanating from accounting regulation and its function in balancing interests between corporate constituencies. They, in turn, determine how socially important sets of accounts are regulated. The welfare-state approach provides the chance to reach a more comprehensive and general understanding of the causality and evolution of divergence. This is especially the case for the relationship between the state and accounting.

The welfare-state types are captured by a dichotomous classification in residual and institutional welfare states. It will become apparent that residual welfare states emphasise the allocative (efficiency) function and leave regulation to private bodies, while institutional welfare states emphasise the distributive (preserving) nature of accounting and allocate the regulation to the state. Convergence occurs only in the area that is irrelevant for the regulatory impetus of the welfare state: that is, group accounts, as they do not serve a legally binding function.

The chapter is organised as follows: it begins with a consideration of the two basic welfare-state types as well as their empirical detectability and stability. The next section connects the welfare state with accounting by outlining its social role and the influence that the welfare-state type exerts on accounting regulation. Based on this, we will provide brief case studies of welfare-state types and accounting, referring to the empirical examples of Germany and the UK as well as the special case of Canada, to substantiate the additional explanatory power of the welfare-state approach.

## 10.2 National differences in delivery: Characteristics of residual and institutional welfare states

States are multifaceted constructs with a multitude of activities. From a functional perspective, a state consists of four intersecting dimensions: the resource dimension, the legal dimension, the legitimatory dimension and the welfare dimension (Zürn and Leibfried 2005). Central importance is attached to the welfare dimension, which had been emphasised strongly in OECD countries by the end of the 1970s (Hurrelmann et al. 2008). The welfare dimension refers to the state as interventionist in order to ensure the well being of its citizens by facilitating economic growth and enabling social equality. The term 'welfare state', however, is difficult to define, as it is an umbrella term incorporating a variety of governmental measures with distinctive characteristics (Pierson 2001). In general, the welfare dimension depicts a dimension that extends the standard economic rationale for state interventions – that is, cushioning external effects and providing public goods – into a distributive rationale.

Welfare activities are observable in all OECD countries, but structural variations in the organisational and institutional features of welfare states exist. This results in significantly different frameworks of state interventions in economic processes. The specific execution of interventionist policies varies, for instance, with regard to the scope and range of state activities as well as the mix of instruments established to implement welfare activities (Alber 1988). Typically, welfare states can be distinguished as belonging to either a 'residual' or an 'institutional' type (Wilensky and Lebeaux 1965; Titmuss 1975; Alber 1988).

Commitment to market sovereignty is specific to the residual types of welfare state. Markets are understood as mechanisms that lead to the optimal distribution of social welfare. This is in line with the assumption that the market is the most efficient means of allocating resources in the traditional economic sphere. The role that the state plays in the distribution of welfare by active intervention in markets and societal processes is simultaneously seen as limited, or rather subordinated. The focus of welfare policies is typically related to the residual part of the society which is unable to take care of itself. Services are means-tested, and their supply is temporary. The residual welfare-state concept rests on the individualistic notion that the vast majority of society can take care of their own well being without state intervention. Therefore, the state assumes responsibility for undertaking corrective actions only if the primary mechanism of welfare distribution – the market – collapses. Consequently, state interventions in residual welfare-state types take place within strict, narrowly defined boundaries.

The boundaries of state intervention in the institutional welfare-state type are less precisely drawn. The institutional type is more encompassing than the residual welfare type; eligibility is universal. Basically, citizens are all entitled to at least a modest standard of living as well as social rights, and an adequate social standing should be guaranteed to everybody without reserve. Moreover, the institutional concept of welfare state understands welfare not as an individualistic notion but as a collective social responsibility: the social collective has a duty to assist individual members. Welfare services are therefore addressed to all citizens and have a strongly redistributive character. In an extensive form social rights have a similar legal standing as property rights (Reich 1964). Owing to the pursuit of far-reaching (re-)distributive aims, the effectiveness of the market as distributive nexus of welfare that secures the optimal distribution is challenged. Limitations or partial displacements of market mechanisms will take place. The state exercises more distributive power.

The residual and institutional types of welfare state are diametrically opposed in their view of the scope of distributive measures and therefore about the state as a corrective actor. In the residual type, interventions take the form of frameworks to sustain the general distributive function of the market and to prevent market failures. By contrast, in the institutional type, state interferences correct the (primary) market distribution by means of policies and different forms of risk absorption. Existing welfare states do not assume the definite shape of one of the two extremes; rather, they combine elements of both, which resolves the dichotomy into a continuum between these two types of welfare state (Kvist 2007).

The general differentiation of welfare states into residual and institutional types has been extended and has led to the establishment of more sophisticated taxonomies. The most prominent is the typology of Esping-Andersen (1990), who distinguishes between liberal, conservative and social-democratic types of welfare state. However, these other taxonomies have not fundamentally challenged the general notion of welfare state types, whose structural features point in the direction of either the residual or the institutional welfare state-type (Kvist 2007). The affiliation of the three types to the classical type notion is unequivocally possible. Liberal welfare types clearly emphasise residual principles: market compared to state solutions of welfare distributions are favoured, as well as the idea of self-reliant individualism (Esping-Andersen and Korpi 1987). The conservative and social-democratic types have marked similarities with the notion of the institutional welfare type. The social-democratic type is almost completely consistent with the institutional type. The conservative type describes a sagging form of the institutional welfare state not granting but protecting the economic position of individuals. Common to both types is that the state is placed in the foreground in order to suppress the market as a distributive nexus of welfare.

The variation of welfare states with respect to structural features is empirically measurable by the degree of de-commodification, which also determines the development of the institutional dimension (Korpi 1980). It also measures the degree to which social policies sustain the market logic and vice versa. De-commodification captures how well individuals are able to maintain an adequate level of well-being independently of their participation in the labour market. Policies demonstrate a de-commodifying effect if (social) rights grant the provision of (social) benefits, which equates to the decoupling of (social) security from the market. A high degree of de-commodification is therefore characteristic of the institutional kind of welfare state, while a low one is characteristic of the residual type. Another possible way of measuring de-commodification is to measure the range of (social) policies that satisfy the needs of individuals (Flora and Heidenheimer 1981). This dimension mainly looks at the scope of (social) policies that are

*Table 10.1* Typical attributes of residual and institutional welfare states

| **Characteristics** | **Residual welfare state** | **Institutional welfare state** |
|---|---|---|
| Commitment to ... | Market sovereignty | State sovereignty |
| Welfare eligibility criteria | Means-tested | Previous status/equality |
| Distribution of welfare | Market-driven | State-driven |
| Social status | Not preserved | Preserved |
| Welfare conception rests on ... | Self-reliance, self-responsibility | Social/political responsibility |
| Focus of state intervention | Sustaining market efficiency | Correcting market distribution |
| De-commodification effect of policies | Marginal | Central |
| Scope of welfare policies | Basic services | Comprehensive services |
| Public–Private Mix | Private arrangements/ market provisions | Political arrangements/ non-market provisions |

*Source*: Own contribution.

transferred from the market to political responsibility: that is, the scope of market versus non-market (political) provisions. Institutional welfare states will limit private arrangements more extensively, whereas residual welfare states will only provide a core of basic welfare services. Table 10.1 summarises the characteristics of the different types of welfare states.

Differences between nation states can be related to different policy traditions (Alber 1988) and consequent ideas of distribution and social justice. The corresponding ideals and values of a society serve as a benchmark for evaluating the extent to which distribution is perceived as fitting and legitimate (Mau 1997). In this regard, welfare states not only reflect the principle of providing social security, but also show that the extent of allocative and distributive activities is determined by societal–political ideals and values. That is, welfare state types also stand for different ideologies of the state. Residual welfare states are built on the moral concept of freedom (Siegel 2007). The principle of subsidiarity that emphasises self-responsible actions and self-determination by individuals is prominent (Seliger 2001). Subsidiarity postulates that that individual freedom should only be minimally curtailed through social constraints, as market forces will generally lead to an adequate coordination of interests. Therefore, the extension and protection of the freedom of the individual dominates state activities. In contrast, institutional welfare states are characterised by a paternalistic state tradition as well as by the ideal of social justice, which in some societies takes on a universalistic conception of the state dominated by the ideal of equality (Peters 2002). In institutional welfare states it is assumed that the allocative mechanism of the market – even when it functions efficiently – does not lead to an equitable distribution.

These motives and values constitute a society's foundations. The sphere of influence of the ideological concepts therefore can be seen as not purely restricted to the area of social security. Social security can be established by a variety of other state activities unless these policies aim at disconnecting and buffering income streams from market outcomes (Schwartz 2001). Accordingly, it is not far-fetched to say that type-specific societal values and motives also determine the demand and supply of state interventions in other policy fields, such as accounting regulation. Society's expectations about the quality of state intervention will rely on these ideals and determine the role accounting plays in society as well as the extent of state intervention in accounting regulation.

### 10.2.1 Empirical form and stability of welfare states

The approach to building welfare-state typologies is subject to criticism, which mostly refers to methodological aspects of typology formation and the lack of detailed analysis with which states are classified into just a very small number of categories (Crouch 2005).[1] Despite their problems, typologies deliver a systematic approach to examine programmatic differences between welfare states (Castles 2001). Moreover, they help to identify and explain (system-specific) pathways of adjustments in the provision of welfare services. However, the main purpose of a welfare-state typology approach has to be seen in its usefulness for analysing whether differences between welfare states disappear or persist, and in which direction they might move.

Questions also arise about the stability of the welfare-state types. Owing to driving forces of all kinds, it has been claimed that the nature of welfare provision is changing and that welfare states are converging towards the residual welfare-state type. Empirical studies have examined these claims: results are mixed and very heterogeneous, but the detected convergence process of welfare indicators is by and large marginal (for a summary see Starke et al. (2008)). Therefore, the hypothesis that welfare states are converging towards the residual type cannot be supported. Further, the de-commodification indicator has not changed substantially over time, which means that the types of welfare have remained fairly static (Scruggs 2004; Starke et al. 2008). This could be demonstrated for the 1970s as well as for later decades, when the

*Table 10.2* Country classification according to Esping-Andersen (1990)

| | Residual welfare state | Institutional welfare state |
|---|---|---|
| Classification based on Esping-Andersen (1990) | Australia, Canada, Ireland, New Zealand, UK, US | Austria, Belgium, France, Germany, Italy, Japan, Netherlands, Switzerland, Denmark, Finland, Norway, Sweden |

*Source*: Esping-Andersen (1990).

*Table 10.3* Distribution among the clusters for the six largest OECD countries

| | **Residual welfare state** | **Institutional welfare state** |
|---|---|---|
| Corresponding legal and financial system | UK, US | Germany, France |
| Not corresponding legal and/or financial system | Canada | Japan |

*Sources*: Demirguc-Kunt and Levine (1999); Calmès (2004); Nobes and Parker (2008).

rhetoric of dismantling social services dominated the discourse of political practice rather than practice itself (Esping-Andersen 1997). Table 10.2 shows the classification on the basis of the degree of de-commodification according to Esping-Andersen (1990).

The appearance of the legal and financial system tends to have strong parallels with the type of welfare state. Welfare states tending to the residual end of the continuum (e.g., the UK or the US) usually exhibit a market-based financial system and belong to the common-law tradition (Jang 2005). By contrast, welfare states tending to be more institutional (e.g., France or Germany) usually exhibit a credit-based financial system and belong to the code-law tradition. Table 10.3 shows the categories of welfare states as well as legal and financial systems for our sample countries using today's classification of welfare states. Canada and Japan are outliers from the base case, as their legal and financial systems do not correspond.

This opens up the discussion about the influence of different welfare-state types on accounting regulation. Discussing the welfare-distributing roles of accounting and relating them to general societal values and motives captured by welfare states allows us to contrast more strongly the fundamental ideas underlying accounting in different countries. More specifically, the inclusion of social motives broadens our perspective on the (qualitative) demand for state intervention in accounting regulation, which is largely neglected by the legal and financial system approach.

## 10.3 Consequences for accounting: Its welfare-distributing roles

The representation of the financial history of a firm is driven by value judgements determining, first, which parts of the corporate reality are shown, and second, how that reality is presented (Hines 1988). Thus, the process of transforming qualitative business transactions into quantitative numbers is always driven by the decision as to which transactions are recognised in financial accounts and how these activities are valued.

In many ways, decisions about valuation methods gain special importance as they can affect major corporate constituencies either positively or negatively (Zeff 1978). The (social) consequences of accounting are also pronounced by Ordelheide (2004), who emphasises, among other things, that accounting-driven actions have an influence on the welfare of society.

The above demonstrates that normative decisions in accounting give rise to a protective as well as a welfare-distributing character, which makes it similar to social policy. Like social policy, accounting can be ascribed two functions: an enabling function and a preserving function. Regarding the enabling function, accounting information serves the allocation of economic resources in markets and advances market efficiency, or it helps in writing individual contracts to control behaviour. The approaches of accounting information for decision-making and accounting as a device for efficient contracting are normally discussed in this context. Regarding the preserving function, accounting divides income between corporate constituencies, and it balances interests directly. As will become apparent, the two approaches to accounting show differences in the way individuals are made responsible for themselves, and furthermore they imply different perceptions of social welfare. Technically, the state will use securities law or corporate law to assign these roles to accounting. How this is done was discussed in Chapter 8.

Regarding the enabling function, the dissemination of accounting information and accounting-based contracts are seen as ways of overcoming market inefficiencies (Fields et al. 2001). Market participants use accounting information to evaluate the past and future performance of the reporting entity and reach economic decisions on this basis. From this perspective, accounting plays a key role in transmitting information that enables market participants to decide whether to join the 'nexus' of the company. This taps the company as a source of income, which is why accounting-based decisions also (positively or negatively) affect individual-related welfare.

Although the dissemination of accounting information is essential, the mere provision of information may not suffice to protect the economic well-being of many economic actors, in particular in (long-term) contractual relationships between market participants and the company. Creditors compared with shareholders have, for instance, an asymmetric loss function (Watts 2003). Because of their fixed claims, they do not benefit from an exceedingly good performance of a firm, but they are fully affected by negative events (e.g., tight liquidity positions or insolvencies) as their claims are curtailed.

In this regard, accounting-based contracts are one way to mitigate agency conflicts and their costs. Accounting information is used by claimholders to set (performance) incentives but also, and more importantly, to secure their entitlements against expropriation by others (Ahmed et al. 2002). Such contracts typically contain precautionary measures that should prevent the exploitation and erosion of anticipated future claims. Sometimes contracts directly include stipulations about valuation requirements in order to tie up liquidity within the corporation. The contractual perspective on accounting highlights the fact that the employment of accounting information is decisive in enabling efficient contractual relationships. That is, accounting stabilises corporate relationships as individual relationships are structured, which is especially important for corporate constituencies that cannot easily resign from the corporate 'nexus'.

From the contracting perspective the protective nature of accounting largely rests on self-responsible actions of individuals. They are put in a position to protect themselves explicitly on the basis of accounting information. Some corporate constituencies cannot be certain that their claims are assured against others without individually backing up their claims by accounting-based contracts. In this vein, the enabling function of accounting abstracts from individuals and their status. Contracting, indeed, is concerned with the relations of individuals, but finally relates to market efficiency. Accounting-based financing contracts, for instance, underpin the individual relationship between lenders and debtors. The argument eventually is one about the efficiency of the contractual relationship. Individual contracting provides efficiency where efficiency cannot be ensured by the dissemination of accounting information alone. Welfare is understood as an aggregation of the individuals' welfare rather than that of society as a whole (Cooper and Sherer 1984).

The preserving function of accounting relates directly to the relationships of corporate constituencies and balances the interests of individual economic actors. Owing to their asymmetrical loss function, creditors will give the securing of their claims a higher priority than the informational protection by accounting. Similar in design are the claims of other constituencies (e.g., supplier and employees). Employees' wages might be reduced or contracts terminated, which would affect their welfare. Their interest also lies in assuring the longevity of the company and the preservation of the company as a source of income. These constituencies will have a propensity to demand safeguards that restrict financial outflows (to shareholders) and maintain capital.

In this respect, the major function of accounting is the division of income between corporate constituencies (Oguri 2005). Accounting is used to define or measure the payout potential of firms (profit) and to calculate the amount of money that can be distributed to the shareholders. If the distribution rules link to accounting, the design of valuation rules have a strong societal importance as they must balance conflicting interests between corporate members. Fixed or long-term-oriented claimants, for instance, will demand conservatively measured profits, while short-term shareholders will demand the opposite, as their dividends dependent on the calculated profit (Moxter 1984). Consequently, there needs to be a balance between restricting and securing payouts to include the varying interests. Depending on the valuation rules, a more or less fixed relationship status is institutionalised. In this respect, valuation rules serve as a common moderating mean to generate stability between related corporate constituencies. Chapter 8 demonstrated how this could be achieved technically.

Without a clear hierarchy of preferences, accounting will resemble a compromise view of what is socially desirable, and the point of reference will be not market efficiency but other criteria. These criteria might be the protection of corporate constituencies with a low level of expertise or the adjustment of unequal distribution of (economic) power. This perspective of accounting emphasises the stabilising and preserving effect of accounting, and protective measures are directly institutionalised into accounting rules. That is, the allocation of claims is directly handled using accounting numbers. Individuals can rely on predetermined conditions that govern the relationship with other stakeholders. Accounting rules establish an implicit protection, and the responsibility to install safeguards for individual claims by means of contracting has been removed by intervention.

In this case, the primary condition for improving welfare rests not on market efficiency but on a societal idea of desirability, because the preserving dimension of accounting focuses on distributive goals rather than on the optimal allocation of economic resources. The individually optimal distribution of profits is subordinated to the socially desired distribution expressed through accounting rules. Accordingly, welfare from the preserving perspective can be understood, rather, as the welfare of society as a whole than as the aggregation of individuals' welfare: it is not the individually efficient answer that is prioritised but the one that is desirable for society.

A summary view indicates that there is a demand for the information function of accounting as well as for its function in distributing and protecting claims in society. The former extends to the enabling function of accounting and the latter to the preserving function. However, there exists a trade-off between the two societal functions of accounting: they are non-complementary and cannot be fulfilled simultaneously. Accounting regulation must emphasise either an enabling or a preserving regulative approach of accounting. Therefore, for the purpose of accounting regulation, the main task will be to weigh the two alternatives against each other and to decide which function is given more support. Each and any form of weighting induces different distributive effects between corporate constituencies and might privilege a certain group.

The normative judgements behind this can be explained by the dominant welfare-state type, which can be regarded as an emanation of the societal will. Similarly, the decision about which primary role accounting fulfils in a welfare state can be understood as an equilibrated outcome. Thus, the demand for and intensity of state intervention as well as the supply of state regulation in accounting will depend on the social judgements expressed in the shape of the prevalent welfare-state type. In the following, we demonstrate how thinking about the welfare state and accounting regulation hang together. In this context, accounting regulation is understood as the general regulative approach of accounting pursued in the welfare-state types. It extends to two aspects. The first concerns the elements of accounting, which were discussed in Chapter 3. The welfare-state type deals with both the question of unified representation (information accounting) versus prudence, as well as the emphasis on group or company accounts. The second aspect concerns state intervention in standard-setting.

### 10.3.1 Accounting regulation in the residual welfare state

The model of accounting that corresponds to the residual welfare state will rest mainly on the information function and combines unbiased representation with an emphasis of group accounts. This follows from the specific characteristics of state interventions embodied in residual welfare states: policies promote market sovereignty and the rationality and responsibilities of individual actors. Accentuating the informational role of accounting supports the self-determination of individuals in reaching rational decisions. All stakeholders rely on the same information; and shareholders are the dominant type. Other stakeholders will not receive a different treatment. The informational role would be consistent with the socio-political attitude that interventions should only occur after a means test, which seems difficult to construct in the case of information so that all participants are treated alike.

The securing of claims has to be done on an individual basis by means of contracts. Economic actors have to advocate their own claims and interests, as their status is not maintained by any institutionalised rules: state interventions would curtail individual freedom, which would be inconsistent with the notion of individualism in residual welfare states. An intervention would also reach beyond securing allocative efficiency. Thus, privately contracted arrangements will be given prominence as they provide a high degree of flexibility and the desired leeway for self-dependent agreements. Consequently, accounting and its regulation in residual welfare states will have a clear intention to enable market participants to make informed decisions. These informed decisions increase the efficiency of markets. This would extend to company laws with a high number of dispensable rules, as discussed in Chapter 8.

The predominance of the efficiency-supporting function presupposes the priority of group over company accounts, as the information function is better fulfilled by this set of accounts as they refer to the economic entity. Group accounts are more informative than the parent's single accounts, as the unified presentation of the financial situation of all related legal entities allows the best assessment of future returns or of the riskiness of an investment. As the state focuses on market efficiency, single accounts will escape the attention of the regulator. If single accounts are mandatory in residual welfare states, they will also fulfil an informational role. Over all, similar accounting standards will be applicable to both types of accounts and all companies.

The standard-setting process for the prominent set of group accounts will be left to private experts. Interventions will only occur in order to improve standard-setting and to make the advantages of common accounting standards available to the society. These interventions could be justified: safeguarding the production of accounting rules serves the purpose of setting up an efficiency framework for markets. Furthermore, private experts stand out with market-specific expertise which helps in furthering market efficiency. Experts have the specific know-how for subject-based accounting solutions (Watrin 2001). At the maximum level of intervention, this might result in a private standard-setter under state supervision.

### 10.3.2 Accounting regulation in the institutional welfare state

The aggregated demand of economic agents in institutional welfare states will require the balancing of interests as a corresponding model of accounting, and the information function will play only an auxiliary role. In institutional welfare states, the societal volition rests on the assumption that even fully efficient market processes do not lead to a fair provision for all interests. To compensate for uneven distribution within society, balancing mechanisms take care of all constituents and not only for the disadvantaged. Relationships among corporate constituencies can be configured by accounting rules; moreover, certain groups could be explicitly protected. Furthermore, accounting can be used to define payout restrictions that maintain the status of individuals by maintaining the existence of the firm from which the status is derived. This makes prudence, as discussed in Chapter 3, a common feature in institutional welfare states. Individual interests are curtailed in favour of a more societal solution. This standardised solution is in line with the collective approach of institutional welfare states.

In institutional welfare states accounting standards will be mainly set for single accounts. Single accounts are necessary for the preserving function of accounting, as they are the legally decisive set of accounts since company law regulations are based on them. They refer to the legal entity, making them a useful regulatory instrument to coordinate legal claims. Therefore, single accounts offer an appropriate interface for the balancing of interests, as only legally justified interests require a balancing. Setting other standards for group accounts – for example, to implement the information function in order to satisfy the particular interest of shareholders – would not cause a conflict between goals. Group accounts are not enmeshed in the regulatory framework and do not have any other function beyond providing information. Consequently, the two functions can co-exist in institutional welfare states as the societally demanded function in balancing interests remains unchanged. Hybridisation of accounting regulation would be the likely outcome.

To incorporate the different interests tied to accounting, the rules will be set for the most part by state authorities, as the political process appears to be the most legitimate way forward if the principal goal is to solve the conflicts of interest between corporate stakeholders in a universal fashion. State authorities are then able to act as 'referee' between corporate constituencies or find a compromise solution for the balancing of interests (Schildbach 1986; Feldhoff 1994). Therefore, the definition of rules and standard-setting at large will be generally state-organised in institutional welfare states. Referring to the co-existence of the two accounting functions in institutional welfare states, the responsibility of standard-setting for group accounts can be delegated (e.g., to private experts) if the state sticks to setting rules for single accounts, as the societal core of accounting regulation would not be jeopardised.

In the described case of state-organised standard-setting, the contractual allocation of claims would be anticipated by the state. However, such a 'state contract' for the coordination of interests requires the restriction of individual discretion and flexibility granted in the private contractual dimensioning of claims. Besides, they would have to be generally and mandatorily valid for everyone to preserve an equitable balance of interests in the society. The strength of demand for such a 'state contract' might be so distinct within society that the rules would make private arrangements dispensable. To some extent, this could end up in a crowding-out of private contracts that use accounting information for allocating and securing claims.

State intervention into accounting regulation will be also demanded by society as the institutional welfare state depends on reliable information about the development and stability of the corporate sector (Kirchhof 2000). The stability of companies is important, as companies are an essential pillar of the social system. The survival of companies and their preservation as perpetual source of income protects the economic status of individuals. But more importantly, their preservation as an employer serves to a large extent the financing of the social system, as the financing largely depends on the contributions of the workforce. Therefore the restriction of capital outflows could also be regarded as a policy instrument that maintains the stability of the corporate sector and, at the same time, of the social system.

Table 10.4 summarises the key characteristics of the corresponding type of accounting regulation pointed out for the two welfare state types. It shows that the type of welfare state presupposes a specific type of accounting regulation, as each accounting approach can be unequivocally assigned to a particular type of welfare state.

*Table 10.4* Ideal type of accounting regulation in residual and institutional types of welfare state

| | **Residual welfare state** | **Institutional welfare state** |
|---|---|---|
| Regulative function of accounting | Enabling | Preserving |
| Main aim pursuit with accounting | Market efficiency/ information function | Distribution/balancing of interests |
| Claim allocation/securing | Privately arranged | State-prescribed |
| Societally important set of accounts | Group accounts | Single accounts |
| Organisation of standard-setting | Private experts | State authorities/political process |

*Source*: Own contribution.

## 10.4 Accounting regulation from a welfare perspective: The UK, Germany and Canada compared

In order to consider the impact that the type of welfare state has on the comparative dynamics of accounting regulation, we will sketch a brief history of the accounting regulation in the UK, Germany and Canada. The UK and Germany are typical examples of a residual and an institutional welfare state respectively. Even though the UK turned from being a leader in the decommodification field in 1950 to a laggard in the 1980s (Hicks 1999), the provision of social security has always been less legally protected and less tax-financed than in institutional welfare states (Schmid 2000). The UK has historically been dominated by the ideals and motives prevalent in residual welfare states (Esping-Andersen 1990; Cumming and MacIntosh 2002).

The UK and Germany were subject to considerable harmonisation efforts at the EU level, which led to the implementation of non-system elements in both countries (Zimmermann 2010b). Most pertinent to accounting regulation as understood here are the Fourth Directive on single accounts (78/660/ECC), the Seventh Directive on consolidated accounts (83/349/ECC) and the IAS-Regulation (No. 1606/2002). But with a difference in welfare styles, notable differences in accounting should remain. Canada is a special case concerning the context variables. Compared to the UK and Germany, the welfare-state type, the legal system and the financial system are not correlated in all respects. Canada is, therefore, the control check of our argument, which isolates and substantiates the influence of the societal motives and values emanating from the welfare-state type on accounting regulation.

### 10.4.1 Accounting requirements in the UK and Germany

In the UK accounting is predominantly used to provide corporate constituencies with decision-useful information, as Chapter 4 shows. The overriding principle for the preparation of accounts is the requirement to present a 'true and fair view' of the company's prospects, with a strong focus on the information needs of investors (Walton 1993). This principle is consistent with the prevailing opinion that the sophisticated information needs of investors also satisfy the requirements of other stakeholders. The 'true-and-fair-view' principle is relevant for the preparation of all types of financial accounts, and the concept of unbiased representation applies to single and group accounts. Financial accounts in the UK, therefore, have a clear information purpose, while single accounts have only some relevance for the calculation of the distributable company profit. Owing to the once very liberal approach to accounting regulation, a strong professionally organised accounting sector developed in the UK (Nobes 2004). The profession assumes responsibility for adopting and enforcing accounting standards, which leaves the accounting sector to virtual self-regulation. Thus, necessary adjustments are specified not by state institutions but by authoritative guidelines of professional bodies. The state keeps out of intervening in distributional issues, but is interested in market efficiency and in enabling a basis for efficient contracting.

In Germany the priority in accounting is given to determine distributable income. German company law refers directly to financial accounts for the calculation of dividends and other payouts. The mandatory accounting rules to calculate the distributable profit are designed according to the prudence principle, which the legislator introduced with the intention to limit the distribution of dividends from capital to protect mainly creditors (Eierle 2005). The 'true-and-fair-view' concept plays only a subordinate role, which is also expressed in the higher relevance of single accounts compared with group accounts. For a considerable time the accounting rules that applied to group accounts were based on the same standards as single accounts. The two types of accounts thus tended not to differ with regard to content (Zimmermann et al. 2008a). However, historical developments as described in Chapter 4 have led to a hybridisation of the German accounting system. Group accounts now have a clear informational purpose and focus on the information desires of investors. The rules have been decoupled from the rules for single accounts in order to mitigate the (informational) drawbacks of the prudence principle. With the hybridisation of the accounting regulation, allocative (efficiency) and distributive (preserving) aspects of accounting now co-exist in Germany. The hybridisation of sets of rules accompanied also a hybridisation in the organisation of standard-setting. While the rules for single accounts are still set by state authorities, standard-setting for group accounts has been delegated to the accounting profession, which in former times played only a minor role.

### 10.4.2 Preliminary findings

The UK, classified as residual welfare state, resembles by and large the ideal type of accounting regulation hypothesised for residual welfare states. That is, the dominant regulative function of accounting is enabling rather than preserving. The informational role of accounting is central, owing to the dominance of the 'true-and-fair-view' principle. The integral acceptance of and convergence to IFRS described in Chapter 4 also confirms this perspective. Thus the efficiency of (capital) markets is in the foreground. A balancing of interests is not intended by the UK accounting regulation. Corporate constituencies cannot rely on implicit protection mechanisms but must protect their claims on the basis of individual contracts. Analogously, group accounts constitute the societally important sets of accounts. The degree of state intervention in accounting is traditionally rather low, as accounting standards have been set by private experts. The legislator has always tried to keep the influence of accounting to a minimum, apart from intervention due to interference from the EU.

In Germany state involvement in accounting is more comprehensive, which is in line with the societal motives and values of institutional welfare states. The regulative aim of accounting is of a preserving nature, and the balancing of interests by distribution is a primary aim of accounting regulation. Moreover, the socially relevant parts of accounting, which are concerned with distributional issues, are derived from the political process and have legal backing. Even though the informational role of accounting has increased in importance in recent years, the distributional aspects of accounting are still fundamental to accounting in Germany. The main function of accounting is still the balancing of interests. Therefore, single accounts are the more important set of accounts societally. This is also borne out by the organisation for standard-setting. While standard-setting for group accounts has been delegated to private actors, standard-setting for single accounts remains at the state level.

These findings argue not only for a hypothetical but also for an empirical relationship between accounting regulation and the welfare-state type. More precisely, the regulative aim of accounting and the preferred method of standard-setting are related to the prevalent welfare-state type, which determines the degree of state intervention.

### 10.4.3 Additional analysis: Canadian accounting regulation

The UK and Germany exhibit typical characteristics: welfare state type, legal system and financial system display the usual correlation. Like other Anglo-Saxon countries, Canada belongs to the common-law group, but it differs from them with regard to its financial system. Demirguc-Kunt and Levine (1999) as well as Calmès (2004) show that from the 1970s until the early 1990s bank loans were the main external source of finance for Canadian companies. Since then, the Canadian financial system has undergone structural changes and has become more market-based. The market share of loans, although still meaningful, has declined, and banks have changed their traditional operations by offering financial instruments that are closer to direct market financing. Nevertheless, the banking sector still has major relevance for corporate financing, as Canadian banks have kept their role as financial intermediaries (Calmès 2004).

The make-up of the financial system would suggest that Canadian accounting regulation resembles the accounting system of bank-based countries (e.g., France or Germany) rather than that of market-based countries (e.g., the UK or the US). However, Canada follows the Anglo-Saxon accounting philosophy (Baylin et al. 1996). The early development of Canadian accounting practices is based mainly on the British accounting tradition. Since the 1920s, US accounting has exerted a strong influence on Canadian GAAP owing to the increasing economic relationship between both countries, and since the 1970s the Canadian standard-setter has also considered IAS issued by the IASC in developing new and revaluating existing Canadian standards. This influence contributes to the view that Canadian accounting standards are seen as most suitable for stakeholders of larger listed companies and primarily focus on investor rather than on creditor needs (Campbell 1984; Rennie and Senkow 2009).

Scott (2009) notices that the existing Canadian GAAP have been developed against a background of the efficient capital market hypothesis, and they pursue to provide relevant information to these markets. This is supported by the preference for substance over form, which should improve the fair presentation of companies and decision-usefulness of accounting information (Nobes 2004). In line with the emphasis on market efficiency is the fact that the distribution of company profits relies on solvency tests. The solvency tests required by Canadian company law neither build on a GAAP test, nor is there any reference made by the legislator to specific accounting methods that should be used (KPMG 2006). Accordingly, accounting and the distribution of company profits are completely decoupled in Canada. Further, consolidated accounts have long been accepted practice in Canada, while single accounts are virtually non-existent.

Taken together, the focus of accounting in Canada lies on providing decision-useful information about the economic entity to safeguard capital market efficiency. Payout issues of the legal entity are not addressed, and conflicts of interests between corporate constituencies are not balanced by accounting. Therefore it is the responsibility of the individuals to negotiate individual contracts to protect their claims. This shows that, first and foremost, Canadian accounting regulation follows an enabling approach. This stands, however, in contrast to the make-up of the Canadian financial system and the (usual) implication for accounting regulation. The financial system would imply, rather, an accounting system that is more strongly oriented towards the accounting requirements of creditors than of investors.

Instead, the welfare-state type has a stronger influence on accounting regulation. The regulative approach of accounting in Canada is congruent with the prevalent welfare-state type, namely the residual welfare state. This shows not only that the effect of the welfare-state type on accounting regulation can be isolated from other explanatory variables but also that societal motives and values really matter for accounting regulation.

## 10.5 Conclusion

Differences in the regulation of accounting persist. They are based on different motives underpinning accounting and different degrees of state intervention. Both can be linked to the welfare state as an emanation of the societal will. Generally, two types of welfare state can be distinguished: the residual and institutional welfare state. The types of welfare state can be regarded as different emanations of the societal will, from which different demands for state intervention and the legitimised supply of state regulation derive. They account for different forms and functions of policies as well as intensities of state intervention.

Accounting does not only serve as a capital market instrument; its function goes beyond the mere protection of market efficiency. Other regulatory aims can be pursued, which largely concern distributional issues. In this regard, the function of accounting extends to the balancing of interests between corporate constituencies. This differentiation made it possible to distinguish between the regulatory functions of accounting by reference to an enabling (allocation efficiency) and a preserving accounting function (balancing of interests).

On the basis of the social motives and values immanent in the types of welfare state, the regulatory functions of accounting can be theoretically and empirically assigned to the two welfare-state types. Besides explaining the underlying intention of accounting in welfare states, this approach explains also how claim allocation takes place, which set of account is societally important and the degree of state influence on the regulation of the societally important set of accounts. The explanations of these issues also help to explain the process of convergence and the persistence of differences between countries.

# Part V
# Conclusion

Accounting is more than just a technical matter. It is an important activity for the functioning of businesses and markets; it is an essential ingredient for our overall welfare. Over time, different constellations of accounting regulation have developed in OECD countries: countries with a Continental European imprint traditionally relied on extensive legal and hierarchical regulation dominated by governmental actors, and Anglo Saxon countries featured more collaborative governance modes – that is, a type of regulation in which private actors (most prominently private standard-setters and other professional organisations) were embedded in the regulatory frameworks. Over the last two decades national accounting regimes have experienced international harmonisation. Chapter 2 showed the accounting revolution for group accounts of listed companies and the advent of an internationally harmonised set of standards. Today the IFRS – issued by the transnational IASB – are the mandatory set of rules for group accounts in over 90 countries; listed companies around the world prepare their consolidated accounts in compliance with this single set of international rules. With its focus on unbiased representation, they mark a shift in content of accounting rules, not only in their governance, particularly for countries that had formerly relied on a strong state, such as France, Germany or Japan.

However, the 'IFRS revolution' is not a total one: single accounts prepared on the basis of prudent national GAAPs are still a central element of the accounting model of Continental European countries. For them, the calculation of corporate payouts is still an important role of accounting, and for this purpose standard-setting remains state-driven. The extent of professional self-regulation increases only where accounting is used for the supply of information. This also holds for the issue of internationalisation. The conclusion of Part II was that accounting for group accounts of listed companies has converged, but also that some differences in the worldwide accounting landscape persist. The outcome is a hybridisation of accounting regulation.

Parts III and IV showed that the more recent developments are not random but can be explained by causal chains. In a world free of institutions and transaction costs there should be no differences between national accounting regimes. In this case changes in the constellation of accounting regulation should be explained solely by reactions to exogenous developments. In reality, institutions matter, and institutions are not similar across countries. As existing institutions shape patterns of change, history matters. This induces path dependencies that explain why national peculiarities persist even when economic factors suggest convergence of economic systems. The literature has identified several causes of path dependencies, including switching costs, the existence of local or multiple equilibriums, rent-seeking of agents as well as complementarity and consistency of properties of economic or societal systems. The explanatory approach used in this book suggests that the recent changes to accounting systems can be explained as follows. Economic agents react to exogenous 'shocks' such as globalisation. This leads to changes in the national accounting systems. Bounded rationality suggests that these changes are motivated by mimicking, normative pressure or coercion. When reconfiguring institutions, existing national arrangements matter, as they have a bearing on agents' decisions. The consequence is that the exogenous 'shocks' have different consequences for different national systems, which are determined by the existing institutional frameworks.

Summarising our findings from Parts III to IV, there are two major conclusions for the hybridisation of accounting. Based on the theory of institutional learning, our first conclusion is that generic driving forces such as globalisation, scandals and crises as well as normative ideas generally contribute to a convergence of accounting systems as economic actors try to adapt to the new global challenges. This explains why some elements of accounting regulation converged fairly quickly. However, it is also observable that other elements in accounting regulation did not. Our second conclusion is that driving forces are moderated by country-specific institutional frameworks, which still differ across nation states. These frameworks, in terms of the national legal and financial system and the prevalent social values, have an impact on the decisions of economic actors in regards to system change, as the institutional structures shape the regulatory demands of actors within the system. Chapter 11 presents the conclusions for the developments of accounting regulation in greater detail.

# 11
# The Hybridisation of Accounting

## 11.1 Global convergence from triggering events

According to our first conclusion, generic driving forces such as globalisation, corporate crises and network structures contribute to a convergence of accounting systems. In chapters 5 to 7 we showed how isomorphic pressure explains why accounting regulation for listed group accounts has converged during the last decades. In particular, we looked at three driving forces and assessed how they contribute to the emergence of convergence. We identified three types of isomorphism driving convergence: coercive, mimetic and normative.

### 11.1.1 Coercive isomorphism triggered by financial globalisation

The coercive aspect was discussed in Chapter 5, where we showed that competitive pressures, initiated by financial globalisation, are an important trigger for the changes in accounting regulation. Globalisation has altered the shape of markets and curtailed the scope for state intervention. Since the 1980s companies have taken advantage by doing business outside their country of incorporation, and they have implemented economies of scale and experienced the positive effects of diversification. Global expansion has increased capital needs, which could be met only by raising funds outside domestic markets. Moreover, advances in information technology such as the automation of trading processes, have facilitated securities trading around the world and increased the integration of capital markets. These developments have had a significant influence on the demand for and supply of financial reports. Investors, companies and national regulators all have an interest in the diffusion of comparable, high-quality accounting standards such as the IFRS or the US GAAP. Capital suppliers demand information accounting in order to be able to use financial reports as a device for entry and exit investment strategies. And, very importantly, international investors need a high transparency and standardised financial reports to lower analysis costs.

Competition for funds put coercive pressure on firms to fulfil equity investors' demands for information. Companies began to model their accounting systems on the systems of other companies that had been successful in raising capital. Where this was not immediately possible, the preparers of financial reports lobbied for information-accounting sets of rules to reduce their cost of capital and transaction costs. The large stock exchanges have supported and propelled the move to information accounting out of their own interest to increase liquidity on the markets that they organise. Some segments such as the AIM at the LSE began to require companies to prepare financial reports on the basis of international standards early on, to make their markets more liquid and thus more attractive to the supply and demand for funds alike. The pressure to accept information-accounting sets of rules also extended to regulatory authorities. They are interested in strengthening the national capital market and in supporting firms in the international competition to increase countries' welfare. The changes in accounting regulation stemming from pressures of financial globalisation are a form of coercive isomorphism which has led to a global convergence of accounting regulation. This point was underscored in Chapter 5 by a globalisation index that demonstrated the concurrence of globalisation and accounting harmonisation.

### 11.1.2 Mimetic isomorphism triggered by scandals and crises

Chapter 6 showed that accounting scandals and corporate crises are an important driver of change and convergence in accounting regulation. Crises and scandals occur – more or less frequently – in many countries, and their impact on the well-being of societies can have either national or international consequences. In many cases crises and scandals are triggering events that reveal deficits of regulatory systems and raise uncertainty about the best way to respond to these events. Generally speaking, scandals and crises initiate mimicking, which is a process of regulatory learning from others. Chapter 6 highlights that the learning process from national and international crises and scandals furthered convergence between national accounting systems, and convergence is explained by the mimicry behaviour of national regulators. In times of crisis, as Chapter 6 showed, regulators usually imitate elements of other accounting systems because they are uncertain about the quality of their own. Japan, for instance, adapted its regulatory system to international best practice after crises in the late 1970s and 1990s. The Japanese regulator introduced mandatory group accounts as well as information-accounting requirements and finally established a private standard-setter, the ASBJ, which develops accounting standards in line with international standards such as IFRS or US GAAP. The adaptations took place in the style of Anglo-Saxon accounting practices. Similar mimetic changes, beginning with KonTraG in 1998, occurred in Germany after the financial system had been shaken by a series of accounting scandals around the 1990s.

Both examples show accounting convergence as an outcome of mimetic regulatory learning. However, the most striking evidence for convergence through mimetic isomorphism in our country sample is the 'diffusion' of a US regulatory innovation: the Sarbanes-Oxley Act. The Act was a role model for improvements of corporate governance and amendments to capital market regulations in almost all the sample countries. In general, Chapter 6 highlights the fact that crises and scandals trigger institutional learning through mimetic behaviour by regulators; an increasing similarity between national regulatory systems ensued. This type of behaviour has its limits: the global financial crisis, which began in 2007, shows that learning from others reaches its limits when the crisis is acted out on a global scale. In such a case, mutual regulatory learning does not happen, as national solutions cannot simply be transferred to an international level.

### 11.1.3 Normative isomorphism triggered by networks

Chapter 2 showed the diffusion of IFRS as global standards for accounting of capital market firms. The diffusion comes with the dissemination of two overarching normative ideas in accounting regulation: first, financial accounting should be information-oriented in such a way that it serves the efficiency and integration of (capital) markets; and second, standard-setting for financial accounting should be professionally self-regulated. These two ideas resemble, broadly speaking, the Anglo-Saxon approach to accounting regulation. The diffusion of IFRS thus describes an outcome of normative isomorphism, the adaptation to a new regulative idea. As is argued in Chapter 7, the process of normative change is mediated by networks through which normative pressure is exerted. We showed that the accounting profession initiated the normative pressure, which was then reinforced by building an effective network of professionals who articulated their opinions. The accounting profession was instrumental in establishing the IASC as the linchpin for transnational accounting regulation. The eventual emergence of transnational standards made it possible to realise economic self-interest and was at the same time a protective measure to secure the profession's influence on accounting regulation, which has a significant impact on the supply of their services.

The network analysis in Chapter 7 also showed that the development of the network took its time. The IASC, or rather the profession, had to establish relationships to legitimising actors to become effective in disseminating their ideas about accounting standard-setting and to gain acceptance as the transnational standard-setter. At the international level, the IASC's successor managed to gain acceptance for its ideas from pertinent actors such as IOSCO or EFRAG. At the national level, the dichotomy of the two archetypes in accounting regulation was dissolved in countries with a Continental European tradition of accounting regulation. Furthermore, the link between the national and international levels of accounting regulation changed. The direct link between national accounting associations and the transnational standard-setting institution was replaced by a direct link to state actor or those that are close to the state actors: that is, the respective national standard-setting body (for consolidated accounts). The engagement with partners from the national scene with stronger legitimising properties strengthened the IASB's effectiveness. The changes in the relationship between actors in the network thus point to a process of social learning, which eventually culminated in the diffusion of IFRS. In this vein, the IASB network served as a mechanism that stimulated the national self-transformation and mediated change towards (policy) convergence in the long run.

To sum up, coercive, mimetic and normative pressures have had a continuing and pervasive effect, especially on the accounting regulation for larger, capital-market-oriented companies. Some of the pressures continue to exert an influence on accounting systems – for example, globalisation and networks – and others, such as accounting scandals and corporate crises, produce episodic changes. It becomes obvious that neither of the forces has exclusive explanatory power for convergence in accounting regulation. It was, rather, the interaction of all kinds of isomorphic pressure that challenged national standalone accounting solutions and forced them to react to these pressures. By adopting or converging to IFRS, the Anglo-Saxon paradigm of 'information accounting' has become the dominating paradigm for financial reporting at the global level.

## 11.2 The moderating effects of change in accounting regulation

Convergence is restricted to those parts of national accounting regulation that deal with information accounting. The reasons are the institutional frameworks in which accounting operates. Our second conclusion, drawn from Chapters 8 to 10, shows that the driving forces are moderated by country-specific institutional frameworks which still differ across countries. There is still variation in all accounting regulation that is not primarily concerned with providing information. Persisting variation is not just rigidity, as the institutional structures that explain the divergence are relatively stable over time.

The institutional frameworks contain elements to which existing accounting regulation is complementary. The frameworks therefore have an impact on the decisions of economic actors in regards to system changes in accounting, as the institutional structures shape the regulatory demands for certain features of accounting rule sets of actors within the system. Complementarities and system fit explain why there are only incremental changes in those parts of the accounting regulation that deal with functions other than the mere information function. Differences persist most visibly in the regulation of single accounts and non-listed companies. In the following, we summarise our evidence on the moderating effects of our examined institutional frameworks: the legal and financial systems and national values and ideas, encapsulated in the type of welfare state.

### 11.2.1 Influence of the legal system

The legal backing of equity investors is organised differently in OECD countries. Legislators use diverse legal instruments to mitigate conflicts in business relationships. Civil-law countries focus on protecting investors by giving them participation and monitoring rights in company law. By contrast, investor protection in common-law countries focuses on the disclosure of information to equity investors and relies on market forces. Here the legislator ensures supply of information by the provisions of securities law. Based on the rights stipulated by the respective laws, investors can use the options of voice or exit if they are dissatisfied with the performance of the company. Traditionally, investors in civil-law countries have a stronger voice opportunity and investors in common-law countries have a stronger exit opportunity.

As Chapter 8 showed, legal systems have changed over time, which is especially true for the legal system of civil-law countries. In civil-law countries, securities law, especially its mandatory disclosure provisions, have been expanded for listed entities. This expansion strengthened the exit opportunity and made it more similar to that of common-law countries. Such a move made the adoption of corresponding accounting rules necessary, and it supported the use of information accounting standards. Today these rules fit into the regulatory system of listed entities in civil-law countries. In this context the legal system had virtually no decelerating effect on the harmonisation of accounting standards for consolidated financial statements of listed firms.

However, we also showed that the situation is different for private entities, and for non-information issues of accounting, which are regulated through single accounts. The country-specific institutional protection mechanisms still have a moderating effect on the convergence of accounting rules. The standardised contracts provided by binding clauses from company law are supported by prudent accounting rules, which restrict payouts, maintain legal capital and support the long-term stability of companies. Prudent accounting rules set by the state are an essential detail of standard contracts. They emphasise the opportunity of investors to make themselves heard (voice option). The calculation of corporate payouts remains an important accounting function and a complementary element in civil-law countries. This is one important reason why the extent of professional self-regulation and the degree of internationalisation have not increased in this field. Only in common-law countries, where the exit option is the prevailing protection mechanism, is the legal system no obstacle to further change.

### 11.2.2 Influence of the financial system

The financial system of a country – or, more precisely, the persisting differences in financial systems between countries – is another important factor why accounting regimes have not fully converged. Countries can still be differentiated into market-based systems and bank-based systems. Different information asymmetries between the suppliers of capital and the company prevail, and thus accounting has a different function and preconception in the respective system type. In the market-based countries the focus of financial reporting is on reducing information asymmetries between outside investors and the management. Hence unbiased representation is the preconception of accounting rules. In contrast, owing to the different ownership structure and the dominant role of banks, the basic objective of accounting in bank-based economies is to support relationship-based financing. As a result of the prevailing form of financing in an economy, each system shows a specific configuration of different actors with dissimilar interests in the regulation of accounting.

Despite financial globalisation, our data presented in Chapter 9 do not point to a convergence of bank-based and market-based economies. Some indicators suggest that bank- and market-based economies are moving closer together, but we cannot speak of a convergence of the two systems. In market-based economies equity capital is still more important than debt capital, and debt raised on markets is more important than credit raised through banks. In bank-based systems the majority of the companies still rely on non-public debt finance. Banks remain the most important source of funds. Moreover, the number of listed companies per inhabitant stays relatively constant over time.

As a consequence, the financial systems remain a barrier to accounting harmonisation. Firms and stakeholders from bank-based systems do not demand information-accounting rule sets to the same extent as their counterparts in market-based economies. On the contrary, they need accounting rules that stabilise lending relationships. This contributes to an understanding of why the convergence of accounting regimes is limited to the regulation and reporting of listed groups. Chapter 9 provided evidence for three moderating effects: the different demands of investors and lenders in general (e.g., the asymmetric loss function of creditors and the information demand of shareholders); the closer relationship between debt holders and lending entities in bank-based economies; and the different demands of short-term and long-term investors.

### 11.2.3 Influence of national values and ideals

Legal and financial systems have important implications for the persistence of differences in accounting regulation. But both variables leave an explanatory gap concerning the (still) differing state involvement in accounting regulation. In particular, the different intensities and intentions of state intervention in accounting regulation cannot be fully understood in terms of legal and financial systems. In Chapter 10 we therefore introduced a new variable of a country's institutional framework into our explanatory model. National differences in the system of values and ideas, which shape differences in political institutions between countries, are used to explain the causality and evolution of differences between accounting systems in a more general way. We captured values and ideas by the type of welfare state, classified into a residual and an institutional type. Welfare-state types prove to be a good proxy for national values and indicate to what extent society demands and legitimises allocative and distributive actions by state actors. In this regard, welfare states also explain different degrees of state intervention.

To relate accounting to welfare states, the welfare-distributing roles of accounting were examined. We identified two regulatory functions of accounting: an enabling and a preserving function. The enabling function describes accounting's role in protecting the efficiency of (capital) markets and assisting individuals to protect themselves on the basis of accounting information. The preserving function highlights the ability to structure corporate relationships and to regulate distributional issues through accounting. By virtue of specific ideals and values encapsulated in the welfare state, the two regulatory functions of accounting can be theoretically and empirically assigned to the two types of welfare state. Institutional welfare states rank the role of accounting in balancing interests higher than its informational role. In comparison, residual welfare states emphasise information accounting as it improves allocation efficiency. The different intentions of accounting regulation explain why the societal importance of single and consolidated accounts differs between countries, as shown in Chapter 10.

More importantly, the inclusion of national values explains the causality for and persistence of some different modes of governance in the regulation of accounting: that is, different degrees of state intervention. Chapter 10 showed that the mode of governance and the purpose of accounting regulation are largely intertwined. While allocation efficiency is best supported by delegating the standard-setting task to private experts, the preserving function can only be suitably provided by a state authority. Only state actors are publicly legitimised to solve distributional conflicts between corporate constituencies, because the process of finding a conflict resolution presupposes finding a compromise between the diverging interests of corporate constituencies. Thus a societal perspective on accounting regulation also explains why different degrees of state intervention have occurred and might persist in the future as national systems of values and ideals remain fairly stable. Partial convergence can still be explained: from the perspective of institutional welfare states convergence occurs only in the area that is irrelevant for their regulatory impetus. That is, the regulation of group accounts can be delegated to a private transnational standard-setter such as the IASB, as they do not serve a distributional function.

The institutional framework of countries, represented by the financial and legal system and the type of welfare state, help to explain why national peculiarities in accounting persist throughout OECD countries. The institutional structure of countries is a barrier to global accounting harmonisation.

Figure 11.1 summarises the explanatory framework that we have used throughout this book to analyse and explain the recent changes in financial accounting regulation. The exogenous forces, globalisation, accounting scandals and crises as well as network structures put pressure on national solutions and expedite a convergence of the constellation of different

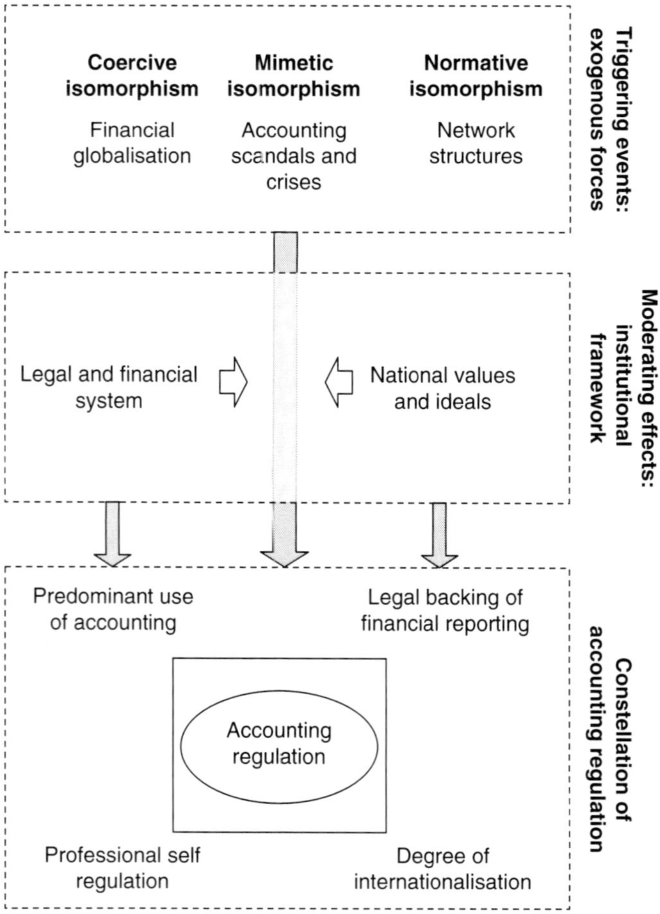


*Figure 11.1* The explanatory model for changes in accounting regulation
*Source*: Authors' own.

systems of accounting regulation. Thus, accounting regulation has become more similar throughout the OECD. However, this development is moderated by institutional frameworks, which still differ substantially between countries. This slows the process of convergence or blocks it totally in some areas. As long as differences in the institutional infrastructure of countries persist, it is unlikely that we will experience a global convergence of accounting systems.

# Notes

## 1 Explaining the Evolution of a New Accounting Framework

1. From a juridical point of view, a corporation is an incorporated legal entity that may be obliged to prepare (individual) accounts to inform outsiders. However, it is quite common for several individual companies to form corporate groups, usually led by a holding (or parent) company which exerts control over its subsidiaries, particularly when the holding company holds a significant proportion of shares of its subsidiaries. As a consequence, consolidated financial statements are very often more informative for outsiders than financial reports being prepared by the individual companies in the group as they are adjusted for intra-group transactions and prepared as if the economic group were a single company.

## 2 Information Accounting: The Global IFRS Revolution

1. At this point it will refrain from a more precise presentation of the interdependences and in particular the interdependences and mechanisms that lead to convergence in accounting standard-setting. Part III deals with these in detail.
2. In 1987 the Fédération des Experts Comptables Européens took over the responsibilities of the UEC and the Groupe d'Etudes.
3. As before, the office of the IASB remained in London. However, the umbrella organisation, the IASCF, was incorporated in the US state of Delaware. Taking into consideration that Delaware is often criticised for its loose legal requirements, especially with regard to corporate law, it is surprising that an organisation committed to issuing high-quality accounting standards should choose it as its corporate base.
4. In 1997 the conceptual framework was revised, and since then it has broadly corresponded to the adopted framework of the FASB.
5. Cf. public comment letters of the BIG-4 auditing firms on SEC Release No. 33–8831, available at www.sec.gov/comments/s7-20-07/s72007.shtml (accessed September 15, 2011).

## 3 Variations in Function: A Barrier to Harmonisation

1. As originally expressed by the architect Louis Sullivan in 1896.
2. The complex matters of employment are often regulated in a different legal setting. They need not be discussed in the context of accounting regulation.
3. In some cases the alignment of interests between managers and owners is affected by accounting outcomes: for instance, when managers receive a part of their income dependent on annual earnings. But these executive compensation contracts are privately negotiable and have little to do with company law.
4. For a comprehensive overview of existent insider trading regulations, see Abée (2012).
5. Theoretically six cases exist, but second-order dominations are ignored here.

## 4 The Transformation of Accounting Regimes: Six National Case Studies

1. Even though the 'true-and-fair-view' concept was formally adopted, the German legislator adjusted the concept to its own accounting tradition, resulting in a very different application from, for example, the UK (Ordelheide 1996).
2. The domination of the CNC over the CRC becomes clear with the statutory composition of the committee, where 8 out of 15 members are assigned by the CNC.
3. For a detailed description of the ANC's structure see Hoarau (2009).
4. The remaining four professional bodies are: the Institute of Chartered Accountants of Scotland (ICAS), the Institute of Chartered Accountants in Ireland (ICAI), the Chartered Institute of Management Accountants (CIMA) and the Chartered Institute of Public Finance and Accountancy (CIPFA).
5. For more detail see Roberts et al. (2005).
6. These efforts were related to the following bodies: the Committee on Accounting Procedure (CAP; 1936–59); and the Accounting Principles Board (APB; 1959–73).
7. For detail see Baylin et al. (1996).
8. At its foundation the institute was named the Dominion Association of Canadian Accountants (DACA); it has operated under its current name since 1951.

## 5 Coercive Isomorphism: Reporting Demands in a Globalised World

1. The United Nations Conference on Trade and Development (UNCDAT) speaks of transnational corporations (TNCs). However, the terms 'MNE' and 'TNC' are often used interchangeably in the literature, and are defined similarly in most cases (Dunning and Lundan 2008).
2. The first electronic stock market was the National Association of Securities Dealers Automated (NASDAQ), set up in 1971.
3. Transport of 1 ton of cargo over 1 sea mile.
4. Owing to country specific institutional arrangements (inducing path dependencies), persistence in nation-specific regulation for individual financial statements can be observed (Heine and Kerber 2002). This can be traced back to deviant demands of private and public firms and different economic functions of single and group accounts (Goncharov et al. 2009). These issues are discussed in Part IV.
5. Owing to limited data, not all proxies are available in every year. For the years 1970–1987 the growth value only consists of FDI growth rates.

## 6 Mimetic Isomorphism: Crisis as a Driver of Change and Convergence

1. Audits may occur because of specific reasons, at the demand of BaFin or in the context of spot checks. Spot checks of companies listed in the DAX, SDAX, MDAX or TecDAX are to be carried out once every four or five years by FERP. All other capital-market-oriented companies have to be audited once every eight or ten years.

2. See http://www.senat.fr/seances/s200303/s20030318/s20030318003.html, accessed on 20 May 2011.
3. See http://webarchive.nationalarchives.gov.uk, accessed on 18 May 2011.

## 7 Normative Isomorphism: The Role of International Networks for Convergence in Accounting Regulation

1. As in, e.g., Kern (2000) and Tews (2002), the terms policy diffusion and policy transfer are used interchangeably in this chapter.
2. Deloitte, Dever, Griffiths & Co. was renamed Deloitte, Plender, Griffiths & Co. in 1905.
3. Cf. Chapter 6.

## 8 Legal Backing of Equity Investment

1. The civil-law countries can be further subdivided into three distinct groups: Roman law (e.g., France, Italy, Spain), Germanic law (e.g., Germany, Greece, Japan) and Scandinavian law (e.g., Denmark, Finland, Sweden). These relatively broad categories are in some cases problematic and have been criticised by other scholars (Zetzsche 2004). However, in terms of the influence of the legal system on accounting regulation, the categories of common and civil law are suitable and helpful for the further analysis.
2. Hirschman added loyalty as a third concept alongside the exit and voice elements and connecting them. In his view the element of loyalty moderates the use of the exit option and shifts attention towards the expression of voice (Hirschman 1970). In this sense loyalty activates the shareholder's voice and prevents exit; hence it serves as an explanation for the change-over from one strategy to the other in a situation where exit would be a rational choice (Kostant 1999).
3. This is contrary to the index from Lele and Siems (2007), who change variables if other regulations have an influence on a variable. The index from Lele and Siems (2007) is available online: http://www.cbr.cam.ac.uk/pdf/Shareholder%20protection%20index%20references%205%20countries.pdf.
4. As will be discussed in Section 3 below, US securities law has been built up by the SEC and the US Supreme Court to a kind of compensatory federal corporate law (Hellgardt and Ringe 2009).
5. Data available online at: http://mba.tuck.dartmouth.edu/pages/faculty/rafael.laporta/working_papers/WhatWorksInSecuritiesLaws/securities%20for%20the%20web.xls.
6. For greater detail see, for example, Zimmermann et al. (2008a), as well as Gadinis and Jackson (2007) or Hammermeister and Zimmermann (2010).
7. We did not display the years 1991–1994 because there were no changes in regulation over this period.
8. In this context we specifically talk about delta convergence, meaning that securities law approaches the US model (Heichel et al. 2005; Werner 2008).

## 9 Financial Systems and Corporate Credit Arrangements

1. The importance of the *Hausbanken-System* is declining for MNE in Germany. However, the majority of SME in Germany still have a close relationship with a main bank (Schmidt 2007).

## 10 National Values and Political Systems

1. The criticism mostly concerns Esping-Andersen's typology approach, owing to its high relevance in welfare-state research (Arts and Gelissen 2002). His typology is criticised for its methodological aspects (e.g., Pitruzello 1999) as well as for the ignorance of the diversity and richness of social policies between countries (e.g., Leibfried 1992). However, a finer taxonomy would not be helpful for the development of our argument, as only two principal accounting functions are distinguished.

# References


Abée, S., *DieNeubestimmung des öffentlichen und privaten Interesses auf Kapitalmärkten* (Frankfurt am Main: Peter Lang, 2012).

AcSB, 'Global Positioning: The New Direction' (Available at: http://www.cica.ca/multimedia/Download_Library/Standards/Accounting/English/e_Strategic DirectionsBulletin1.pdf, 2006a).

AcSB, 'Public Companies and the Move to International Accounting: Getting There from Here' (Available at: http://www.acsbcanada.org/download.cfm?ci_id=33627&la_id=1&re_id=0, 2006b).

Ahmed, A. S., Billings, B. K., Morton, R. M. and Stanford-Harris, M., 'The Role of Accounting Conservatism in Mitigating Bondholder-Shareholder Conflicts over Dividend Policy and in Reducing Debt Costs', *Accounting Review* 77:4 (2002) 867–890.

Akerlof, G. A., 'The Market for "Lemons": Quality Uncertainty and the Market Mechanism', *Quarterly Journal of Economics* 84:3 (1970) 488–500.

Alber, J., 'Continuities and Changes in the Idea of the Welfare State', *Politics Society* 16:4 (1988) 451–468.

Alexander, G. J., Eun, C. S. and Janakiramanan, S., 'Asset Pricing and Dual Listing on Foreign Capital Markets: A Note', *Journal of Finance* 42:1 (1987) 151–158.

Ali, A. and Hwang, L.-S., 'Country-Specific Factors Related to Financial Reporting and the Value Relevance of Accounting Data', *Journal of Accounting Research* 38:1 (2000) 1–21.

Anderson, C. W. and Campbell Ii, T. L., 'Restructuring the Japanese Banking System: Has Japan Gone Far Enough?', *International Review of Financial Analysis* 9:2 (2000) 197–218.

Antzoulatos, A. A., Thanopoulos, J. and Tsoumas, C., 'Financial System Structure and Change: 1986–2005 Evidence from the OECD Countries', *Journal of Economic Integration* 23:4 (2008) 977–1001.

Armour, J., 'Legal Capital: An Outdated Concept?', in: H. Eidenmüller and W. Schön (eds.), *The Law and Economics of Creditor Protection: A Transatlantic Perspective* (The Hague: Asser Press, 2006).

Arts, W. and Gelissen, J., 'Three Worlds of Welfare or More? A State-of-the-Art Report', *Journal of European Social Policy* 12:2 (2002) 137–158.

Accounting Standards Board of Japan, 'The ASBJ and the IASB Announce Tokyo Agreement on Achieving Convergence of Accounting Standards by 2011' (Available at: https://www.asb.or.jp/asb/asb_e/asbj/pressrelease/pressrelease_20070808_e.jsp, 2007).

Baker, C. R. and Barbu, E. M., 'Trends in Research on International Accounting Harmonization', *The International Journal of Accounting* 42:3 (2007) 272–304.

Ball, R., 'Infrastructure Requirements for an Economically Efficient System of Public Financial Reporting and Disclosure', in: R. E. Litan and R. Herring (eds.), *Brookings: Wharton Papers on Financial Services* (Washington: Brookings Institution Press, 2001).

Ball, R., 'International Financial Reporting Standards (IFRS): Pros and Cons for Investors', *Accounting & Business Research* 36 (2006) 5–27.

Ball, R., 'Market and Political/Regulatory Perspectives on the Recent Accounting Scandals', *Journal of Accounting Research* 47:2 (2009) 277–323.

Ball, R., Kothari, S. and Robin, A., 'The Effect of International Institutional Factors on Properties of Accounting Earnings', *Journal of Accounting and Economics* 29 (2000) 1–51.

Ball, R. and Shivakumar, L., 'Earnings Quality in UK Private Firms: Comparative Loss Recognition Timeliness', *Journal of Accounting and Economics* 39:1 (2005) 83–128.

Barreto, I. and Baden-Fuller, C., 'To Conform or to Perform? Mimetic Behaviour, Legitimacy-Based Groups and Performance Consequences', *Journal of Management Studies* 43:7 (2006) 1559–1581.

Barth, M. E., *Research, Standard Setting, and Global Financial Reporting* (Hanover, MA: New Publishers, 2007).

Barth, M. E., Landsman, W. R. and Lang, M. H., 'International Accounting Standards and Accounting Quality', *Journal of Accounting Research* 46:3 (2008) 467–498.

Baskerville, R. F., 'Hofstede Never Studied Culture', *Accounting, Organizations & Society* 28:1 (2003) 1–14.

Basu, S., 'The Conservatism Principle and the Asymmetric Timeliness of Earnings', *Journal of Accounting & Economics* 24:1 (1997) 3–37.

Basu, S., 'Discussion of "Conditional and Unconditional Conservatism: Concepts and Modeling" ', *Review of Accounting Studies* 10:2/3 (2005) 311–321.

Basu, S. and Waymire, G. B., 'Recordkeeping and Human Evolution', *Accounting Horizons* 20:3 (2006) 201–229.

Baylin, G., MacDonald, L. and Richardson, A. J., 'Accounting Standard-Setting in Canada, 1864–1992: A Theoretical Analysis of Structural Evolution', *Journal of International Accounting, Auditing and Taxation* 5:1 (1996) 113–131.

Beaver, W. H., 'What Sould Be the FASB's Objectives', *Journal of Accountancy* 141:1 (1973) 49–56.

Beaver, W. H. and Ryan, S. G., 'Conditional and Unconditional Conservatism: Concepts and Modeling', *Review of Accounting Studies* 10:2/3 (2005) 269–309.

Beck, T. and Demirgüç-Kunt, A., 'Financial Institutions and Markets across Countries and over Time: Data and Analysis', *World Bank Policy Research Working Paper* No. 4943 (2009).

Becker, F., *Kooperative und konsensuale Strukturen in der Normensetzung* (Tübingen: Mohr Siebeck, 2005).

Bekaert, G. and Harvey, C. R., 'Capital Markets: An Engine for Economic Growth', *The Brown Journal of World Affairs* 5:2 (1998) 33–53.

Benner, T., Reinicke, W. H. and Witte, J. M., 'Multisectoral Networks in Global Governance: Towards a Pluralistic System of Accountability', *Government and Opposition* 39:2 (2004) 191–210.

Bennett, C. J., 'What Is Policy Convergence and What Causes It?', *British Journal of Political Science* 21:2 (1991) 215–233.

Benos, E. and Weisbach, M. S., 'Private Benefits and Cross-Listings in the United States', *Emerging Markets Review* 5:2 (2004) 217–240.

Benson, H., 'The Story of International Accounting Standards', *Accountancy Magazine* 87:995 (1976) 34–39.

Benston, G. J., Bromwich, M., Litan, R. E. and Wagenhofer, A., *Worldwide Financial Reporting: The Development and Future of Accounting Standards* (Oxford: Oxford University Press, 2006a).

Benston, G. J., Bromwich, M. and Wagenhofer, A., 'Principles- versus Rules-Based Accounting Standards: The FASB's Standard Setting Strategy', *Abacus* 42:2 (2006b) 165–188.

Benston, G. J. and Hartgraves, A. L., 'Enron: What Happened and What We Can Learn from It', *Journal of Accounting and Public Policy* 21:2 (2002) 105–127.

Benzacar, K., 'IFRS: The Next Accounting Revolution', *CMA Management* 82:4 (2008) 26–30.

Beresford, D. R., 'Accounting and Disclosure', in: *An Unpublished Address to a Meeting of the Western Hemisphere Securities Authorities (quoted in Thorell and Whittington (1994)). Financial Accounting Standards Board* (1992).

Berglöf, E., 'A Note on the Typology of Financial Systems', in: K. Hopt and E. Wymeersch (eds.), *Comparative Corporate Governance: Essays and Materials* (Berlin: de Gruyter, 1997).

Berglöf, E. and Thadden, E.-L. v., 'Short-Term versus Long-Term Interests: Capital Structure with Multiple Investors', *The Quarterly Journal of Economics* 109:4 (1994) 1055–1084.

Berle, A. A. and Means, G. C., *The Modern Corporation and Private Property* (New York: Commerce Clearing House, 1932).

Bhimani, A., 'Mapping Methodological Frontiers in Cross-National Management Control Research', *Accounting, Organizations & Society* 24:4–5 (1999) 413–440.

Birkland, T. A., 'Learning and Policy Improvement after Disaster', *American Behavioral Scientist* 48:3 (2004) 341–364.

Born, K., *Rechnungslegung International, Einzel- und Konzernabschlüsse nach IAS, US-GAAP, HGB und EG-Richtlinien*, 3rd ed. (Stuttgart: Schäffer-Poeschel, 2002).

Botzem, S., *Standards der Globalisierung: Die grenzüberschreitende Regulierung der Unternehmensrechnungslegung als Pfadgestaltung* (Berlin: Freie Universität Berlin, Available at: http://www.diss.fu-berlin.de/diss/receive/FUDISS_thesis_000000016627, 2010).

Botzem, S. and Quack, S., 'Contested Rules and Shifting Boundaries: International Standard Setting in Accounting', in: *Discussion Paper SP III 2005-201* (Berlin: Wissenschaftszentrum Berlin für Sozialforschung, 2005a).

Botzem, S. and Quack, S., 'Contested Rules and Shifting Boundaries: International Standard Setting in Accounting', *Discussion Paper SP III 2005–2010* (2005b) 1–23, published in: S. Djelic, and K. Sahlin-Anderson (eds.), *Transnational Governance: Institutional Dynamics of Regulation* (Cambridge: Cambridge University Press, 2006) 266–286.

Bowker, G. C. and Star, S. L., *Sorting Things Out: Classification and Its Consequences* (Cambridge, MA: MIT Press, 2000).

Brackney, K. S. and Witmer, P. R., 'The European Union's Role in International Standards Setting: Will Bumps in the Road to Convergence Affect the SEC's Plans?', *CPA Journal* 75:11 (2005) 18–27.

Bradley, M., Desai, A. and Kim, E. H., 'Synergistic Gains from Corporate Acquisitions and Their Division between the Stockholders of Target and Acquiring Firms', *Journal of Financial Economics* 21:1 (1988) 3–40.

Brennan, G. and Buchanan, J. M., *The Power to Tax: Analytical Foundations of a Fiscal Constitution* (Indianapolis: Liberty Fund, 1980).

Brunsson, N. and Jacobsson, B., *A World of Standards* (Oxford: Oxford University Press, 2000).

Bryer, R., 'The Laws of Accounting in the Late Ninteenth Century Britain', *Accounting History* 3:1 (1998) 55–94.

Bundesverband der Deutschen Industrie (BDI): Außenwirtschafts-Report 04/2002.

Burkart, M. and Panunzi, F., 'Agency Conflicts, Ownership Concentration, and Legal Shareholder Protection', *Journal of Financial Intermediation* 15:1 (2006) 1–31.

Burt, R. S., *Structural Holes: The Social Structure of Competition* (Cambridge, MA: Harvard University Press, 1995).

Burt, R. S., 'Structural Holes and Good Ideas', *The American Journal of Sociology* 110:2 (2004) 349–399.

Busch, P. O. and Jörgens, H., 'The International Sources of Policy Convergence: Explaining the Spread of Environmental Policy Innovations', *Journal of European Public Policy* 12 (2005) 860–884.

Bush, G. W., Merkel, A. and Barrosso, J. M., 'Framework for Advancing Transatlantic Economic Integration between the United States and the European Union' (Available at: http://georgewbush-whitehouse.archives.gov/news/releases/2007/04/20070430-4.html, 2007).

Bushman, R. M., Engel, E. and Smith, A., 'An Analysis of the Relation between the Stewardship and Valuation Roles of Earnings', *Journal of Accounting Research* 44:1 (2006) 53–83.

Bushman, R. M., Piotroski, J. D. and Smith, A. J., 'What Determines Corporate Transparency?', *Journal of Accounting Research* 42:2 (2004) 207–252.

Busse, Matthias, 'Transaktionskosten und Wettbewerbspolitik', Hamburg: HWWA Discussion Paper No. 116. (2001).

Busse von Colbe, W., 'Accounting and the Business Economics Tradition in Germany', *European Accounting Review* 5:3 (1996) 413–434.

Calmès, C., 'Regulatory Changes and Financial Structure: The Case of Canada', *Schweizerische Zeitschrift für Volkswirtschaft und Statistik* 140:1 (2004) 1–35.

Camfferman, K. and Zeff, S. A., *Financial Reporting and Global Capital Markets: A History of the International Accounting Standards Committee, 1973–2000* (Oxford: Oxford University Press, 2007).

Campbell, J., 'An Application Protocol Analysis to the "Little GAAP" Controversy', *Accounting, Organizations and Society* 9:3–4 (1984) 329–342.

Cascini, K., 'The EU Has Accepted IAS for Listed Companies: Will the U.S. Follow?', *International Business and Economics Research* 7:4 (2008) 11–20.

Castles, F., 'Reflections on the Methodology of Comparative Type Constructions: Three Worlds or Real Worlds?', *Acta Politica* 36:3 (2001) 141–154.

Chandler, A. D., 'Managerial Enterprise and Competitive Capabilities', *Business History* 34:1 (1992) 11–41.

Cheffins, B. R., 'Does Law Matter? The Separation of Ownership and Control in the United Kingdom', *Journal of Legal Studies* 30:2 (2001) 459–484.

Cheffins, B. R., *Company Law: Theory, Structure, and Operation* (Oxford: Clarendon Press, 2006).

Cherry, P., 'Time for Common Accounting Standards', *CAmagazine* 141:3 (2008b) 16–17.

Choi, F. D. S. and Meek, G. K., *International Accounting*, 6th ed. (New Jersey: Pearson, 2008).

Choi, F. D. S. and Meek, G. K., *International Accounting* (New Jersey: Pearson, 2011).

Christensen, J. A. and Demski, J., *Accounting Theory: An Information Content Perspective* (Boston, MA: McGraw-Hill, 2003).

Chua, W. F. and Taylor, S. L., 'The Rise and Rise of IFRS: An Examination of IFRS Diffusion', *Journal of Accounting and Public Policy* 27:6 (2008) 462–473.

Coase, R. H., 'The Nature of the Firm', *Economica* 4:16 (1937) 386–405.

Coenenberg, A. D., *Jahresabschluss und Jahresabschlussanalyse, Betriebswirtschaftliche, handelsrechtliche, steuerrechtliche und internationale Grundsaetze – HGB, IFRS und US-GAAP*, 20th ed. (Stuttgart: Schäffer-Poeschel, 2005).

Coenenberg, A. D. and Marten, K.-U., 'Der Wechsel des Abschlußprüfers', *Der Betrieb* 46:3 (1993) 101–110.

Coffee, J. C., Jr., 'Convergence and Its Critics: What Are the Preconditions to the Separation of Ownership and Control?', *Columbia Law and Economics Working Paper No. 179* (Available at: http://ssrn.com/abstract=241782, 2000a).

Coffee, J. C., Jr., 'The Rise of Dispersed Ownership: The Role of Law in the Separation of Ownership and Control', *The Yale Law Journal Company* 111:1 (2001) 1–82. Published by: The Yale Law Journal Company, Inc.Stable. URL: http://www.jstor.org/stable/797515.

Coffee, J. C., Jr., 'Racing Towards the Top?: The Impact of Cross-Listings and Stock Market Competition on International Corporate Governance', *Columbia Law and Economics Working Paper No. 205* (Available at: http://ssrn.com/paper=315840, 2002).

Colasse, B. and Pochet, C., 'The Genesis of the 2007 *Conseil Natioinal de la Comptabilité*: A Case of Institutional Isomorphism?', *Accounting in Europe* 6:1–2 (2009) 25–57.

Colasse, B. and Standish, P., 'State versus Market: Contending Interests in the Struggle to Control French Accounting Standardisation', in: McLeay, S. and Riccaboni, A. (Ed.): *Contemporary Issues in Accounting Regulation* (Wales, Siena, Springer Science + Business Media, 2001) 1–39.

Cooke, T. E., 'The Evolution of Financial Reporting in Japan: A Shame Culture Perspective', *Accounting, Business & Financial History* 1:3 (1991) 251–277.

Cooke, T. E., 'The Influence of the Keiretsu in Japanese Corporate Disclosure', *Journal of International Financial Management & Accounting* 7:3 (1996) 191–214.

Cooke, T. E. and Wallace, O., 'Financial Disclosure Regulation and Its Environment: A Review and Further Analysis', *Journal of Accounting and Public Policy* 9:2 (1990) 79–110.

Cooper, D. J. and Sherer, M. J., 'The Value of Corporate Accounting Reports: Arguments for a Political Economy of Accounting', *Accounting, Organizations and Society* 9:3–4 (1984) 207–232.

Cooter, R. D. and Ginsburg, T., 'Leximetrics: Why the Same Laws are Longer in Some Countries than Others', *University of Illinois Law & Economics Research Paper No. LE03-012* (Available at: http://ssrn.com/abstract=456520,June 2003).

Covrig, V. M., Defond, M. L. and Hung, M., 'Home Bias, Foreign Mutual Fund Holdings, and the Voluntary Adoption of International Accounting Standards', *Journal of Accounting Research* 45:1 (2007) 41–70.

Crouch, C., *Capitalist Diversity and Change: Recombinant Governance and Institutional Entrepreneurs*, 1st ed. (Oxford: Oxford University Press, 2005).

Csigó, M., *Institutioneller Wandel durch Lernprozesse: Eine neo-institutionalistische Perspektive* (Wiesbaden: VS Verlag für Sozialwissenschaften, 2006).

Cumming, D. J. and MacIntosh, J. G., 'The Rationales Underlying Reincorporation and Implications Canadian Corporations', *International Review of Law and Economics* 22:3 (2002) 277–330.

Cyert, R. M. and March, J. G., *A Behavioral Theory of the Firm* (Englewood Cliffs, NJ: Prentice-Hall, 1963).

DAI-Factbook 2009: Statistiken, Analysen und Graphiken zu Aktionären, Aktiengesellschaften und Börsen (Frankfurt, M: Deutsches Aktieninstitut, 2009).

Daniels, P. W., Thrift, N. J. and Leyshon, A., 'Internationalisation of Professional Producer Services: Accountancy Conglomerates', in: P. Enderwick (ed.), *Multinational Service Firms* (London: Routledge, 1989).

Daske, H., Hail, L., Leuz, C. and Verdi, R., 'Mandatory IFRS Reporting around the World: Early Evidence on the Economic Consequences', *Journal of Accounting Research* 46:5 (2008) 1085–1142.

David, R. and Brierley, J. E. C., *Major Legal Systems in the World Today: An Introduction to the Comparative Study of Law*, 3rd ed. (London: Stevens, 1996).

Davies, P., *Introduction to Company Law* (Oxford: Oxford University Press, 2002).

De Lange, P. and Howieson, B., 'International Accounting Standards Setting and U. S. Exceptionalism', *Critical Perspective on Accounting* 17:8 (2006) 1007–1032.

Decker, F., 'Governance Beyond the Nation-State. Reflections on the Democratic Deficit of the European Union.', *Journal of European Public Policy* 9:2 (2002) 256–272.

Defliese, P. L., 'British Standards in a World Setting', in: R. Leach and E. Stamp (eds.), *British Accounting Standards: The First 10 Years* (Cambridge: Woodhead-Faulkner, 1981).

Delvaille, P., Ebbers, G. and Saccon, C., 'International Financial Reporting Convergence: Evidence from Three Continental European Countries', *Accounting in Europe* 2:1 (2005) 137–164.

Demirguc-Kunt, A. and Levine, R., 'Bank-Based and Market-Based Financial Systems – Cross-Country Comparisons', *Working Paper* (The World Bank, 1999).

Demski, J. S. and Christensen, J. A., *Accounting Theory – An Information Content Perspective* (Boston: Kluwer Academic Publishers, 2003).

Desai, M. A., Foley, C. F. and Hines, J. J. R., 'A Multinational Perspective on Capital Structure Choice and Internal Capital Markets', *Journal of Finance* 59:6 (2004) 2451–2487.

Devine, C. T., 'The Rule of Conversation Reexamined', *Journal of Accounting Research* 1:2 (1963) 127–138.

Dewing, I. P. and Russell, P. O., 'Regulation of UK Corporate Governance: Lessons from Accounting, Audit and Financial Services', *Corporate Governance: An International Review* 12:1 (2004) 107–115.

DiMaggio, P. J. and Powell, W. W., 'The Iron Cage Revisited: Institutional Isomorphism and Collective Rationality in Organizational Fields', *American Sociological Review* 48:2 (1983) 147–160.

Djelic, M.-L., *Exporting the American Model: The Post-War Transformation of European Business* (Oxford: Oxford University Press, 2001).

Djelic, M.-L. and Quack, S., 'Overcoming Path Dependency: Path Generation in Open Systems', *Theory and Society* 36:2 (2007) 161–186.

Dobler, M., 'Notes from Germany on Section 404', *Journal of Accountancy* 197:3 (2004) 16–17.

Dolowitz, D. P., 'British Employment Policy in the 1980s: Learning from the American Experience', *Governance* 10:1 (1997) 23–42.

Dolowitz, D. P. and Marsh, D., 'Who Learns What from Whom? A Review of Policy Transfer Literature', *Political Studies* 44:2 (1996) 343–357.

Domowitz, I., Glen, J. and Madhavan, A., 'International Cross-Listing and Order Flow Migration: Evidence from an Emerging Market', *Journal of Finance* 53:6 (1998) 2001–2027.

Dragneva, R. and Millan, E., 'Transposing the "True and Fair View" Concept in the Legislation of Hungary and Poland in the Context of EU Enlargement', *Review of Central and East European Law* 28:2 (2002) 183–209.

Drezner, D. W., 'Globalisation and Policy Convergence', *International Studies Review* 3:1 (2001) 53–78.

Dunning, J. H. and Lundan, S. M., *Multinational Enterprises and the Global Economy* (Cheltenham: Elgar, 2008).

Dutzi, A., *Der Aufsichtsrat als Instrument der Corporate Governance: Ökonomische Analyse der Veränderungen im Corporate-Governance-System börsennotierter Aktiengesellschaften* (Wiesbaden: Deutscher Universitäts-Verlag, 2005).

Easterbrook, F. H. and Fischel, D. R., 'Corporate Control Transactions', *Yale Law Journal* 91 (1982) 698–737.

Easterbrook, F. H. and Fischel, D. R., 'The Corporate Contract', *Columbia Law Review* 89:7 (1989) 1416–1448.

Easterbrook, F. H. and Fischel, D. R., *The Economic Strucure of Corporate Law* (Cambridge, MA: Harvard University Press, 1998).

Eberhartinger, E. L. E., 'The Impact of Tax Rules on Financial Reporting in Germany, France and the UK', *The International Journal of Accounting* 34:1 (1999) 93–119.

Eccles, T. and Holt, A., 'Financial Statements and Corporate Accounts: The Conceptual Framework', *Property Management* 23:5 (2005) 374–387.

Eierle, B., 'Differential Reporting in Germany– A Historical Analysis', *Accounting, Business and Financial History* 15:3 (2005) 279–315.

Eitzen, B. v., *Der Wirtschaftsprüfer im internationalen Umfeld. Eine statistische Untersuchung zum Berufstand des Wirtschaftsprüfers, Probleme bei seiner Internationalisierung sowie bei der Harmonisierung von Ausbildung, Rechnungslegung und Prüfung* (Freiburg, 1996).

El-Gazzar, S. and Pastena, V., 'Negotiating Accounting Rules in Private Financial Contracts', *Journal of Accounting & Economics* 12:4 (1990) 381–396.

Elkins, Z. and Simmons, B., 'On Waves, Clusters, and Diffusion: A Conceptual Framework', *The ANNALS of the American Academy of Political and Social Science* 598:1 (2005) 33–51.

Engel, E., Hayes, R. M. and Wang, X., 'The Sarbanes-Oxley Act and Firms' Going-Private Decisions', *Journal of Accounting & Economics* 44:1/2 (2007) 116–145.

Errunza, V. and Losq, E., 'International Asset Pricing under Mild Segmentation: Theory and Test', *The Journal of Finance* 40:1 (1985) 105–124.

Esping-Andersen, G., *The Three Worlds of Welfare Capitalism*, 1st ed. (Princeton, NJ: Princeton University Press, 1990).

Esping-Andersen, G., 'Towards a Post-Industrial Welfare State', *Internationale Politik und Gesellschaft* 51:3 (1997) 237–245.

Esping-Andersen, G. and Korpi, W., 'From Poor Relief to Institutional Welfare States: The Development of Scandinavian Social Policy', in: R. Erikson and E. J. Hansen (eds.), *The Scandinavian Model: Welfare States and Welfare Research: Welfare States and Welfare Research* (Armonk, NY: Sharpe, 1987).

EU, *Implementation of the IAS Regulation (1606/2002) in the EU and EEA* (Available at: http://ec.europa.eu/internal_market/accounting/docs/ias/ias-use-of-options_en.pdf, 2008).

Expert Panel on Securities Regulation, *Final Report and Recommendations* (Available at: http://www.expertpanel.ca/eng/documents/Expert_Panel_Final_Report_And_Recommendations.pdf, 2009).

Fama, E. F. and Miller, M. H., *The Theory of Finance* (New York: Holt Rinehart and Winston, 1972).

FASB and IASB, 'Memorandum of Understanding "The Norwalk Agreement"' (Available at: http://www.fasb.org/cs/BlobServer?blobkey=id&blobwhere=1175819018817&blobheader=application%2Fpdf&blobcol=urldata&blobtable=MungoBlobs, 2002).

Fearnley, S. and Beattie, V. A., 'The Reform of the UK's Auditor Independence Framework after the Enron Collapse: An Example of Evidence-Based Policy Making', *International Journal of Auditing* 8:2 (2004) 117–138.

Feldhoff, M., 'Staat und Rechnungslegung – eine regulierungstheoretische Perspektive', *Die Wirtschaftsprüfung* 47:15–16 (1994) 529–536.

Feltham, G. A. and Ohlson, J. A., 'Valuation and Clean Surplus Accounting for Operating and Financial Activities', *Contemporary Accounting Research* 11:2 (1995) 689–731.

Fields, T. D., Lys, T. Z. and Vincent, L., 'Empirical Research on Accounting Choice', *Journal of Accounting and Economics* 31:1–3 (2001) 255–307.

Fisher, J. and Bewsey, J., *The Law of Investor Protection*, 2nd ed. (London: Sweet & Maxwell, 2003).

Flora, P. and Heidenheimer, A. J., *The Development of Welfare States in Europe and America*, 1st ed. (New Brunswick, NJ: Transaction Books, 1981).

Flower, J., 'The Future Shape of Harmonization: The EU versus the IASC versus the SEC', *The European Accounting Review* 6:2 (1997) 281–303.

Flower, J., *European Financial Reporting: Adapting to a Changing World* (Basingstoke: Palgrave MacMillan, 2004).

Flower, J. and Ebbers, G., *Global Financial Reporting* (Houndmills: Palgrave, 2002).

Fogarty, T., Magnan, M. L., Markarian, G. and Bohdjalian, S., 'Inside Agency: The Rise and Fall of Nortel', *Journal of Business Ethics* 84:2 (2008) 165–187.

Franks, J. and Mayer, C., 'Corporate Control: A Comparison of Insider and Outsider Systems', *Working Paper* (London Business School, 1994).

Freeman, L. C., 'A Set of Measures of Centrality Based on Betweenness', *Sociometry* 40:1 (1977) 35–41.

Freeman, L. C., 'Centrality in Social Networks: Conceptual Clarification', *Social Networks* 1:3 (1979) 215–239.

Fülbier, R. U., Gassen, J. and Sellhorn, T., 'Vorsichtige Rechnungslegung– Theoretische Erklärung und empirische Evidenz', *Zeitschrift für Betriebswirtschaft* 78:12 (2008) 1317–1341.

Gadinis, S. and Jackson, H. E., 'Markets as Regulators: A Survey', *Southern California Law Review* 80:6 (2007) 1239–1382.

Gallhofer, S. and Haslam, J., 'Exploring Social, Political and Economic Dimensions of Accounting in the Global Context: The International Accounting Standards Board and Accounting Disaggregation', *Socio-Economic Review* 5:4 (2007) 633–664.

Garcia Lara, J. M. and Mora, A., 'Balance Sheet versus Earnings Conservatism in Europe', *European Accounting Review* 13:2 (2004) 261–292.

Garrido, P., Léon, Á. and Zorio, A., 'Measurement of Formal Harmonization Progress: The IASC Experience', *The International Journal of Accounting* 37:1 (2002) 1–26.

Giner, B. and Rees, W., 'On the Asymmetric Recognition of Good and Bad News in France, Germany and the United Kingdom', *Journal of Business Finance & Accounting* 28:9/10 (2001) 1285–1350.

Goncharov, I., Werner, J. R. and Zimmermann, J., 'Legislative Demands and Economic Realities: Company and Group Accounts Compared', *The International Journal of Accounting* 44:4 (2009) 334–362.

Gordon, W. D., 'A Critical Evaluation of Japanese Accounting Changes since 1997', *Working Paper* (University of Sheffield, School of East Asian Studies, Available at: http://wgordon.web.wesleyan.edu/papers/japacct.pdf,1999).

Gornik-Tomaszewski, S., 'Antecendents and Expected Outcomes of the New Accounting Regulation in the European Union', *Research in Accounting Regulation* 18:1 (2005) 69–103.

Goshen, Z., 'The Impact of Insider Trading Rules on Company Law', in: K. Hopt and E. Wymeersch (eds.), *Capital Markets and Company Law* (Oxford: Oxford University Press, 2003).

Gray, V., 'Innovation in the States: A Diffusion Study', *The American Political Science Review* 67:4 (1973) 1174–1185.

Grewe, T., *Professional Service Firms in einer globalisierten Welt: Eine strategische Analyse am Beispiel von Wirtschaftsprüfungsgesellschaften und Unternehmensberatungen*, Gabler ed. (Wiesbaden: Wissenschaft, Unternehmensführung und Controlling, Gabler Verlag/GWV Fachverlage GmbH, Wiesbaden, 2008).

Grey, J., 'Home-grown Accounting Scandals', *Canadian Business* 75:6 (2002) 32–34.

Grundfest, J., 'Securities Regulation', in: Newman, P. (ed.), *The New Palgrave Dictionary of Economics and the Law* (London: Macmillan, 1998).

Guay, W., 'Conservative Financial Reporting, Debt Covenants, and the Agency Costs of Debt', *Journal of Accounting & Economics* 45:2–3 (2008) 175–180.

Gwilliam, D. and Jackson, R. H. G., 'Creative Accounting: The UK Experience', in: M. Jones (ed.), *Fraud and International Accounting Scandals* (Chichester: John Wiley, 2011).

Haas, J. and Malang, T., 'Beziehungen und Kanten', in: C. Stegbauer and R. Häußling (eds.), *Handbuch Netzwerkforschung* (Wiesbaden: VS Verlag für Sozialwissenschaften, 2010).

Haas, P. M., 'Introduction: Epistemic Communities and International Policy Coordination', *International Organization* 46:1 (1992) 1–36.

Habermas, J., *Legitimation Crisis* (Boston: Beacon Press, 1973).

Hachmeister, D., *Wirtschaftsprüfungsgesellschaften im Prüfungsmarkt: eine ökonomische Analyse zur Konzentration auf dem Prüfungsmarkt und zur Entwicklung großer Prüfungsgesellschaften* (Munich: Schäffer-Poeschel, 2001).

Hackethal, A. and Schmidt, R. H., 'Finanzsystem und Komplementarität', in: H.-H. Francke, E. Ketzel and H.-H. Kotz (eds.), *Finanzmärkte im Umbruch* (Berlin: Duncker & Humblot, 2000).

Hackethal, A., Schmidt, R. H. and Tyrell, M., 'The Transformation of the German Financial System', *Revue D'Economie Politique* 117:4 (2006) 433–456.

Hail, L. and Leuz, C., 'International Differences in the Cost of Equity Capital: Do Legal Institutions and Securities Regulation Matter?', *Journal of Accounting Research* 44:3 (2006) 485–531.

Hall, P. A., 'Policy Paradigm, Experts and the State: The Case of Economic Policy Making in Britain', *Comparative Politics* 25:3 (1993) 275–296.

Hall, P. A. and Soskice, D., 'An Introduction to Varieties of Capitalism', in: P. A. Hall and D. Soskice (eds.), *Varieties of Capitalism: The Institutional Foundations of Comparative Advantage* (Oxford: Oxford University Press, 2001).

Haller, A., 'The Relationship of Financial and Tax Accounting in Germany: A Major Reason for Accounting Disharmony in Europe', *International Journal of Accounting* 27:4 (1992) 310–323.

Haller, A., 'Financial Accounting Developments in the European Union: Past Events and Future Prospects', *European Accounting Review* 11:1 (2002) 153–190.

Haller, A., Raffournier, B. and Walton, P., *Unternehmenspublizität im internationalen Wettbewerb* (Stuttgart: Schäffer-Poeschel, 2000).

Hammermeister, J.-H. and Werner, J. R., 'Conditional Conservatism, Debt Markets and Financial Structure: Further Evidence from the United Kingdom', *Working Paper* (University of Bremen, 2010).

Hammermeister, J.-H. and Zimmermann, J., 'Financial Reporting Demands in a Globalised World: The Harmonisation of Accounting Rules', *Sfb597 "Staatlichkeit im Wandel" – TranState Working Papers No. 125* (University of Bremen, 2010).

Hammermeister, J.-H. and Zimmermann, J., 'Die Rolle von Nationalstaaten auf OECD-Kapitalmärkten', in: M. Beisheim, T. Börzel, P. Genschel and B. Zangl (eds.), *Wozu Staat?: Governance in Räumen begrenzter und konsolidierter Staatlichkeit* (Baden-Baden: Nomos Reihe 'Weltpolitik im 21. Jahrhundert', 2011).
Hansmann, H. and Kraakman, R., 'The End of History for Corporate Law', *Georgetown Law Journal* 89:2 (2001) 439–469.
Healy, P. M. and Palepu, K. G., 'Information Asymmetry, Corporate Disclosure, and the Capital Markets: A Review of the Empirical Disclosure Literature', *Journal of Accounting and Economics* 31:1–3 (2001) 405–440.
Healy, P. M. and Palepu, K. G., 'The Fall of Enron', *Journal of Economic Perspectives* 17:2 (2003) 3–24.
Healy, P. M. and Wahlen, J. M., 'A Review of the Earnings Management Literature and Its Implications for Standard Setting', *Accounting Horizons* 13:4 (1999) 365–383.
Heichel, S., Pape, J. and Sommerer, T., 'Is There Convergence in Convergence Research? An Overview of Empirical Studies on Policy Convergence', *Journal of European Public Policy* 12:5 (2005) 817–840.
Heine, K. and Kerber, W., 'European Corporate Laws, Regulatory Competition and Path Dependence', *European Journal of Law and Economics* 13:1 (2002) 47–71.
Heiser, K., 'Can Capital Market Law Approaches Be Harmonised with Essential Principles of Company Law?', *European Business Law Review* 11:2 (2000) 60–82.
Hellgardt, A. and Ringe, W.-G., 'Internationale Kapitalmarkthaftung als Corporate Governance', *Zeitschrift für das gesamte Handelsrecht und Wirtschaftsrecht* 173:6 (2009) 802–838.
Hendriksen, E. S., *Accounting Theory*, 3rd ed. (Homewood: Irwin, 1977).
Henselmann, K. and Hofmann, S., 'Vivendi Universal (France, 2002)', in: K. Henselmann and S. Hofmann (eds.), *Accounting Fraud: Case Studies and Practical Implications* (Berlin: Erich Schmidt, 2010).
Herz, R. H. and Petrone, K. R., 'International Convergence of Accounting Standards – Perspectives from the FASB on Challenges and Opportunities', *Northwestern Journal of International Law and Business* 25:3 (2005) 631–659.
Hicks, A., *Social Democracy and Welfare Capitalism* (New York: Cornell University Press, 1999).
Hines, R. D., 'Financial Accounting: In Communicating Reality, We Construct Reality', *Accounting, Organizations and Society* 13:3 (1988) 251–261.
Hirschman, A. O., *Exit, Voice, and Loyalty: Responses to Decline in Firms, Organizations, and States* (Cambridge, MA: Harvard University Press, 1970).
Hitz, J.-M., 'The Decision Usefulness of Fair-Value Accounting – A Theoretical Perspective', *European Accounting Review* 16:2 (2007) 323–362.
Hoarau, C., 'Accounting in France', in: P. Walton, A. Haller and B. Raffournier (eds.), *International Accounting* (London: Thomson Business Press, 1998).
Hoarau, C., 'Frankreich', in: A. Haller, B. Raffournier and P. Walton (eds.), *Unternehmenspublizität im internationalen Wettbewerb* (Stuttgart: Schäffer-Poeschel, 2000).
Hoarau, C., 'The Reform of the French Standard-Setting System: Its Peculiarities, Limits and Political Context', *Accounting in Europe* 6:2 (2009) 127–148.
Hoffmann, S., 'Aktuelle Informationen zum BilMoG: Diskussion der handelsbilanzrechtlichen Kernpunkte im Rechtsausschuss des Deutschen Bundestags', *Zeitschrift für Corporate Governance* 4:1 (2009) 38–41.
Holzinger, K., Jörgens, H. and Knill, C., 'Transfer, Diffusion und Konvergenz: Konzepte und Kausalmechanismen', in: K. Holzinger, H. Jörgens and C. Knill

(eds.), *Transfer, Diffusion und Konvergenz von Politiken* (Wiesbaden: VS Verlag für Sozialwissenschaften, 2007).

Holzinger, K. and Knill, C., 'Causes and Conditions of Cross-National Policy Convergence', *Journal of European Public Policy* 12:5 (2005) 775–796.

Honda, E., 'Financial Deregulation in Japan', *Japan and the World Economy* 15:1 (2003) 135–140.

Hopwood, A. G., 'Some Reflections on the Harmonizing of Accounting within the EU', *European Accounting Review* 3:2 (1994) 241–253.

Hoshi, T. and Kashyap, A. K., *Corporate Financing and Governance in Japan: The Road to the Future* (Cambridge, MA and London: MIT Press, 2001).

Hudack, L. R. and McAllister, B. C., 'International Accounting Standards: A Status Report (1995)', *CPA Journal* 65:6 (1995) 54–57.

Hurrelmann, A., Leibfried, S., Martens, K. and Mayer, P., 'Die Zerfaserung des Nationalstaates: Ein analytischer Rahmen', in: A. Hurrelmann, S. Leibfried, K. Martens and P. Mayer (eds.), *Zerfasert der Nationalstaat? Die Internationalsierung politischer Verantwortung* (Frankfurt: Campus, 2008).

IASB, 'The ASBJ and the IASB Announce Tokyo Agreement on Achieving Convergence of Accounting Standards by 2011', *Press Release*, (August 2007).

IASCF, *Changes in the IASCF Constitution: Report of the IASC Foundation Trustees* (London: IASCF, 2005).

Ito, T. and Melvin, M., *Japan's Big Bang and the Transformation of Financial Markets* (Cambridge, MA: National Bureau of Economic Research, 1999).

Jaafar, A. and McLeay, S., 'Country Effects and Sector Effects on the Harmonisation of Accounting Policy Choice', *Abacus* 43:2 (2007) 156–189.

Jang, Y. S., 'The Expansion of Modern Accounting as a Global and Institutional Practice', *International Journal of Comparative Sociology* 46:4 (2005) 297–326.

Jansen, D., *Einführung in die Netzwerkanalyse: Grundlagen, Methoden, Forschungsbeispiele*, 3rd. rev. ed. (Wiesbaden: Verlag für Sozialwissenschaften, 2006).

Jayaraman, N., Shastri, K. and Tandon, K., 'The Impact of International Cross Listings on Risk and Return', *Journal of Banking & Finance* 17:1 (1993) 91–103.

Jensen, M. and Meckling, W., 'Theory of the Firm: Managerial Behavior, Agency Costs, and Ownership Structure', *Journal of Financial Economics* 3:4 (1976) 305–360.

Jesover, F. and Kirkpatrick, G., 'The Revised OECD Principles of Corporate Governance and Their Relevance to Non-OECD Countries', *Corporate Governance: An International Review* 13:2 (2005) 127–136.

Jetuah, D., 'Citigroup Lays Out IFRS-US GAAP Gulf', *Accountancy Age* (August 2007) 9.

Katz, M. L. and Shapiro, C., 'Network Externalities, Competition, and Compatibility', *American Economic Review* 75:3 (1985) 424–440.

Kern, K., *Die Diffusion von Politikinnovationen. Umweltpolitische Innovationen im Mehrebenensystem der USA* (Opladen: Laseke and Budrich, 2000).

Kerr, C., *The Future of Industrial Societies: Convergence or Continuing Diversity?* (Cambridge, MA: Harvard University Press, 1983).

Kikuya, M., 'International Harmonization of Japanese Accounting Standards', *Accounting, Business & Financial History* 11:3 (2001) 349–368.

Kilian, J.-P., *Rechnungslegung als Instrument des Gläubigerschutzes: Stabilität und Wandel im internationalen Vergleich* (Frankfurt am Main: Peter Lang, 2011).

Kirchhof, P., 'Gesetzgebung und private Regelsetzung als Geltungsgrund für Rechnungslegungspflichten?', *Zeitschrift für Unternehmens- und Gesellschaftsrecht* 29:4–5 (2000) 681–692.

Kleekämper, H., 'Aktuelle Entwicklungen beim IASC', *Betriebswirtschaftliche Forschung und Praxis* 47:4 (1995) 414–431.

Knill, C., 'Introduction: Cross-National Policy Convergence: Concepts, Approaches and Explanatory Factors', *Journal of European Public Policy* 12:5 (2005) 764–774.

Knoepfel, P. and Kissling-Näf, I., 'Social Learning in Policy Networks', *Policy and Politics* 26:3 (1998) 343–367.

Knoke, D. and Yang, S., *Social Network Analysis: Quantitative Applications in the Social Sciences*, 2nd ed. (Los Angeles: Sage Publication, 2008).

Konishi, T., 'Fraud by Certified Public Accountants in Japan and the United States', *Asian Journal of Criminology* 5:2 (2010) 99–107.

Korpi, W., 'Social Policy and Distributional Conflict in the Capitalist Democracies', *West European Politics* 3:3 (1980) 296–316.

Kostant, P. C., 'Exit, Voice and Loyalty in the Course of Corporate Governance and Counsel's Changing Role', *The Journal of Socio-Economics* 28:3 (1999) 203–266.

KPMG, 'Feasibility Study on Capital Maintenance– Main Report' (Available at: http://ec.europa.eu/internal_market/company/docs/capital/feasbility/study_en.pdf, 2006).

KPMG, 'Feasibility Study on an Alternative to the Capital Maintenance Regime Established by the Second Company Law Directive' (Available at: http://ec.europa.eu/internal_market/company/docs/capital/feasbility/study_en.pdf, 2008).

Krahnen, J. P. and Schmidt, R. H., 'Taking Stock and Looking Ahead: The German Financial System at the Crossroads?', in: J. P. Krahnen and R. H. Schmidt (eds.), *The German Financial System* (Oxford: Oxford University Press, 2004).

Küting, K. and Kaiser, T., 'Fair-Value-Accounting – Zu komplex für den Kapitalmarkt?', *Corporate Finance* 1:6 (2010) 375–386.

Kvist, J., 'Fuzzy Set Ideal Type Analysis', *Journal of Business Research* 60:5 (2007) 474–481.

La Porta, R., Lopez-De-Silanes, F. and Shleifer, A., 'Law and Finance', *Journal of Political Economy* 106:6 (1998) 1113–1155.

La Porta, R., Lopez-De-Silanes, F. and Shleifer, A., 'What Works in Securities Laws?', *Journal of Finance* 61:1 (2006) 1–32.

La Porta, R., Lopez-De-Silanes, F., Shleifer, A. and Vishny, R. W., 'Legal Determinants of External Finance', *Journal of Finance* 52:3 (1997) 1131–1150.

Lamb, M., 'The Relationship between Accounting and Taxation: The United Kingdom', *European Accounting Review* 5 (1996) 933–949.

Lamb, M., Nobes, C. and Roberts, A., 'International Variations in the Connections between Tax and Financial Reporting', *Accounting and Business Research* 28:3 (1998) 173–188.

Lee, G. A., 'Accounting in the United Kingdom', in: H. P. Holzer and D. T. Bailey (eds.), *International Accounting* (New York: Harper and Row, 1984).

Lee, I. B., 'Balancing and Its Alternatives: Jurisprudential Choice, Federal Securities Legislation and the Trade and Commerce Power', *Canadian Business Law Journal* 50:1 (2011) 95–128.

Leibfried, S., 'Towards a European Welfare State? Integrating Poverty Regimes into the European Community', in: S. Ferge and J. E. Kolberg (eds.), *Social Policy in a Changing Europe* (Boulder, CO: Westview, 1992).

Lele, P. P. and Siems, M. M., 'Shareholder Protection: A Leximetric Approach', *CBR Working Paper No. 324* (University of Cambridge, 2007).

Lenz, H., 'Accounting Scandals in Germany', in: M. Jones (ed.), *Fraud and International Accounting Scandals* (Chichester: John Wiley, 2011).

Leuz, C., 'The Role of Accrual Accounting in Restricting Dividends to Shareholders', *European Accounting Review* 7:4 (1998) 579–604.

Leuz, C., 'Different Approaches to Corporate Reporting Regulation: How Jurisdictions Differ and Why', *Accounting & Business Research* 40:3 (2010) 229–256.

Leuz, C., Deller, D. and Stubenrath, M., 'An International Comparison of Accounting-Based Payout Restrictions in the United States, United Kingdom and Germany', *Accounting & Business Research* 28:2 (1998) 111–129.

Leuz, C. and Wüstemann, J., 'The Role of Accounting in the German Financial System', in: J. P. Krahnen and R. H. Schmidt (eds.), *The German Financial System* (Oxford: Oxford University Press, 2004).

Levine, R. and Zervos, S., 'Stock Markets, Banks, and Growth', *American Economic Review* 88:3 (1998) 537–558.

Levitt, T., 'The Globalization of Markets', *Harvard Business Review* 61:3 (1983) 92–102.

Littleton, A. C., 'A Genealogy for "Cost or Market"', *Accounting Review* 16:2 (1941) 161–167.

Lodge, M., 'The Importance of Being Modern: International Benchmarking and National Regulatory Innovation', *Journal of European Public Policy* 12:4 (2005) 649–667.

Loft, A. and Humphrey, C., 'The Complex World of International Auditing Regulation', *QFinance: The Ultimate Financial Ressource* 2nd ed. (London: Bloomsbury, 2011) 271–274 (Available at: http://www.qfinance.com/auditing-best-practice/the-complex-world-of-international-auditing-regulation?).

Lück, W. and Holzer, H. P., 'Multinationale Wirtschaftsprüfungsgesellschaften', *Der Betrieb* 34:33 (1981) 1989–1993.

Luthardt, U. and Zimmermann, J., 'A European View on the Legitimacy of Accounting Procedures: Towards a Deliberative-Accountability Framework for Analysis', *Research in Accounting Regulation* 21:2 (2009) 79–88.

Maltby, J., 'The Origins of Prudence in Accounting', *Critical Perspectives on Accounting* 11:1 (2000) 51–70.

Mandler, U., 'Wirtschaftsprüfung im Umbruch: Harmonisierung der Rechnungslegung und Globalisierung der Unternehmensstrukturen', *Zeitschrift für Betriebswirtschaft* 64:2 (1994) 167–188.

Mandler, U., 'Theorie internationaler Wirtschaftspruefungsorganisationen: Qualitaetskonstanz und Reputation', *Die Betriebswirtschaft* 55:1 (1995) 31–44.

Mandler, U., 'Die Internationalisierung von Wirtschaftsprüfungsgesellschaften', in: F. Giesel and M. Glaum (eds.), *Globalisierung: Herausforderung an die Unternehmensführung zu Beginn des 21. Jahrhunderts* (Munich: Beck, 1999).

Manne, H. G., 'Our Two Corporation Systems: Law and Economics', *Virginia Law Review* 53:2 (1967) 259–284.

Marosi, A. and Massoud, N., 'Why Do Firms Go Dark?', *Journal of Financial & Quantitative Analysis* 42:2 (2007) 421–442.

Marten, K.-U., Quick, R. and Ruhnke, K., *Wirtschaftsprüfung: Grundlagen des betriebswirtschaftlichen Prüfungswesens nach nationalen und internationalen Normen*, 2nd ed. (Stuttgart: Schäffer-Poeschel, 2003).

Martinez-Diaz, L., 'Strategic Experts and Improvising Regulators: Explaining the IASC's Rise to Global Influence, 1973–2001', *Business and Politics* 7:3 (2005) 1–25.

Mau, S., 'Ungleichheits- und Gerechtigkeitsorientierung in modernen Wohlfahrtsstaaten: Ein Vergleich der Länder Schweden, Großbritannien und der Bundesrepublik Deutschland', *Discussion Paper FS-III 97-401* (Berlin: Wissenschaftszentrum Berlin, 1997).

McKinnon, J. L., 'Application of Anglo-American Principles of Consolidation to Corporate Financial Disclosure in Japan', *Abacus* 20:1 (1984) 16–33.

Mennicken, A. and Heßling, A., 'Welt(en) regulierter Zahlenproduktion zwischen Globalität und Lokalität: Reflexion zu globalen Standards in der Rechnungslegung und Wirtschaftprüfung', in: A. Mennicken and H. Vollmer (eds.), *Zahlenwerk: Kalkulation, Organisation und Gesellschaft* (Wiesbaden: VS Verlag für Sozialwissenschaft, 2007).

Merton, R. C., 'A Simple Model of Capital Market Equilibrium with Incomplete Information', *Journal of Finance* 42:3 (1987) 483–510.

Mittoo, U. R. and Zhang, Z., 'The Capital Sstructure of Multinational Corporations: Canadian versus U.S. Eevidence', *Journal of Corporate Finance* 14:5 (2008) 706–720.

Mizruchi, M. S. and Fein, L. C., 'The Social Construction of Organizational Knowledge: A Study of the Uses of Coercive, Mimetic, and Normative Isomorphism', *Administrative Science Quarterly* 44:4 (1999) 653–683.

Modigliani, F. and Miller, M. H., 'The Cost of Capital, Corporation Finance and the Theory of Investment', *American Economic Review* 48:3 (1958) 261.

Morgan, M. and Previts, G. J., 'The SEC and the Profession, 1934–84: The Realities of Self-Regulation', *Journal of Accountancy* 158:1 (1984) 68–80.

Moshirian, F., 'The Global Financial Crisis and the Evolution of Markets, Institutions and Regulation', *Journal of Banking & Finance* 35:3 (2011) 502–511.

Moxter, A., *Bilanzlehre Band 1: Einführung in die Bilanztheorie*, 3rd ed. (Wiesbaden: Gabler, 1984).

Müller-Stewens, G., Drolshammer, J. and Kriegmeier, J., 'Professional Service Firms: Branchenmerkmale und Gestaltungsfelder des Managements', in: G. Müller-Stewens, J. Drolshammer and J. Kriegmeier (eds.), *Professional Service Firms: Wie sich multinationale Dienstleister positionieren* (Frankfurt am Main: Frankfurter Allgemeine Buch, 1999).

Murinde, V., Agung, J. and Mullineux, A., 'Patterns of Corporate Financing and Financial System Convergence in Europe', *Review of International Economics* 12:4 (2004) 693–705.

Nachum, L., 'Does Nationality of Ownership Make Any Difference and, if so, under What Circumstances?: Professional Service MNEs in Global Competition', *Journal of International Management* 9:1 (2003) 1–32.

Newman, D. P., 'The SEC's Influence on Accounting Standards: The Power of the Veto', *Journal of Accounting Research* 19 (1981) 134–156.

Nicholls, C., 'The Characteristics of Canada's Capital Markets and the Illustrative Case of Canada's Legislative Regulatory Response to Sarbanes–Oxley', in: Task Force to Modernize Securities Legislation in Canada (ed.), *Canada Steps Up: Final Report* (Toronto: Task Force, Available at: http://www.tfmsl.ca, 2006).

Nicolaisen, D. T., 'A Securities Regulator Looks at Convergence', *Northwestern Journal of International Law & Business* 25:3 (2005) 661–686.

Niskanen, J., Kinnunen, J. and Kasanen, E., 'A Note on the Information Content of Parent Company versus Consolidated Earnings in Finland', *European Accounting Review* 7:1 (1998) 31–40.

Nobes, C. W., 'Towards a General Model of the Reasons for International Differences in Financial Reporting', *Abacus* 34:2 (1998) 162–187.

Nobes, C. W., 'On Accounting Classification and the International Harmonisation Debate', *Accounting, Organizations & Society* 29:2 (2004) 189–200.

Nobes, C. W., 'The Survival of International Differences Under IFRS: Towards a Research Agenda', *Accounting and Business Research* 36:3 (2006) 233–245.

Nobes, C. W. and Parker, R. H., '"True and Fair": A Survey of UK Financial Directors', *Journal of Business Finance & Accounting* 18:3 (1991) 359–375.

Nobes, C. W. and Parker, R. H., *Comparative International Accounting*, 9th ed. (Harlow: Prentice Hall, 2006).
Nobes, C. W. and Parker, R. H., *Comparative International Accounting*, 10th ed. (Harlow: Financial Times Prentice Hall, 2008).
Nobes, C. W. and Parker, R. H., *Comparative International Accounting*, 11th ed. (Harlow: Pearson, 2010).
Nobes, C. W. and Zeff, S. A., 'Auditors' Affirmations of Compliance with IFRS around the World: An Exploratory Study', *Accounting Perspectives* 7:4 (2008) 279–292.
Nöelke, A., 'Introduction to the Special Issue: The Globalization of Accounting Standards', *Business & Politics* 7:3 (2005) 1–7.
North, D. C., *Institutions, Institutional Change and Economic Performance* (Cambridge, MA: Cambridge University Press, 1990).
Nusbaumer, J., *The Services Economy. Lever to Growth* (Boston, MA: Kluwer, 1987).
Obstfeld, M. and Taylor, A. M., *Global Capital Markets: Integration, Crisis, and Growth* (Cambridge, MA: Cambridge University Press, 2004).
OEC/CNCC, *Developments in French Accounting and Auditing 1998* (Paris: Expert Comptable Média, 1999).
Oehr, T. and Zimmermann, J., 'Accounting and the Welfare State: The Missing Link', *Critical Perspectives on Accounting* 23:2 (2012) 134–152.
Oguri, T., 'Functions of Accounting and Accounting Regulation: Alternative Perspectives Based on Marxian Economics', *Critical Perspectives on Accounting* 16:2 (2005) 77–94.
Oguri, T. and Hara, Y., 'A Critical Examination of Accounting Regulation in Japan', *Accounting, Auditing & Accountability Journal* 3:2 (1990) 37–51.
Olivier, H., 'Challenges Facing the Accountancy Profession', *European Accounting Review* 9:4 (2001) 603–624.
Ordelheide, D., 'True and Fair View: A European and a German Perspective II', *European Accounting Review* 5:3 (1996) 495–506.
Ordelheide, D., 'Germany', in: S. McLeay (ed.), *Accounting Regulation in Europe* (Basingstoke: Macmillan, 1999).
Ordelheide, D., 'The Politics of Accounting: A Framework', in: C. Leuz, D. Pfaff and A. Hopwood (eds.), *The Economics and Politics of Accounting: International Perspectives on Research Trends, Policy, and Practice* (Oxford: Oxford University Press, 2004).
Osugi, K., 'Companies Act – Overview', in: *Fukuoka: Group for International Corporate Law* (Fukuoka: Kyushu University, 2010).
Parker, C., 'Reinventing Regulation within the Corporation', *Administration & Society* 32:5 (2000) 529–565.
Pellens, B., Fülbier, R. U., Gassen, J. and Sellhorn, T., *Internationale Rechnungslegung*, 8th rev. ed. (Stuttgart: Schäffer-Poeschel, 2011).
Perridon, L. and Steiner, M., *Finanzwirtschaft der Unternehmung*, 15th ed. (Munich: Vahlen, 2009).
Perry, J. and Nöelke, A., 'International Accounting Standard Setting: A Network Approach', *Business & Politics* 7:3 (2005) 1–32.
Perry, J. and Nöelke, A., 'The Political Economy of International Accounting Standards', *Review of International Political Economy* 13:4 (2006) 559–586.
Peters, H. R., *Wirtschaftssystemtheorie und Allgemeine Ordnungspolitik*, 4th ed. (Munich: Oldenbourg, 2002).
Pierson, P., *The New Politics of the Welfare State*, 1st ed. (Oxford: Oxford University Press, 2001).

Pitruzello, S., *Decommodification and the Worlds of Welfare Capitalism: A Cluster Analysis*, 1st ed. (Florence: European University Institute, 1999).

Pong, C. K. M. and Whittington, G., 'The Withdrawal of Current Cost Accounting in the United Kingdom: A Study of the Accounting Standards Committee', *Abacus* 32:1 (1996) 30–53.

Portes, A. and Yeo, S., *Think-net: The CEPR Model of a Research Network*, Center for Economic Policy Research (Available at: http://www.cepr.org/aboutcepr/cepr/cepr_think.pdf, 2001).

Posner, E. and Veron, N., 'The EU and Financial Regulation: Power without Purpose?', *Journal of European Public Policy* 17:3 (2010) 400–415.

Puxty, A. G., Willmott, H. C., Cooper, D. J. and Lowe, T., 'Modes of Regulation in Advanced Capitalism: Locating Accountancy in Four Countries', *Accounting, Organizations & Society* 12:3 (1987) 273–291.

Qi, Y. and Wald, J., 'State Laws and Debt Covenants', *Journal of Law & Economics* 51:1 (2008) 179–207.

Radebaugh, L. H., Gebhardt, G. and Gray, S. J., 'Foreign Stock Exchange Listinge: A Case Study of Daimler Benz', *Journal of International Financial Management and Accounting* 6:2 (1995) 158–192.

Radebaugh, L. H. and Gray, S. J., *International Accounting and Multinational Enterprises*, 5th ed. (New York: John Wiley & Sons, 2002).

Ramanna, K. and Sletten, E., 'Why Do Countries Adopt International Financial Reporting Standards?', in: *Harvard Business School Accounting & Management Unit Working Paper No. 09-102* (Available at: http://www.hbs.edu/faculty/Publication%20Files/09-102.pdf, 2009).

Raskop, J., *Der Deutsche Corporate Governance Kodex als Instrument zur Reduzierung der Kapitalkosten deutscher Publikumsaktiengesellschaften?: Eine institutionenökonomische Analyse im Spannungsfeld zwischen Markt, Organisation und Norm* (Bayreuth: Verlag PCO, 2004).

Reich, C. A., 'The New Property', *Yale Law Journal* 73:5 (1964) 733–787.

Rennie, M. D. and Senkow, D. W., 'Financial Reporting for Private Companies', *Accounting Perspectives* 8:1 (2009) 43–68.

Rhodes, R. A. W., 'Foreword', in: W. J. M. Kicker, E.-H. Klijn and J. F. M. Koppenjan (eds.), *Managing Complex Networks: Strategies for the Public Sector* (London: Sage, 1997).

Richardson, A. J., 'Regulatory Networks for Accounting and Auditing Standards: A Social Network Analysis of Canadian and International Standard-Setting', *Accounting, Organizations and Society* 34:5 (2009) 571–588.

Roberts, C., Weetman, P. and Gordon, P., *International Financial Accounting: A Comparative Approach*, 3rd ed. (Harlow: Prentice Hall, 2005).

Roberts, C. B., Salter, S. B. and Kantor, J., 'The IASC Comparability Project and Current Financial Reporting Reality: An Empirical Study of Reporting in Europe', *British Accounting Review* 28:1 (1996) 1–22.

Rodrigues, L. L. and Craig, R., 'Assessing International Accounting Harmonization Using Hegelian Dialectic, Isomorphism and Foucault', *Critical Perspectives on Accounting* 18:6 (2007) 739–757.

Rogers, M. E., *Diffusion of Innovations* (New York: Free Press, 1995).

Rosen, H. S. and Gayer, T., *Public Finance*, 8 th. ed. (New York: McGraw-Hill, 2008).

Rosenthal, U. and Kouzmin, A., 'Crises and Crisis Management: Toward Comprehensive Government Decision Making', *Journal of Public Administration Research & Theory* 7:2 (1997) 277–304.

Ruder, D. S., Canfield, C. T. and Hollister, H. T., 'Creation of World Wide Accounting Standards: Convergence and Independence', *Northwestern Journal of International Law & Business* 25:3 (2005) 513–588.

Rutz, D., *Strukturwandel im französischen Finanzsystem: Privatisierung und Strukturveränderungen auf den französischen Finanz- und Kapitalmärkten* (Frankfurt: Peter Lang, 1998).

Rybczynski, T. M., 'Industrial Finance System in Europe, U.S. and Japan', *Journal of Economic Behavior & Organization* 5:3–4 (1984) 275–286.

Samuels, J. M. and Piper, A. G., *International Accounting: A Survey* (London: Croom Helm, 1985).

Schaub, A., 'The Use of International Accounting Standards in the European Union', *Northwestern Journal of International Law & Business* 25:3 (2005) 609–629.

Schildbach, T., *Jahresabschluß und Markt*, 1st ed. (Berlin: Heidelberger betriebswirtschaftliche Studien, 1986).

Schildbach, T., *US-GAAP, Amerikanische Rechnungslegung und ihre Grundlagen*, 2nd ed. (Munich: Vahlen, 2002).

Schipper, K., 'Principles-Based Accounting Standards', *Accounting Horizons* 17:1 (2003) 61–72.

Schipper, K., 'The Introduction of International Accounting Standards in Europe: Implications for International Convergence', *European Accounting Review* 14:1 (2005) 101–126.

Schmid, J., 'Wohlfahrtsstaaten im Vergleich: Bestandsaufnahme und aktuelle Diskussion', *Gegenwartskunde* 4:49 (2000) 517–536.

Schmidt, R. H., 'Die Transformation des deutschen Finanzsystems und der Corporate Governance deutscher Unternehmen', in: M. Glaum, U. Hommel and D. Thomaschewski (eds.), *Internationalisierung und Unternehmenserfolg: Wettbewerb, organisatorischer Wandel und Corporate Governance* (Stuttgart: Schäffer-Poeschel, 2007).

Schmidt, R. H., Hackethal, A. and Tyrell, M., 'Disintermediation and the Role of Banks in Europe: An International Comparison', *Journal of Financial Intermediation* 8:1–2 (1999) 36–67.

Schmidt, R. H. and Spindler, G., 'Path Dependence, Corporate Governance and Complementarity', *International Finance* 5:3 (2002) 311–333.

Schön, W., *Steuerliche Maßgeblichkeit in Deutschland und Europa* (Cologne: Verlag Dr. Ottto Schmidt, 2005).

Schruff, W., 'Die Rolle des Hauptfachausschusses (HFA) des IDW', *Die Wirtschaftsprüfung* 59 1–2 (2006) 1–8.

Schwartz, H., 'Round Up the Usual Suspects!: Globalization, Domestic Poltics, and Welfare State Changes', in: P. Pierson (ed.), *The New Politics of the Welfare State* (Oxford: Oxford University Press, 2001).

Scott, J., *Social Network Analysis: A Handbook*, 2nd ed. repr. ed. (London: Sage, 2005).

Scott, W. R., *Financial Accounting Theory*, 5th ed. (Toronto: Pearson Education Canada, 2009).

Scruggs, L., *Welfare State Entitlements Data Set: A Comparative Institutional Analysis of Eighteen Welfare States*, 1st ed. (Storrs, CT: University of Connecticut, 2004).

SEC, 'Concept Release on Allowing U.S. Issuers to Prepare Financial Statements in Accordance with International Financial Reporting Standards (Corrected), August 7' (Available at: http://www.sec.gov/rules/concept/2007/2033-8831a.pdf, 2007a).

SEC, 'SEC Announces Next Steps Relating to International Financial Reporting Standards, *Press Release*, April 24' (Available at: http://www.sec.gov/news/press/2007/2007-72.htm, 2007b).

Seliger, B., 'Die Krise der sozialen Sicherung und die Globalisierung: Politische Mythen und ordnungspolitische Wirklichkeit', *ORDO: Jahrbuch für die Ordnung von Wirtschaft und Gesellschaft* 52:1 (2001) 215–238.

Shiba, K., ' "Accounting Big Bang" and Corporate Behaviour in Japan', *Kansai University Review of Business and Commerce* 6:6 (2004) 43–74.

Shiba, K. and Shiba, L., 'Japan', in: R. Ma (ed.), *Financial Reporting in the Pacific Asia Region* (Singapore: Singapore Institute of Management 1997).

Shleifer, A. and Vishny, R. W., 'Large Shareholders and Corporate Control', *Journal of Political Economy* 94:3 (1986) 461–488.

Siegel, N. A., 'Welten des Wohlfahrtskapitalismus und Typen wohlfahrtsstaatlicher Politik', in: M. G. Schmidt, T. Ostheim, N. A. Siegel and R. Zohlnhöfer (eds.), *Der Wohlfahrtsstaat: Eine Einführung in den historischen und internationalen Vergleich* (Wiesbaden: VS Verlag für Sozialwissenschaften, 2007).

Siems, M. M., *Die Konvergenz der Rechtssysteme im Recht der Aktionäre: ein Beitrag zur vergleichenden Corporate Governance in Zeiten der Globalisierung* (Tübingen: Mohr Siebeck, 2005a).

Siems, M. M., 'Numerical Comparative Law: Do We Need Statistical Evidence in Law in Order to Reduce Complexity?', *Cardozo Journal of International and Comparative Law* 13:2 (2005b) 521–540.

Sikka, P., 'Regulation of Accountancy and the Power of Capital: Some Observations', *Critical Perspectives on Accounting* 12:2 (2001) 199–211.

Sikka, P. and Willmott, H., 'The Power of "Independence": Defending and Extending the Jurisdiction of Accounting in the United Kingdom', *Accounting, Organizations & Society* 20:6 (1995) 547–581.

Simmons, B. A. and Elkins, Z., 'The Globalization of Liberalization: Policy Diffusion in the International Political Economy', *American Political Science Review* 98:1 (2004) 171–189.

Simons, D., *Internationalisierung von Rechnungslegung, Prüfung und Corporate Governance* (Wiesbaden: Gabler, 2005).

Smith, A., *An Inquiry into the Nature and Causes of the Wealth of Nations* (London: W. Strahan and T. Cadell, 1776).

Smith, P., 'Riding Out the Global Storm', *Accountancy Age* (2009) 9–11.

Soderstrom, N. S. and Sun, K. J., 'IFRS Adoption and Accounting Quality: A Review', *European Accounting Review* 16:4 (2007) 675–702.

Spreen, M., 'Rare Populations, Hidden Populations, and Link-Tracing Designs: What and Why?', *Bulletin de Méthodologie Sociologique* 36:1 (1992) 34–58.

Stapleton, R. C. and Subrahmanyam, M. G., 'Market Imperfections, Capital Market Equilibrium and Corporation Finance', *The Journal of Finance* 32:2 (1977) 307–319.

Starke, P., Obinger, H. and Castles, F. G., 'Convergence Towards Where: In What Ways, If Any, Are Welfare States Becoming More Similar?', *Journal of European Public Policy* 15:7 (2008) 975–1000.

Stern, E., 'Crisis and Learning: A Conceptual Balance Sheet', *Journal of Contingencies & Crisis Management* 5:2 (1997) 69–86.

Stigler, G. J., 'The Theory of Economic Regulation', *Bell Journal of Economics and Management Science* 2:3 (1971) 3–21.

Stolowy, H., 'Nothing Like the Enron Affair Could Happen in France (!)', *European Accounting Review* 14:2 (2005) 405–415.

Stone, D. L., 'Transfer Agents and Global Networks in the "Transnationalisation" of Policy', *Journal of European Public Policy* 11:3 (2004) 545–566.
Street, D. L., 'The G4's Role in the Evolution of the International Accounting Standard Setting Process and Partnership with the IASB', *Journal of International Accounting, Auditing and Taxation* 15:1 (2006) 109–126.
Street, D. L., 'The Impact in the United States of Global Adoption of IFRS', *Australian Accounting Review* 18:3 (2008) 199–208.
Street, D. L. and Linthicum, C. L., 'IFRS in the US: It May Come Sooner than You Think', *Journal of International Accounting Research* 6:1 (2007) xi-xvii.
Street, D. L. and Shaughnessy, K. A., 'The Evolution of the G4 + 1 and its Impact on International Harmonization of Accounting Standards', *Journal of International Accounting, Auditing and Taxation* 7:2 (1998) 131–161.
Suda, K., 'Creative Accounting and Accounting Scandals in Japan', in: M. J. Jones (ed.), *Creative Accounting, Fraud and International Accounting Scandals* (Chichester: Wiley, 2011).
Sunder, S., 'Regulatory Competition for Low Cost-of-Capital Accounting Rules', *Journal of Accounting & Public Policy* 21:2 (2002) 147–149.
Tamm Hallström, K., *Organizing International Standardization: ISO and the IASC in Quest of Authority* (Cheltenham: Edward Elgar Publishing, 2004).
Taylor, P., *Consolidated Financial Reporting* (London: Paul Chapman, 1996).
Tews, Kerstin, 'Politiktransfer: Phänomen zwischen Policy-Lernen und Oktroi. Überlegungen zu unfreiwilligen Umweltpolitikimporten am Beispiel der EU-osterweiterung', *Zeitschrift für Umweltpolitik & Umweltrecht* 25:2 (2002) 173–201.
Thiele, S. and Tschesche, F., 'Zur Bilanzierungspraxis der DAX-Unternehmen im Geschäftsjahr 1996 – Mehr "Einblick" durch internationale Rechnungslegungsnormen?', *Der Betrieb* 50:50 (1997) 2497–2502.
Thorell, P. and Whittington, G., 'The Harmonization of Accounting within the EU', *European Accounting Review* 3:2 (1994) 215–240.
Tinbergen, J., *Economic Policy: Principles and Design* (Amsterdam: North-Holland, 1956).
Titmuss, R. M., *Social Policy: An Introduction* (New York: Pantheon Books, 1975).
Touron, P., 'The Adoption of US GAAP by French Firms before the Creation of the International Accounting Standard Committee: An Institutional Explanation', *Critical Perspectives on Accounting* 16:6 (2005) 851–873.
Tweedie, D. and Seidenstein, T. R., 'Setting a Global Standard: The Case for Accounting Convergence', *Northwestern Journal of International Law & Business* 25:3 (2005) 589–608.
Van Hulle, K., 'Von den Bilanzrichtlinien zu International Accounting Standards', *Die Wirtschaftsprüfung* 56:18 (2003) 213–229.
van Zandt, D., 'Convergence: Challenges, Controversies, and Collaboration', *Northwestern Journal of International Law & Business* 25:3 (2005) 509–512.
Vernimmen, P., *Corporate Finance: Theory and Practice*, 6th rev. ed. (Chichester: John Wiley & Sons, 2005).
Véron, N., 'The Global Accounting Experiment', in: *Bruegel Blueprint Series* (Brussels: Bruegel, 2007).
Volmer, P. B., Werner, J. R. and Zimmermann, J., 'New Governance Modes for Germany's Financial Reporting System: Another Retreat of the Nation State?', *Socioecon Review* 5:3 (2007) 437–465.
Wagenhofer, A., 'Anspruch und Wirklichkeit der IFRS als Global GAAP', in: K. Bock and A. v. Werder (eds.), *Unternehmensübernahme, Unternehmensaufsicht und Unternehmensberichterstattung: Perspektiven für Europa* (Stuttgart: Schäfer-Poeschel, 2008).

Wagenhofer, A., *Internationale Rechnungslegungsstandards - IAS/IFRS*, 6th ed. (Munich: FinanzBuch Verlag, 2009).

Walker, J. L., 'The Diffusion of Innovations among the American States', *The American Political Science Review* 63:3 (1969) 880–899.

Walker, M., 'Accounting for Varieties of Capitalism: The Case against a Single Set of Global Accounting Standards', *The British Accounting Review* 42:3 (2010) 137–152.

Walton, P., 'Introduction: The True and Fair View in British Accounting', *European Accounting Review* 2:1 (1993) 49–58.

Walton, P., 'IAS 39 - Where Different Accounting Models Collide', *Accounting in Europe* 1:1 (2004) 5–16.

Walton, P. J., 'Accountancy: The Most Exciting Profession in the World', in: D. Alexander and C. Nobes (eds.), *International Financial Reporting Standards: Context, Analysis and Comment* (Oxon: Routledge, 2008).

Watrin, C., *Internationale Rechnungslegung und Regulierungstheorie*, (Wiesbaden: Deutscher Universitäts-Verlag, 2001).

Watts, R. L., 'Conservatism in Accounting, Part I: Explanations and Implications', *Accounting Horizons* 17:3 (2003) 207–221.

Watts, R. L. and Zimmerman, J. L., *Positive Accounting Theory* (Englewood Cliffs, NJ: Prentice-Hall, 1986).

Way, C. R., 'Political Insecurity and the Diffusion of Financial Market Regulation', *The ANNALS of the American Academy of Political and Social Science* 598:1 (2005) 125–144.

Werner, J. R., *Unternehmenspublizität und Corporate Governance im Wandel: Staatliche Steuerungsmodelle im internationalen Vergleich* (Frankfurt: Campus Verlag, 2008).

Werner, J. R., 'Conclusions on Hierarchical versus Collaborative Governance in the Finance Sector', in: E. Bohne and C. Karlsson (eds.), *Repositioning Europe and America for Growth: The Role of Governments and Private Actors in Key Policy Areas* (Münster: LIT, 2010).

Werner, J. R. and Zimmermann, J., 'Der Staat und die Internationalisierung von Normen der Rechnungslegung', in: A. Hurrelmann, S. Leibfried, K. Martens and P. Mayer (eds.), *Zerfasert der Nationalstaat: Die Internationalisierung politischer Verantwortung* (Frankfurt: Campus, 2008).

Werner, J. R. and Zimmermann, J., 'Internationaler Vergleich von Rechnungslegungssystemen: Stand und Perspektiven', *Die Betriebswirtschaft* 69:1 (2009) 85–106.

Whittington, G., 'The Adoption of International Accounting Standards in the European Union', *European Accounting Review* 14:1 (2005) 127–153.

Wilensky, H. L. and Lebeaux, C. N., 'Conceptions of Social Welfare', in: M. N. Zald (ed.), *Social Welfare Institutions: A Sociological Reader* (New York: Wiley, 1965).

Williams, D. D., 'The Potential Determinants of Auditor Change', *Journal of Business Finance & Accounting* 15:2 (1988) 243–261.

Williamson, O. E., *Markets and Hierarchies: Analysis and Antitrust Implications* (New York: Free Press, 1975).

Willmott, H., Cooper, D. J. and Puxty, T., 'Maintaining Self-Regulation: Making "Interests" Coincide in Discourses on the Governance of the ICAEW', *Accounting, Auditing & Accountability Journal* 6:4 (1993) 68–93.

Wise, T. A., 'The Very Private World of Peat, Marwick, Mitchell', *Fortune* 74:1 (1966) 88–91.

Witt, U., 'How Evolutionary Is Schumpeter's Theory of Economic Development', *Industry and Innovations* 9:1–2 (2002) 7–22.

Witt, U., 'Evolutionary Economics', in: S. N. Durlauf and L. E. Blume (eds.), *The New Palgrave Dictionary of Economics* (Basingstoke: Palgrave Macmillan, 2008).

World Bank, World development indicators 2010, available online: http://data.worldbank.org/data-catalog/world-development-indicators/wdi-2010.

Wootton, C. W., Wolk, C. M. and Normand, C., 'An Historical Perspective on Mergers and Acquisitions by Major US Accounting Firms', *Accounting History* 8:1 (2003) 25–60.

Wüstemann, J., 'Disclosure Regimes and Corporate Governance', *Journal of Institutional and Theoretical Economics* 159:4 (2003) 717–726.

Zarzeski, M. T., 'Spontaneous Harmonization Effects of Culture and Market Forces on Accounting Disclosure Practices', *Accounting Horizons* 10:1 (1996) 18–37.

Zeff, S. A., 'The Rise of "Economic Consequences" ', *Journal of Accountancy* 146:6 (1978) 56–63.

Zeff, S. A., 'Political Lobbying on Proposed Standards: A Challenge to the IASB', *Accounting Horizons* 16:1 (2002) 43–54.

Zetzsche, D. A., 'Explicit and Implicit System of Corporate Control: A Convergence Theory of Shareholder Rights', *SSRN eLibrary* (Available at: http://ssrn.com/paper=600722, 2004).

Zimmermann, J., 'Ordnungspolitische Fragen zur Unternehmenspublizität nach der Enron-Insolvenz', *Wirtschaftsdienst* 82:5 (2002) 303–312.

Zimmermann, J., 'The Role of the Nation State in the Internationalization of Accounting Regimes', in: A. Hurrelmann, S. Leibfried, K. Martens and P. Mayer (eds.), *Transforming the Golden-Age Nation State* (Basingstoke: Palgrave Macmillan, 2007).

Zimmermann, J., 'Das neue Bilanzrecht: Mode statt Moderne', *Betriebliche Altersversorgung* 64:7 (2009) 579–586.

Zimmermann, J., 'Aufgaben und Bedeutung des Deutschen Rechnungslegungs Standards Committees (DRSC)', in: K. Petersen, C. Zwirner and G. Brösel (eds.), *Handbuch Bilanzrecht: Abschlussprüfung und Sonderfragen in der Rechnungslegung* (Munich: Bundesanzeiger Verlag, 2010a).

Zimmermann, J., 'EU Federalism and the Governance of Financial Reporting', *Publius: The Journal of Federalism* 40:1 (2010b) 200–225.

Zimmermann, J. and Abée, S., 'Do Cross-Listings Drive Regulatory Convergence? Evidence from Germany', *SSRN eLibrary* (Available at: http://ssrn.com/paper=902827, 2006).

Zimmermann, J., Schymczyk, J. and Kilian, J. P., 'Convergence Patterns in Accounting Regulation: Six Country Cases of The Transforming Regulatory Landscape', *Sfb597 'Staatlichkeit im Wandel'–TranState Working Papers No. 119* (Available at: http://econstor.eu/bitstream/10419/32779/1/62600926X.pdf, 2010).

Zimmermann, J., Werner, J. R. and Kilian, J.-P., 'Wie verbreitet sind Covenants?', *Die Bank* 17:7 (2011) 20–25.

Zimmermann, J., Werner, J. R. and Volmer, P. B., *Global Governance in Accounting: Rebalancing Public Power and Private Commitment* (Basingstoke: Palgrave Macmillan, 2008).

Zürn, M. and Leibfried, S., 'A New Perspective on the State: Reconfiguring the National Constellation', *European Review* 13:1 (2005) 1–36.

# Index

Note: Figures and tables in bold